Microsoft Exchange Server 2013 High Availability

Design a highly available Exchange 2013 messaging environment using real-world examples

Nuno Mota

[PACKT] enterprise
PUBLISHING professional expertise distilled

BIRMINGHAM - MUMBAI

Microsoft Exchange Server 2013 High Availability

First published: February 2014

Production Reference: 1120214

Published by Packt Publishing Ltd.
Livery Place
35 Livery Street
Birmingham B3 2PB, UK.

ISBN 978-1-78217-150-8

www.packtpub.com

Cover Image by Vivek Sinha (vs@viveksinha.com)

Credits

Author
Nuno Mota

Reviewers
Michael Collard, I.
Jorrit Mertens
Vivek Vinod Sharma
Oleg Sokolov
Linwood Wright

Acquisition Editor
Owen Roberts

Content Development Editor
Akshay Nair

Technical Editors
Kunal Anil Gaikwad
Pramod Kumavat
Siddhi Rane
Sonali S. Vernekar

Copy Editors
Janbal Dharmaraj
Sayanee Mukherjee
Deepa Nambiar
Alfida Paiva

Project Coordinator
Joel Goveya

Proofreaders
Maria Gould
Paul Hindle

Indexers
Hemangini Bari
Tejal Soni

Graphics
Ronak Dhruv
Valentina Dsilva
Yuvraj Mannari

Production Coordinator
Saiprasad Kadam

Cover Work
Saiprasad Kadam

About the Author

Nuno Mota works as a Senior Microsoft Messaging Consultant for a UK services provider company in London. He is responsible for designing and deploying Exchange and Office 365 solutions for organizations around the UK. He also shares a passion for Lync, Active Directory, and PowerShell.

Besides writing his personal Exchange blog, `http://LetsExchange.blogspot.com`, he is also an author for the `MSExchange.org` website with dozens of published articles, and is a regular contributor in the Exchange TechNet forums.

He has also been awarded Microsoft Most Valuable Professional (MVP) on Exchange since 2012.

I dedicate this book to my parents, Preciosa and António Mota, and my sister, Carla, who are always there for me no matter what, for all their unconditional support, and for teaching me never to give up.

To my beautiful girlfriend Linda for putting up with me and for all her patience and love towards me.

And to my good friend and mentor Sean Treloar; if you hadn't taken a chance on me, I wouldn't be where I am today.

To all of you, a big thank you! Love you.

About the Reviewers

Michael Collard, I. is a computer problem solver. He holds a degree from DeVry University, holds multiple certifications, and has over 25 years of experience with computers. His first computer was a Commodore 64, which was very sensitive to temperature and humidity. Those lessons on environment followed him through his career. While troubleshooting a computer server, program, or installation, he always looks at external factors.

He has been involved in numerous technology startups as a principle or as a consultant. He has also programmed more than 50 Android applications and runs a successful webhosting and web design company.

He lives in Kansas City, MO, with his lovely wife and two great children. He is a distance runner, and has run multiple road races including a marathon.

> I would like to thank my wonderful wife and my kids for being the guidance, the motivation, and my everything in this world.

Jorrit Mertens (MCT, MCSA, MCSE, MCITP, MCITP:MBS) is a consultant, trainer, and speaker. He has experience working with a wide range of Microsoft technologies, focusing on enterprise network infrastructure. He has implemented several large Exchange implementations and migrations from non-Microsoft mail solutions to Exchange and Office 365.

Vivek Vinod Sharma is a Technical Consultant with Microsoft who enables partners to position, sell, and deploy Office 365 and Microsoft Exchange 2010/2013 by providing end-to-end consulting. As a part of the Microsoft Partner Services team, he has worked with partners and customers in North America on Office 365, Exchange 2010/2013, Lync 2010/2013, Exchange Online Protection, Exchange Hosted Encryption, and Exchange Online Archiving. He has a keen interest in PowerShell scripting and loves to work on new technologies that come around.

Oleg Sokolov is an Enterprise Software Engineer with more than 8 years of industry experience in developing embedded systems and desktop software. He lives and works in Nizhny Novgorod, Russia.

Over the last few years, he has been focusing on custom software development based on Microsoft infrastructure solutions, and has good experience in Microsoft products and technologies such as Windows Server, SQL Server, System Center, Exchange, and Hyper-V virtualization.

He is currently working for Uniglass Ltd. and developing software solutions for the integration of industrial measuring systems into enterprise IT environments.

Linwood Wright, since 1997, has been increasing employee productivity and reducing company expenses and labor hours through technology. He has honed his skills through the years with formal education, personal research, and testing.

Throughout his life, he has enjoyed learning and helping people. With his technical and communication skills, he is able to design and implement alternate methods of achieving the required business results that reduce labor hours and/or expenses.

If you are interested in growing your business, contact My Tampa IT at `MyTampaIT.com`.

www.PacktPub.com

Support files, eBooks, discount offers, and more

You might want to visit www.PacktPub.com for support files and downloads related to your book.

Did you know that Packt offers eBook versions of every book published, with PDF and ePub files available? You can upgrade to the eBook version at www.PacktPub.com and as a print book customer, you are entitled to a discount on the eBook copy. Get in touch with us at service@packtpub.com for more details.

At www.PacktPub.com, you can also read a collection of free technical articles, sign up for a range of free newsletters, and receive exclusive discounts and offers on Packt books and eBooks.

![PACKTLIB logo]

http://PacktLib.PacktPub.com

Do you need instant solutions to your IT questions? PacktLib is Packt's online digital book library. Here, you can access, read and search across Packt's entire library of books.

Why Subscribe?

- Fully searchable across every book published by Packt
- Copy and paste, print, and bookmark content
- On demand and accessible via web browser

Free Access for Packt account holders

If you have an account with Packt at www.PacktPub.com, you can use this to access PacktLib today and view nine entirely free books. Simply use your login credentials for immediate access.

Instant Updates on New Packt Books

Get notified! Find out when new books are published by following @PacktEnterprise on Twitter, or the *Packt Enterprise* Facebook page.

Table of Contents

Preface

For most organizations around the world, e-mail is the top mission-critical service. During the course of twenty years of Exchange development, Microsoft has been improving the Exchange platform, making it more user friendly and reliable with each release. From Windows clusters, through Cluster Continuous Replication, to Database Availability Groups, the progress of Exchange in terms of availability and resilience is extraordinary.

Microsoft Exchange Server 2013 High Availability is a hands-on, practical guide that provides you with a number of clear illustrations and concepts that will help you understand how this new version works and how you can achieve the most out of it in terms of availability and resilience.

Throughout this book, you will go through all the roles, components, and features that should be considered when addressing high availability. You will learn to successfully design and configure a highly available Exchange 2013 environment by going through different examples and real-world scenarios, saving you and your company's time, money, and eliminating errors.

With every chapter, you will go through everything you need to know in order to successfully design and configure a highly available Exchange 2013 environment. Each chapter can be used as a reference, or it can be read from the beginning to the end, allowing consultants/administrators to build a solid and highly available Exchange 2013 environment.

What this book covers

Chapter 1, *Getting Started*, covers the differences between a highly available and a resilient solution followed by an introduction to the new architecture of Exchange 2013.

Chapter 2, High Availability with the Client Access Server, explores how to make the CAS role highly available by covering its changes from previous versions, load balancing, and the autodiscover service.

Chapter 3, High Availability with the Mailbox Server, describes how to make the Mailbox server role highly available and lists its improvements and new features, such as automatic reseed, database availability groups, and public folders.

Chapter 4, Achieving Site Resilience, discusses site resilience for both the client access and Mailbox server roles, covering the new global namespace and database availability groups across multiple datacenters.

Chapter 5, Transport High Availability, discusses, the new transport pipeline in Exchange 2013 and the new and improved shadow redundancy and Safety Net features.

Chapter 6, High Availability of Unified Messaging, describes the architectural changes made to Unified Messaging and what is required to achieve high availability for this service.

Chapter 7, Backup and Recovery, explores Windows integrated backup and System Center Data Protection Manager, what needs to be backed up in an Exchange environment, whether database availability groups can fully replace backups, and disaster recovery.

Chapter 8, Monitoring Exchange, focuses on the new Managed Availability monitoring engine, what it brings into Exchange monitoring, and its impact for System Center Operations Manager.

Chapter 9, Underlying Infrastructure, explores key infrastructure components and systems that also need to be made highly available so that they do not affect Exchange's availability. These include, for example, Active Directory, Domain Name System, and virtualization.

What you need for this book

Microsoft Exchange Server 2013 High Availability provides several PowerShell cmdlets that require Microsoft Exchange Server 2013 to run. Every concept explored in this book is Exchange-related and, as such, you do not have to install anything in particular other than Exchange itself.

Note that all cmdlets should be run using the Exchange Management Shell and not the normal Windows PowerShell or command prompt.

Who this book is for

This book is targeted at messaging professionals who want to learn how to design a highly available Exchange 2013 environment. It assumes you have practical experience with Exchange 2013. Although not a definite requirement, practical experience with Exchange 2010 is expected, without being a subject matter expert.

Conventions

In this book, you will find a number of styles of text that distinguish between different kinds of information. Here are some examples of these styles, and an explanation of their meaning.

Code words in text are shown as follows: "This will automatically configure the `ExternalUrl` parameters for all the virtual directories so that we can start load balancing external requests to these services."

Any command-line input or output is written as follows:

```
Set-OutlookProvider EXPR -CertPrincipalName msstd:*.domain.com
```

New terms and **important** words are shown in bold. Words that you see on the screen, in menus or dialog boxes for example, appear in the text like this: "Additionally, the **Exchange Server authentication** checkbox should be disabled to make sure Exchange traffic is not routed through this Receive connector."

> Warnings or important notes appear in a box like this.

> Tips and tricks appear like this.

Reader feedback

Feedback from our readers is always welcome. Let us know what you think about this book—what you liked or may have disliked. Reader feedback is important for us to develop titles that you really get the most out of.

To send us general feedback, simply send an e-mail to feedback@packtpub.com, and mention the book title via the subject of your message.

If there is a topic that you have expertise in and you are interested in either writing or contributing to a book, see our author guide on www.packtpub.com/authors.

Customer support

Now that you are the proud owner of a Packt book, we have a number of things to help you to get the most from your purchase.

Errata

Although we have taken every care to ensure the accuracy of our content, mistakes do happen. If you find a mistake in one of our books — maybe a mistake in the text or the code — we would be grateful if you would report this to us. By doing so, you can save other readers from frustration and help us improve subsequent versions of this book. If you find any errata, please report them by visiting http://www.packtpub.com/submit-errata, selecting your book, clicking on the **errata submission form** link, and entering the details of your errata. Once your errata are verified, your submission will be accepted and the errata will be uploaded on our website, or added to any list of existing errata, under the Errata section of that title. Any existing errata can be viewed by selecting your title from http://www.packtpub.com/support.

Piracy

Piracy of copyright material on the Internet is an ongoing problem across all media. At Packt, we take the protection of our copyright and licenses very seriously. If you come across any illegal copies of our works, in any form, on the Internet, please provide us with the location address or website name immediately so that we can pursue a remedy.

Please contact us at copyright@packtpub.com with a link to the suspected pirated material.

We appreciate your help in protecting our authors, and our ability to bring you valuable content.

Questions

You can contact us at questions@packtpub.com if you are having a problem with any aspect of the book, and we will do our best to address it.

1
Getting Started

For most organizations around the world, e-mail is their top mission-critical service. Throughout nearly 20 years of Exchange development, Microsoft has been improving the Exchange platform, making it more user-friendly and reliable with each release. From Windows clusters to Cluster Continuous Replication to Database Availability Groups and much more, the progress of Exchange in terms of availability and resilience is extraordinary.

In this chapter, we will look at the definitions of availability and resilience, as well as the new architecture of Exchange 2013.

Defining high availability and resilience

Before we delve into how we will make Exchange 2013 a highly available solution, it is important to understand the differences between a highly available solution and a resilient solution.

Availability

According to the Oxford English dictionary, **available** means *able to be used or obtained; at someone's disposal*. From an Exchange perspective, we can interpret availability as the proportion of time that Exchange is accessible to users during normal operations and during planned maintenance or unplanned outages. In simple terms, we are trying to provide service availability, that is, keep the messaging service running and available to users. Remember that uptime and availability are not synonymous; Exchange can be up and running but not available to users, as in the case of a network outage.

The availability of any IT system is often measured using percentages; more commonly, the number of nines in the digits ("class of nines"). The higher the percentage, the higher the availability of the system. As an example, when the business states that the organization's target is 99.9 percent Exchange availability, it is referred to as three nines, or class three. And 99.9 percent sounds excellent, right? Actually, it depends on the organization itself, and its requirements and goals. Looking at the following table, we can see that 99.9 percent of availability means that Exchange is actually down for almost 9 hours in a year, or 10 minutes every week on average. While this might seem acceptable, imagine if the period of downtime was to happen every week during peak utilization hours. The following table gives an overview of the approximate downtime hours for different values of availability, starting from 90 percent and higher:

Availability (%)	Downtime		
	per year (365d)	per month (30d)	per week
90 percent (1 nine)	36.50 days	3.00 days	16.80 hours
95 percent	18.25 days	36.00 hours	8.40 hours
99 percent (2 nines)	3.65 days	7.20 hours	1.68 hours
99.5 percent	1.82 days	3.60 hours	50.40 minutes
99.9 percent (3 nines)	8.76 hours	43.20 minutes	10.08 minutes
99.95 percent	4.38 hours	21.60 minutes	5.04 minutes
99.99 percent (4 nines)	52.56 minutes	4.32 minutes	1.01 minutes
99.999 percent (5 nines)	5.26 minutes	25.92 seconds	6.05 seconds
99.9999 percent (6 nines)	31.54 seconds	2.59 seconds	0.60 seconds

While a typical user would probably be content with an availability of 99.9 percent, users in a financial institution may expect, or even demand, better than 99.99 percent. High levels of availability do not happen naturally or by chance; they are the result of excellent planning, design, and maintenance.

The ideal environment for any Exchange administrator is obviously one that is capable of achieving the highest level of availability possible. However, the higher the level of availability one tries to achieve, the higher the cost and complexity of the requirements that guarantee those extra few minutes or hours of availability.

Furthermore, how does one measure the availability of an Exchange environment? Is it by counting the minutes for which users were unable to access their mailboxes? What if only a subset of the user population was affected? Unfortunately, how availability is measured changes from organization to organization, and sometimes even from administrator to administrator depending on its interpretation. An Exchange environment that has been up for an entire year might have been unavailable to users due to a network failure that lasted for 8 hours. Users, and possibly the business, will see Exchange unavailable while its administrators will still claim 100 percent of availability. If we take the true definition of availability, Exchange was only approximately 99.9 percent available. But is this fair for the Exchange administrator? After all, the reason why Exchange was not available was not because of an issue with Exchange itself, but with the network.

The use of "nines" has been questioned a few times since it does not appropriately reflect the impact of unavailability according to the time of occurrence. If in an entire year, Exchange was only unavailable for 50 minutes during Christmas day at 3 A.M when no one tried to access it, should its availability be quantified as 99.99 percent or 100 percent?

The definition of availability must be properly established and agreed upon. It also needs to be accurately measured, ideally with powerful monitoring tools, such as Microsoft System Center Operations Manager, which are themselves highly available. Only when everyone agrees on a shared interpretation and define how to accurately measure availability, will it actually be useful for the business.

The level of availability that the business expects from Exchange will not be simply expressed as, for example, 99.9 percent. It will be part of a **Service Level Agreement** (**SLA**), which is one of the few ways of ensuring that Exchange meets the business objectives. SLAs differ for every organization, and there is not an established process on how to define one for Exchange. Typically, Exchange SLAs contain five categories:

- **Performance**: An SLA of this category pertains to the delivery and speed of e-mails. An example would be *90% of all e-mails are to be delivered within 10 minutes*. If desired, the SLA might also define the remaining 10 percent.

- **Availability**: An SLA of this category establishes the level of availability of Exchange to the end users using the "class of nines" that we discussed previously.

- **Disaster Recovery**: An SLA of this category defines how long it should take to recover data or restore a service when a disaster occurs. These SLAs typically focus on the service recovery time as well as on more specific targets such as a single server or a mailbox. To help establish these SLAs, two other elements of business continuity are used:

  ◦ **Recovery Time Objective (RTO)**: This element establishes the duration of time in which Exchange must be restored after a disaster. For example, *Exchange must be made available within 4 hours in the secondary datacenter if a major incident happens in the primary datacenter.*

  ◦ **Recovery Point Objective (RPO)**: This element establishes the maximum tolerable period in which data might be lost from Exchange due to a major incident. For example, *in case of a major incident, no more than 1 hour of data can be lost.* In environments where a secondary datacenter is used for disaster recovery, the RPO can be defined as the amount of time taken for the data to be replicated to the secondary datacenter. If a disaster occurs during this time, any data written during that time frame could be lost if the primary datacenter is unrecoverable.

- **Security**: An SLA of this category generally includes assurances regarding malware-detection rate, encryption performance, data at rest and in transit, e-mail-scanning time, and physical security of servers and the datacenter(s) where these are located.

- **Management**: An SLA of this category helps ensure that the messaging solution meets both user and maintenance requirements.

Translating an SLA document by putting it into practice requires administrators to be suitably skilled and to have the necessary infrastructure and tools to achieve the SLA. After SLAs have been planned, developed, and deployed, they must be periodically reviewed to ensure they are being met and are achieving the desired results. It is extremely important to ensure SLAs remain cost-effective and realistic.

Resilience

According to the Oxford English dictionary, the adjective **resilient** means *able to withstand or recover quickly from difficult conditions.*

Resilience, or resiliency as it is sometimes used, is the ability to provide a satisfactory level of service when faced with faults and challenges during normal operation. More specifically, it is the ability of a server, network, or an entire datacenter to recover quickly and continue operating normally during a disruption.

Resilience is usually achieved by installing additional equipment (redundancy) together with careful design to eliminate single points of failure (deploying multiple Hub Transport servers, for example) and well-planned maintenance. Although adding redundant equipment might be straightforward, it can be expensive and, as such, should be done only after considering its costs versus its benefits.

A typical example is one in which when a server's power supply fails, the server also fails, and its services become unavailable until the services are restored to another suitable server or the server itself is repaired. However, if this same server had a redundant power supply, it would keep the server running while the failed power supply was being replaced.

A resilient network infrastructure, for example, is expected to continue operating at or above the minimum service levels, even during localized failures, disruptions, or attacks. Continuing operation, in this example, refers to the service provided by the communications infrastructure. If the routing infrastructure is capable of maintaining its core purpose of routing packets despite local failures or attacks, it is said to be robust or resilient.

The same concept holds true from the server level all the way up to the datacenter facilities. Datacenter resilience is typically guaranteed by using redundant components and/or facilities. When an element experiences a disruption (or fails), its redundant counterpart seamlessly takes over and continues to provide services to the users. For example, datacenters are usually powered by two independent utility feeds from different providers. This way, a backup provider is available in case the other fails. If one is to design a resilient Exchange environment that extends across multiple datacenters, no detail should be overlooked.

Let us briefly throw another term into the mix, **reliability**, which signifies the probability of a component or system to perform for an anticipated period of time without failing. Reliability in itself does not account for any repairs that may take place, but for the time it takes the component (or system) to fail while it is in operation.

Reliability is also an important notion because maintaining a high level of availability with unreliable equipment is unrealistic, as it would require too much effort and a large stock of spares and redundant equipment. A resilient design takes into consideration the reliability of equipment in a redundant topology.

Taking storage as an example, the advertised reliability of the disks used in a storage array might influence the decision between using a RAID 1, RAID 5, RAID 6, or even a RAID 10.

> Designing and implementing a highly available and resilient Exchange 2013 environment is the sole purpose of this book. Although the main focus will be on the Exchange application layer, technologies such as Active Directory, DNS, and virtualization are also covered in some detail in the final chapter.

Introducing the new Exchange architecture

Before we delve into how to design and deploy a highly available Exchange 2013 infrastructure, we need to look at the architecture changes and improvements made over the previous editions of Exchange.

> This is not an extensive list of all the improvements introduced in Exchange 2013. Only the main changes are mentioned as well as those relevant for high availability.

Looking at the past

In the past, Exchange has often been architected and optimized with consideration to a few technological constraints. An example is the key constraint that led to the creation of different server roles in Exchange 2007: CPU performance. A downside of this approach is that server roles in Exchange 2007/2010 are tightly coupled together. They introduce version dependency, geo-affinity (which requires several roles to be present in a specific Active Directory site), session affinity (often requiring a complex and expensive load-balancing solution), and namespace complexity.

Today, memory and CPU are no longer the constraining factors as they are far less expensive. As such, the primary design goals for Exchange 2013 became failure isolation, improved hardware utilization, and simplicity to scale.

Let us start by having a quick look at how things have evolved since Exchange 2000.

Exchange 2000/2003

In Exchange 2000 and 2003, server tasks are distributed among frontend and backend servers, with frontend servers accepting client requests and proxying them for processing by the appropriate backend server. This includes proxying RPC-over-HTTP (known as Outlook Anywhere), HTTP/S (**Outlook Web App (OWA)**), POP, and IMAP clients. However, internal Outlook clients do not use the frontend servers as they connect directly to the backend servers using MAPI-over-RPC.

An advantage of this architecture over Exchange 5.5 is that it allows the use of a single namespace such as `mail.domain.com`. This way, users do not need to know the name of the server hosting their mailbox. Another advantage is the offloading of SSL encryption/decryption to the frontend servers, freeing up the backend servers from this processor-intensive task.

While the frontend server is a specially configured Exchange server, there is no special configuration option to designate a server as a backend server.

High availability was achieved on the frontend servers by using **Network Load Balancing** (**NLB**) and by configuring backend servers in an active/active or active/passive cluster.

Exchange 2007

While in Exchange 2003 the setup process installs all features regardless of which ones the administrators intend to use, in Exchange 2007, Microsoft dramatically changed the server roles architecture by splitting the Exchange functionality into five different server roles:

- **Mailbox server** (**MBX**): This role is responsible for hosting mailbox and public folder data. This role also provides MAPI access for Outlook clients.
- **Client Access Server** (**CAS**): This role is responsible for optimizing the performance of mailbox servers by hosting client protocols such as POP, IMAP, ActiveSync, HTTP/S, and Outlook Anywhere. It also provides the following services: Availability, Autodiscover, and web services. Compared to Exchange 2000 or 2003 frontend servers, this role is not just a proxy server. For example, it processes ActiveSync policies and does OWA segmentation, and it also renders the OWA User Interface. All client connections with the exception of Outlook (MAPI) use the CAS as the connection endpoint, offloading a significant amount of processing that occurs against backend servers in Exchange 2000 or 2003.

- **Unified Messaging Server**: This role is responsible for connecting a Private Branch eXchange (PBX) telephony system to Exchange.
- **Hub Transport Server (HTS)**: This role is responsible for routing e-mails within the Exchange organization.
- **Edge Transport Server**: This role is typically placed in the perimeter of an organization's network topology (DMZ) and is responsible for routing e-mails in and out of the Exchange organization.

Each of these server roles logically group specific features and functions, allowing administrators to choose which ones to install on an Exchange server so that they can configure a server the way they intend to use it. This offers other advantages such as reduced attack surface, simpler installation, full customization of servers to support the business needs, and the ability to designate hardware according to the role since each role has different hardware requirements.

This separation of roles also means that high availability and resilience is achieved using different methods depending on the role: by load-balancing CASs (either using NLB or hardware/software load-balancing solutions), by deploying multiple Unified Messaging and Hub Transport Servers per Active Directory site, and at the Mailbox server level by using Local Continuous Replication, Standby Continuous Replication, or through the cluster technologies of Cluster Continuous Replication or Single Copy Cluster.

Exchange 2010

In terms of server roles, Exchange 2010 has the same architecture, but under the hood, it takes a step further by moving Outlook connections to the CAS role as well. This means there will be no more direct connections to Mailbox servers. This way, all data access occurs over a common and single path, bringing several advantages, such as the following:

- Improved consistency
- Better user experience during switch and fail-over scenarios as Outlook clients are connected to a CAS and not to the mailbox server hosting their mailbox
- Support for more mailboxes per mailbox server
- Support for more concurrent connections

The downside is that this change greatly increases the complexity involved in load-balancing CASs as these devices now need to load-balance RPC traffic as well.

To enable a quicker reconnect time to a different CAS when the server that a client is connected to fails, Microsoft introduced the Client Access array feature, which is typically an array of all CASs in the Active Directory (AD) site where the array is created. Instead of users connecting to the **Fully Qualified Domain Name (FQDN)** of a particular CAS, Outlook clients connect to the FQDN of the CAS array itself, which typically has a generic name such as `outlook.domain.com`.

Exchange 2010 includes many other changes to its core architecture. New features including shadow redundancy and transport dumpster provide increased availability and resilience, but the biggest change of all is the introduction of Database Availability Group (DAG) – the base component of high availability and site resilience of Exchange 2010. A DAG is a group of (up to 16) Mailbox servers that hosts databases and provides automatic database-level recovery by replicating database data between the members of the DAG. As each server in a DAG can host a copy of any database from any other server in the same DAG, each mailbox database is now a unique global object in the Exchange organization, while in Exchange 2007, for example, databases were only unique to the server hosting them. DAGs provide automatic recovery from failures that can go from a single database to an entire server.

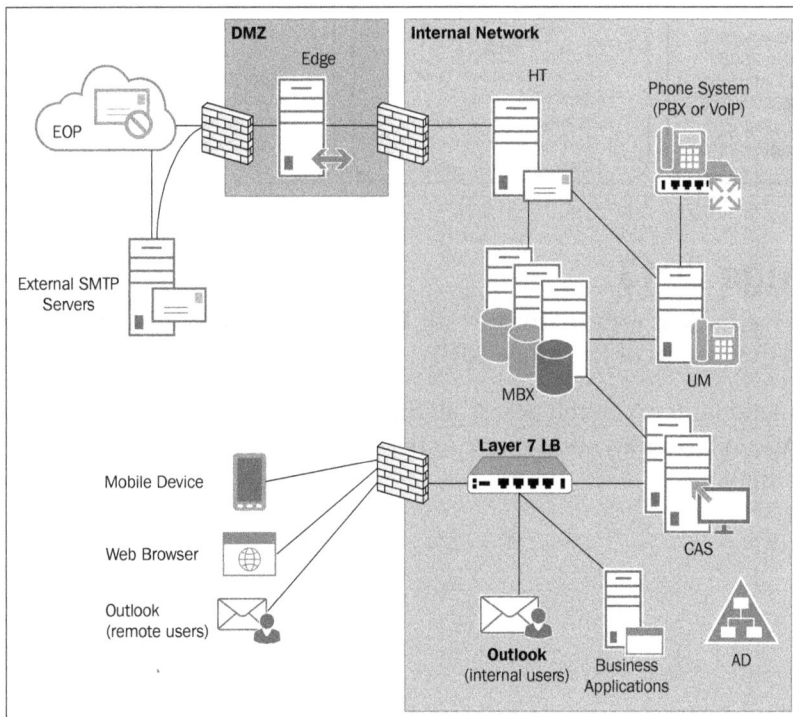

The following diagram provides an overview of the evolution from Exchange 2003 to Exchange 2010:

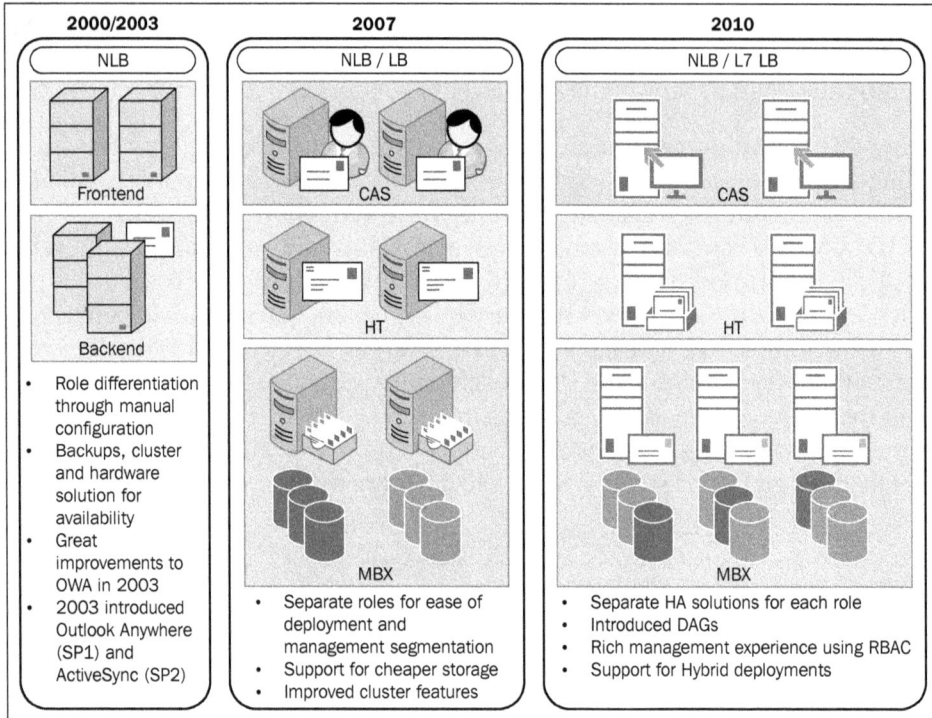

Exchange 2013

While looking back at ways of improving Exchange, Microsoft decided to address three main drawbacks of Exchange 2010:

- Functionality scattered across all different server roles, forcing HTS and CASs to be deployed in every Active Directory site where Mailbox servers are deployed.

- Versioning between different roles, meaning a lower version of HTS or CAS should not communicate with a higher version of the Mailbox server. Versioning restrictions also indicate that administrators cannot simply upgrade a single server role (such as a Mailbox server) without upgrading all first.

- Geographical affinity, where a set of users served by a given Mailbox server is always served by a given set of CAS and HTS servers.

Enter Exchange 2013, which introduces major changes once more, and we seem to be back in the Exchange 2000/2003 era, only in a far improved way as one would expect. In order to address the issues just mentioned, Microsoft introduced impressive architectural changes and investments across the entire product. Hardware expansion was seen as a limiting boundary from a memory and disk perspective. At the same time, CPU power keeps increasing, which a separate role architecture does not take advantage of, thus introducing a potential for the consolidation of server roles once more.

The array of Client Access servers and Database Availability Group are now the only two basic building blocks, each providing high availability and fault tolerance, but now decoupled from one another. When compared with a typical Exchange 2010 design, the differences are clear:

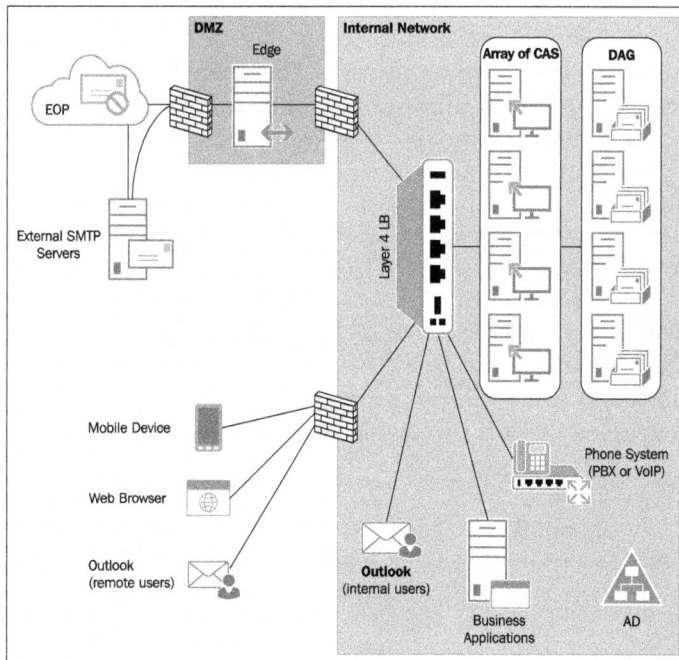

To accomplish this, the number of server roles has been reduced to three, providing an increased simplicity to scale, isolation of failures, and improved hardware utilization:

- The **Mailbox server** role hosts mailbox databases and handles all activity for a given mailbox. In Exchange 2013, it also includes the Transport service (virtually identical to the previous Hub Transport Server role), Client Access protocols, and the Unified Messaging role.

- The **Client Access Server** role includes the new Front End Transport service and provides authentication, proxy, and redirection services without performing any data rendering. This role is now a thin and stateless server which never queues or stores any data. It provides the usual client-access protocols: HTTP (Outlook Anywhere, Web Services, and ActiveSync), IMAP, POP, and SMTP. MAPI is no longer provided as all MAPI connections are now encapsulated using RPC-over-HTTPS.

- The **Edge server** role, added only in Service Pack 1, brings no additional features when compared to a 2010 Edge server. However, it is now only configurable via PowerShell in order to minimize its attack surface, as adding a user interface would require Internet Information Services, virtual directories, opening more ports, and so on.

In this new architecture, the CAS and the Mailbox servers are not as dependent on one another (role affinity) as in the previous versions of Exchange. This is because all mailbox-processing occurs only on the Mailbox server hosting the mailbox. As data rendering is performed local to the active database copy, administrators no longer need to be concerned about incompatibility of different versions between CAS and Mailbox servers (versioning). This also means that a CAS can be upgraded independently to Mailbox servers and in any order.

Encapsulating MAPI connections using RPC-over-HTTPS and changing the CAS role to perform pure connection-proxying means that advanced layer 7 load-balancing is no longer required. As connections are now stateless, CASs only accept connections and forward them to the appropriate mailbox server. Therefore, session affinity is not required at the load-balancer; only layer 4 TCP with source IP load-balancing is required. This means that if a CAS fails, the user session can simply be transferred to another CAS because there is no session affinity to maintain.

> All these improvements bring another great advantage: users no longer need to be serviced by CASs located within the same Active Directory site as that of the Mailbox servers hosting their mailboxes.

Other changes introduced in Exchange 2013 include the relegation of RPC. Now, all Outlook connections are established using RPC-over-HTTP (Outlook Anywhere). With this change, CASs no longer need to have the RPC client-access service, resulting in a reduction from two different namespaces normally required for a site-resilient solution. As we will see in *Chapter 4*, *Achieving Site Resilience*, a site-resilient Exchange infrastructure is deployed across two or more datacenters in a way that it is able to withstand the failure of a datacenter and still continue to provide messaging services to the users.

Outlook clients no longer connect to the FQDN of a CAS or CAS Array. Outlook uses Autodiscover to create a new connection point involving the mailbox GUID, in addition to the @ symbol and the domain portion of the user's primary SMTP address (for example `64c50652-f6a8-411b-94db-add8f975d178@domain.com`). Because the GUID does not change no matter where the mailbox is replicated, restored, or switched over to, there are no client notifications or changes. The GUID abstracts the backend database name and location from the client, resulting in a near elimination of the message *Your administrator has made a change to your mailbox. Please restart Outlook.*

The following diagram shows the client protocol architecture of Exchange 2013:

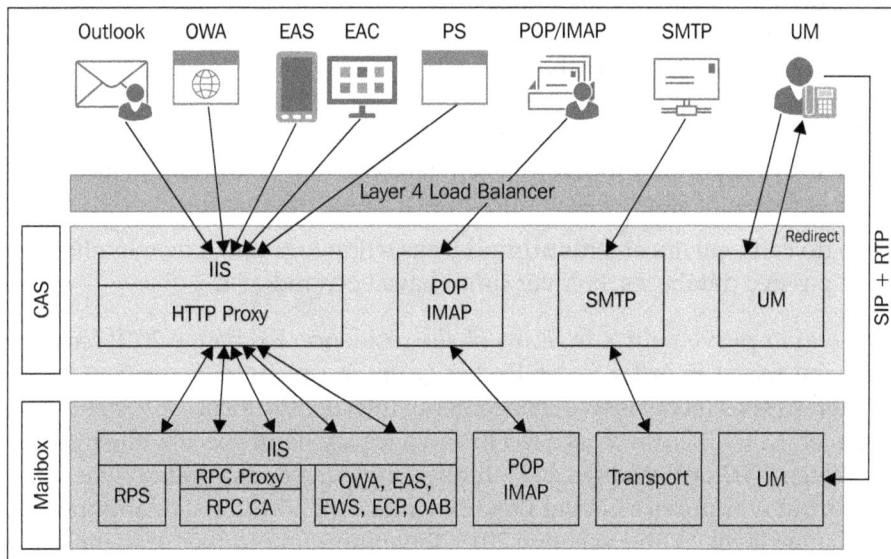

As shown in the preceding diagram, Exchange Unified Messaging (UM) works slightly differently from the other protocols. First, a Session Initiation Protocol (SIP) request is sent to the UM call router residing on a CAS, which answers the request and sends an SIP redirection to the caller, who then connects to the mailbox via SIP and **Real-time Transport Protocol (RTP)** directly. This is due to the fact that the real-time traffic in the RTP media stream is not suitable for proxying.

There are also other great improvements made to Exchange 2013 at the Mailbox server level. The following are some of them:

- Improved archiving and compliance capabilities
- Much better user experience across multiple devices provided by OWA
- New modern public folders that take advantage of the DAG replication model
- 50 percent to 70 percent reduction in IOPS compared to Exchange 2010, and around 99 percent compared to Exchange 2003
- A new search infrastructure called Search Foundation based on the FAST search engine
- The Managed Availability feature and changes made to the Transport pipeline

In terms of high availability, only minor changes have been made to the mailbox component from Exchange 2010 as DAGs are still the technology used. Nonetheless, there have been some big improvements:

- The Exchange Store has been fully rewritten
- There is a separate process for each database that is running, which allows for isolation of storage issues down to a single database
- To do code enhancements around transaction logs and a deeper checkpoint on passive databases, failover times have been reduced

Another great improvement is in terms of site resilience. Exchange 2010 requires multiple namespaces in order for an Exchange environment to be resilient across different sites (such as two datacenters): Internet Protocol, OWA fallback, Autodiscover, RPC Client Access, SMTP, and a legacy namespace while upgrading from Exchange 2003 or Exchange 2007. It does allow the configuration of a single namespace, but it requires a Global Load Balancer and additional configuration at the Exchange level. With Exchange 2013, the minimum number of namespaces was reduced to just two: one for client protocols and one for Autodiscover. While coexisting with Exchange 2007, the legacy hostname is still required, but while coexisting with Exchange 2010, it is not.

This is explored in more depth in *Chapter 4, Achieving Site Resilience*.

Summary

In this first chapter, we had a look at the differences between availability and resilience, as well as an overview of the new architecture of Exchange 2013 and all the improvements it brings over the past editions of Exchange.

Throughout the following chapters, we will explore in depth about all these new availability and resilience features. We will see how to take full advantage of them through the design and configuration of a highly available Exchange 2013 infrastructure, starting with the CAS role in the next chapter.

2
High Availability with the Client Access Server

Although the Exchange 2013 **Client Access Server** (**CAS**) role maintains the same name as in the previous versions of Exchange, it has changed significantly. The CAS role in Exchange 2010 performed proxy/redirection, authentication, and data rendering for Internet Protocols. In Exchange 2013, this role does not perform data rendering; it only performs proxy/redirection and authentication and offers support for the client Internet Protocols, e-mail transport, and part of the Unified Messaging stack (it redirects SIP traffic generated from incoming calls to the Mailbox server). As a result of this architectural change, from a protocol session perspective, the CAS role is now stateless, and because all processing for a mailbox happens on the Mailbox server, it does not matter which CAS receives each client request; that is, there is no session affinity.

Before we start exploring how to achieve high availability for the CAS role, there are two topics that we need to fully understand beforehand: session affinity and outlook connectivity.

Removing session affinity

As we saw in *Chapter 1, Getting Started*, Exchange 2013 does not require session affinity any longer. To understand why this is the case, let us look at how the new CAS role works from a protocol perspective:

1. A client resolves the namespace to a CAS.
2. The CAS authenticates the requests and queries Active Directory for the following pieces of information:
   ° Mailbox version (if the mailbox is hosted on Exchange 2010 or 2013, for example; let us assume a 2013 mailbox)
   ° Mailbox location information such as database and `ExternalURL`
3. The CAS decides if it will redirect or proxy the request to another CAS or array (within the same AD forest).
4. The CAS queries the instance of the Active Manager responsible for the database in order to discover in which Mailbox server the active copy is hosted.
5. The CAS will either proxy the request to the Mailbox server currently hosting the active copy using HTTPS, IMAP, or POP, or, in the case of a telephony request, redirect it to the Mailbox server instead because SIP and RTP sessions need to be established directly with the Mailbox server's Unified Messaging components.

Two changes in the new CAS architecture made it possible to remove session affinity at the load balancer: the fact that data rendering is no longer performed by the CAS and from step 4 that mentions the CAS queries the instance of the Active Manager responsible for the database. For any protocol session, CASs now maintain a relationship of 1:1 with the Mailbox server that hosts the user's mailbox. If an active database copy gets moved to another Mailbox server, the CAS will close the session(s) to the previous server and establish a new session to the new server, meaning that all sessions, independent of their point of origin (CAS), will always terminate at the same place: the Mailbox server that currently hosts the active database copy.

In regards to authentication, **Forms-Based Authentication** (**FBA**) was another reason why session affinity was necessary for OWA in the previous versions of Exchange. This was due to the cookie in FBA using a per-server key for encryption—if the request was received by another CAS, it would not be able to decrypt the session. By using the private key of the certificate installed on the CASs instead, Exchange 2013 no longer has a per-server session key, which enables a logged on user to resume a session on a different CAS without having to reauthenticate. However, it is extremely important that all CASs share the same SSL certificate as this will allow them to decrypt the authentication cookie that clients present.

Connecting to Outlook

Another major change in Exchange 2013 is in the role of Microsoft's RPC-based **Messaging API (MAPI)**. Previously, the Outlook clients used two transport options for RPC traffic: HTTP or TCP. With Exchange 2013, RPC/TCP is no longer supported as a connectivity solution; only RPC/HTTP (also known as Outlook Anywhere) is supported.

Changing the protocols used for communication between the CAS and Mailbox server roles from RPC/TCP to a protocol that is more tolerant to latency and throughput over Internet and WAN connections allows these roles to not be as tied together from a geographical or user affinity perspective as they were before. This change allows CASs in one Active Directory site to authenticate and proxy requests to a Mailbox server located in a different site.

Exchange 2010 introduced the new shared RPC Client Access namespace that Outlook clients use to connect. Exchange 2013, instead of using an FQDN for the RPC endpoint, it uses a mailbox GUID together with a domain suffix in order to support multi-tenant scenarios. As mailbox GUIDs are unique within the entire organization independent of where the database is mounted, CASs can easily determine the location and proxy the request to the right Mailbox server. If a failover/switchover occurs, the CAS will simply proxy the connection to the Mailbox server that now hosts the active database copy, meaning Outlook clients will not require a restart nor receive a notification to restart Outlook, as was the case with Exchange 2010.

A further architectural change is the introduction of external and internal namespaces for Outlook Anywhere, meaning administrators no longer need to deploy split DNS or have Outlook clients using an external firewall because of a change in the MAPI connectivity. This is important in terms of high availability as we will see further in this chapter.

Exchange 2013 SP1, however, has taken Outlook connectivity a step further and has introduced yet another feature called **MAPI-HTTP**, also internally referred by Microsoft as Exchange HTTP Transport or by its internal code name of *Alchemy*. MAPI-HTTP is a new communication protocol for Exchange and Outlook. It adds a new connection option for Outlook, which improves the existing RPC/HTTP protocol. At the time of writing this book, this new protocol is only available in Outlook 2013 SP1 and later clients, but Microsoft plans to add it to Outlook 2010 in a future build.

The plan is for MAPI-HTTP to eventually replace RPC/HTTP in an effort to further improve the reliability and stability of the Outlook/Exchange connection by removing the dependency on the RPC communication mechanism.

But why another change? RPC/HTTP already works great! Well, there are challenges in continuing to depend on the RPC components for Outlook. RPC has been in use for decades and the components are showing their age. At the same time, operating system and networking enhancements make this an opportune time to remove the dependency on RPC. Additionally, the RPC components that are required on both the client and the server add to the complexity of troubleshooting Outlook/Exchange connectivity issues.

> To enable MAPI-HTTP in Exchange 2013 SP1, simply run the following cmdlet: `Set-OrganizationConfig -MapiHttpEnabled $True`.

The following diagram shows how Outlook connects to Exchange using RPC/HTTP and its dependency on the RPC Proxy component in IIS. We can also see that Outlook submits Remote Operations (ROPs) to access and modify the mailbox information on the Exchange server using RPC, which in turn uses HTTP to deliver these commands to Exchange:

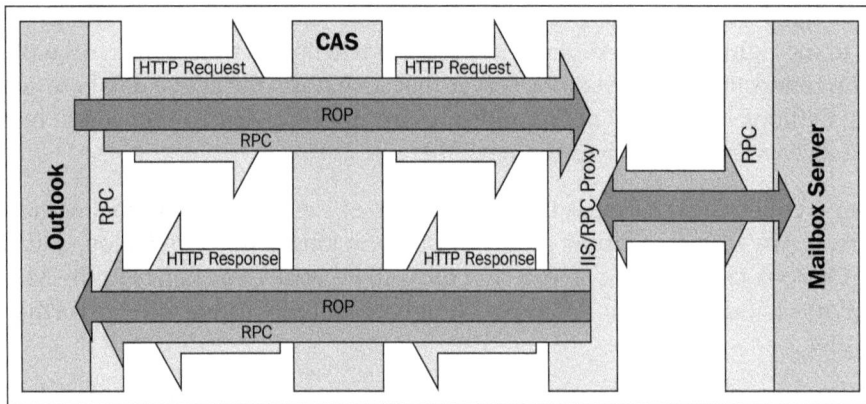

With the new MAPI-HTTP protocol, instead of having the intermediary RPC components, Outlook and Exchange communicate directly using the Secure HTTP (HTTPS) protocol. As shown in the next diagram, Outlook and Exchange bypass the RPC components and use the common HTTP request and response processes instead:

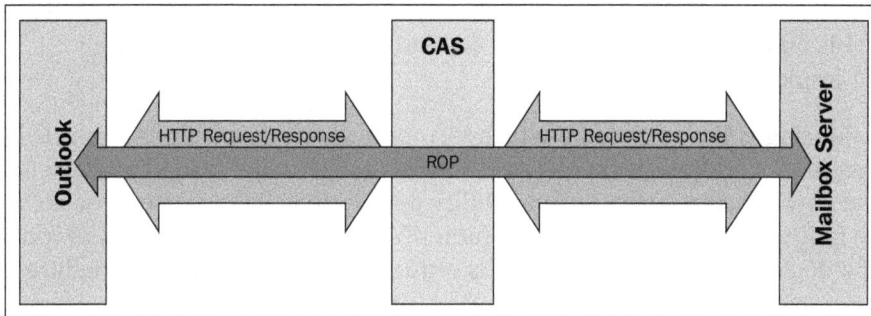

MAPI-HTTP will continue to use Autodiscover, discussed later in this chapter, to initiate the connection between Outlook and Exchange. As Exchange 2013 SP1 will continue to support RPC/HTTP as well as the new MAPI-HTTP connection mechanisms, Outlook informs Exchange that it is capable of connecting using MAPI-HTTP. This is done by sending the new *x-header* x-MapiHttpCapability to Exchange, which in turn provides the MAPI-HTTP URL(s) via Autodiscover, allowing Outlook to connect using MAPI-HTTP instead of RPC/HTTP.

> When using MAPI-HTTP, Outlook connects to the /mapi Virtual Directory for mail and directory, not /rpc as previously. Outlook still uses /EWS, /OAB, /AutoDiscover, and so on for all web service calls; it is only mail and directory that uses /mapi. This means that if you are publishing Outlook to external users using the Microsoft Unified Access Gateway, for example, the easiest method is simply to add the /mapi path to the existing Outlook Anywhere publishing rule.

Load balancing and CAS arrays

In order to achieve a high level of availability for the CAS role, there are two requirements: deploy more than one CAS and use a load balancing solution. Both these requirements have the purpose of decreasing the downtime for users by allowing failover of connections in case of an issue with one or more CASs. This failover is often automatic, depending on the load balancing solution implemented.

Load balancing is the method by which incoming client connections are distributed over a variety of endpoints (in our case, CASs) to ensure the load across all endpoints is similar. In Exchange, from an availability perspective, its main purpose is to provide failover redundancy if one or more CASs fail, ensuring that users continue to be able to access their mailboxes, thus reducing the impact of a CAS failure.

Furthermore, both these advantages are often achieved while presenting a single hostname for clients.

In Exchange 2010, the CAS role handled and processed client connections. This meant that in order to achieve fault tolerance and utilize servers efficiently, both internal and external Outlook connections had to be load balanced across an array of CASs. Because of the different needs of all client protocols in Exchange 2010, it was recommended to use a Layer 7 load balancing solution, also known as application or workload-aware load balancing. This allows the load balancer to decrypt Secure Sockets Layer (SSL) traffic, "read" the traffic passing though, analyze it, and use more complex and "intelligent" rules to determine how to balance/route each request. In this case, if all requests for protocols that required affinity did not end up on the same CAS, the user experience would be affected.

With all the architectural changes we have seen so far, Exchange 2013 CASs now support the use of Layer 4 load balancing, which only takes into account the IP addresses and TCP ports, with requests distributed at the transport layer. Now that session affinity (or protocol affinity, or application level affinity to be clearer) is not required, administrators have more choices when it comes to the load balancing architecture they chose, and it also becomes simpler to deploy it. Load balancing without session affinity increases the capacity of the load balancer as processing is not used to maintain affinity options such as SSL session IDs, cookie-based load balancing, or authentication tokens. Note that TCP session affinity is still maintained, otherwise network connections would simply fail.

It is important to explore the **Client Access array** introduced in Exchange 2010. After a Client Access array (also known as RPC CAS array or simply CAS array) was configured for an Active Directory site (they were site-specific), all CASs in the site automatically became members of the array and were typically load balanced using some sort of load balancing technology. This was configured to provide domain-joined Outlook clients a unified namespace endpoint to connect to, as the group of CASs could be addressed as a single entity with a single IP address and FQDN. CAS arrays did nothing for non-MAPI clients such as OWA or ActiveSync. Also, CAS arrays performed no load balancing—they were simply an AD object with the primary purpose of automatically populating the `RpcClientAccessServer` attribute of any new Exchange 2010 mailbox database created in the same AD site. This was used to tell the Outlook clients during the profile creation process the correct server name they should connect to.

With Exchange 2013, the RPC CAS array is no longer required because of the improvements in Exchange's architectural and Outlook connectivity. Now there is only an array of CASs, simply a group of CASs organized in a load-balanced configuration. Remember that Outlook clients no longer use the FQDN of the CAS array for the RPC endpoint, but they use the mailbox GUID and the URLs for Outlook Anywhere to connect to Exchange which is revealed through Autodiscover. When an incoming client connection reaches a CAS, the CAS performs a query on the directory in order to gather details of the mailbox via the GUID as well as a query to Active Manager to determine where the active copy of the database is currently hosted.

> Remember that in Exchange 2013, a CAS array, or an array of CAS to be more accurate, is just a group of CASs organized in a load-balanced configuration.

The use of load balancers is still supported and recommended for Exchange 2013, although its configuration can now be simplified because of the architectural changes mentioned earlier. Connections to Exchange 2013 CASs can now be simply directed to any available server by the load balancer without the need for an additional configuration and processing of session affinity. A proper load balancing solution is still crucial in providing high availability for Exchange services as it detects when a CAS becomes unavailable and removes it from the set of servers configured to handle inbound connections, thus preventing downtime for users.

The following section describes the four available methods of load balancing Exchange 2013 CASs.

The do nothing method

In any deployment with two or more CASs, Exchange, by default, tries to load balance traffic between all end points to the best it can. This means that typically, the first Outlook request will go to *CAS1*, the second will go to *CAS2*, and so on. While this method can be considered a form of load-balancing, it does not provide high availability. When Outlook connects to a particular CAS, it will continue to try to connect to that server even if the server is down. After a while, it will eventually try to connect to another CAS, but in the meantime, Outlook will be disconnected.

Windows Network Load Balancing (WNLB)

WNLB is a software load balancer solution used for several Microsoft applications, including Exchange. However, you should note that it is not recommended to use WNLB with Exchange because of the following inherent limitations:

- On multi-roled servers where DAGs are also being used, WNLB cannot be used because it is not compatible with Windows failover clustering.

- It does not detect service outages; it only detects server outages based on the IP address. For example, if a particular web service such as OWA fails but the server is still operational, WNLB will not detect the failure and will continue to route requests to the CAS with failed services.

- When a single node is added or removed, all clients have to be reconnected to the Network Load Balancing array.

- It does not scale out very well as it cannot typically load balance more than eight CASs in an array, nor is it recommended to do so, without performance issues.

- The CPU overhead is high on the cluster hosts, as the hosts themselves have to analyze and filter network packets.

Despite all these disadvantages, WNLB remains a decent basic solution for small deployments where a hardware load balancer is not available, and it is certainly better than using DNS Round Robin.

DNS Round Robin

With all these improvements in Exchange 2013, does it mean DNS can finally be used to load balance CASs? In theory, yes, because it is nearly as effective as WNLB. Since clients' connections can now reach a different CAS on each request (remember that authentication is maintained throughout and the session's endpoint remains the same backend Mailbox server), if one CAS fails, then the HTTP client will use DNS Round Robin to select the next server to be accessed.

To configure DNS Round Robin, we simply create multiple entries in DNS for each workload, pointing to each of the servers in the array. In an example of an environment with three CASs, the following screenshot is how DNS would look:

owa	Host (A)	192.168.1.70
owa	Host (A)	192.168.1.71
owa	Host (A)	192.168.1.72

When a client hits DNS requesting for an IP address for an OWA, all IP addresses are returned. When the next request hits DNS, the entries are shifted up a slot. As such, the first request would receive:

1. 192.168.1.70
2. 192.168.1.71
3. 192.168.1.72

The second request would receive:

1. 192.168.1.71
2. 192.168.1.72
3. 192.168.1.70

Similarly, the entries will be shifted up a slot for subsequent requests that hit the DNS. This results in each client connecting to a different CAS first until DNS cycles through the list of all the records.

The problem with this method is when a service or server fails. Since DNS does not perform any health checks, it does not know when to return a specific server's IP address and when not to, resulting in clients trying to connect to a server even if it is not available, thus causing downtime for the user. The only solution in such a scenario is for an administrator to manually remove the record from DNS until the issue is resolved and wait for the client's local DNS cache to expire. If this method of load balancing is selected, it is recommended to set a low **Time-To-Live (TTL)** value for these records such as 300 seconds.

A good thing with this method is that clients such as Outlook, for example, will try the second server on the list if they do not get a response from the first server. Before doing so, it will wait for a timeout (usually 20 seconds), during which users remain disconnected from Exchange. This can be seen as an automatic failover mechanism.

Since everything is handled by DNS, separate monitoring should be in place so that administrators are quickly made aware in case of any issues with a CAS in the array. This will allow them to react and minimize the user impact.

There is no doubt that DNS Round Robin is the most cost-effective method of achieving some high availability in Exchange 2013, but it is not recommended for any environment in which Exchange is considered business-critical, as it is still very limited and does not have all the benefits of the following load balancer solutions.

Hardware/virtual load balancers

Although hardware load balancers are most commonly referenced in documentation, we are starting to see an increase both in the number of vendors developing virtual load balancers as well as their use in the enterprise world. These are typically virtual appliances that run on a dedicated virtual machine and provide the same features as normal hardware load balancers. The decision of which one to choose depends entirely on the organization's specific requirements and budget. Although virtual appliances can leverage the high availability features of a virtual infrastructure, these are sometimes complemented by an additional physical appliance for redundancy. Though virtually unlimited, the performance of a virtual appliance is obviously constrained by the hardware and performance of the virtual infrastructure.

Independent of which type of device is used, in order to achieve a higher level of availability, at least two load balancers should be deployed to prevent single point of failure.

> In this book, I make no distinction between hardware and virtual load balancers.

Let's start with some basic concepts of load balancers. When setting up these devices, the following concepts are always involved:

1. A **Virtual IP** (VIP, also known as virtual service) is configured. The VIP is usually a unique combination of IP address/TCP port, such as 192.168.1.70 and port 443.

2. Each VIP contains a set of rules that define the load balancing logic that it will use (least connections, Round Robin, weighted least connections, least sessions, and so on) and two or more servers to forward the traffic to.

3. Each VIP also contains a health check, which the load balancer executes against each of the servers to determine whether they are available to route traffic or not.

These devices typically operate at two different layers: Layer 4 and Layer 7. With Layer 4, the load balancer operates in a rudimentary way as it is only aware of the destination IP address and the TCP port of the traffic passing through—it has no knowledge of the type of traffic or its content. Therefore, it is only able to route and load balance traffic based on the combination of the destination IP address and the TCP port. As Exchange services are only available in a single combination of IP address/TCP port, Layer 4 load balancers are only able to maintain one health check and persistence per service.

With Layer 7, on the other hand, the load balancer can read packets' data, which allows it to use a load balancing logic not limited to the IP address and port, but also based on its content. This results in the load balancer being able to distinguish between OWA and the Outlook Anywhere traffic, for example, allowing administrators to configure load balancers so that the OWA traffic is sent to one set of servers while Outlook Anywhere traffic is sent to a different set of servers, or implement health checks for different services.

> Because this book is about Exchange 2013 itself, I will not describe how to configure load balancers. Most vendors now provide templates and thorough documentation for load balancing Exchange traffic. I will focus solely on the Exchange configuration.

Let's now look at the three main load balancer configurations for Exchange 2013 CASs.

Layer 4 with a single namespace and IP address

Layer 4 with single namespace and IP address is the simplest and most restricted scenario possible, but it is also the easiest to implement while still achieving high availability. In this case, we use a single namespace to load balance all traffic for the different Exchange workloads (Outlook Anywhere, OWA, ActiveSync, EAC, EWS, and OAB). Although we could configure different namespaces for each workload, in this scenario, they would all be pointing to the same VIP, and this would not bring any additional benefits as we will see shortly.

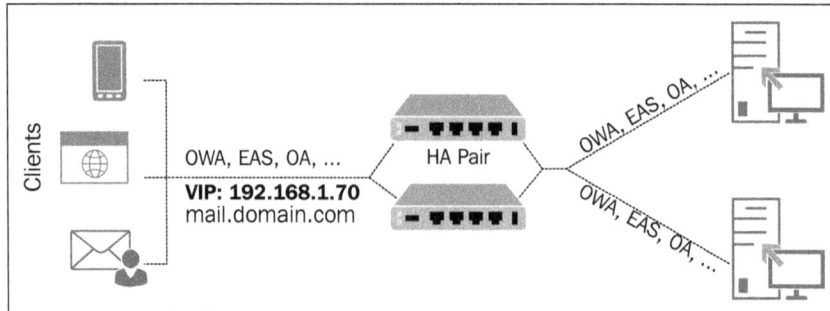

In all the methods that will be described in this section, the Autodiscover service should always have its own namespace (autodiscover. domain.com). In this first method, the DNS record for this namespace points to the same VIP address as the "general" namespace, thus also load balancing Autodiscover requests.

Because this method uses a single IP address and a single namespace, we cannot do health checking or workload-specific load balancing. This means that if a single workload fails, it can impact the end-user experience. For example, let us assume that users are connected to the mail.domain.com namespace and the load balancers are configured to perform a health check using the OWA's URL. If the OWA service fails on a particular server, its health check will fail and the load balancers will remove the entire server from their pool and no longer forward traffic to that server, even though other workloads such as Outlook Anywhere are still working fine. This would be OK if the entire server was down, but in this scenario, we are simply wasting resources.

This becomes a concern if the RPC/HTTP component is the one experiencing a problem. In this case, the OWA health check returns a positive status, meaning load balancers assume the server is in a healthy state. As such, traffic is still sent to the server, even though the Outlook Anywhere clients are unable to connect. This is where a powerful monitoring solution comes in to play so that administrators are aware of any issues as quickly as possible.

To configure this scenario, we start by installing the same certificate across all CASs that have `mail.domain.com` in the **Subject Alternative Name (SAN)** list. This is very important as discussed previously, especially for multi-site deployments as we will see in *Chapter 4, Achieving Site Resilience*.

Next, we configure the chosen namespace in DNS so that it points to our load balancer VIP. In this example, I am using `mail.letsexchange.com` and a VIP of `192.168.1.70` as seen in the following screenshot:

> Do not forget to create a DNS record so that `autodiscover.domain.com` points to the same VIP.

We then configure the load balancers to use Layer 4 load balancing together with the VIP we just added in DNS. After adding all the CASs we want to use to the pool, we configure the load balancers to use the HTTPS protocol to check the `/owa/auth/logon.aspx` URL for the health check of OWA. We typically also have to configure an HTTP to HTTPS redirect rule so that requests to `http://mail.domain.com/owa` are automatically redirected to `https://mail.domain.com/owa` instead.

Now we need to configure all CASs to use this namespace. We can do this using the Shell or the **Exchange Admin Center** (EAC) by navigating to **servers | virtual directories** and then clicking on the **configure external access domain** button, which is shown in the following screenshot:

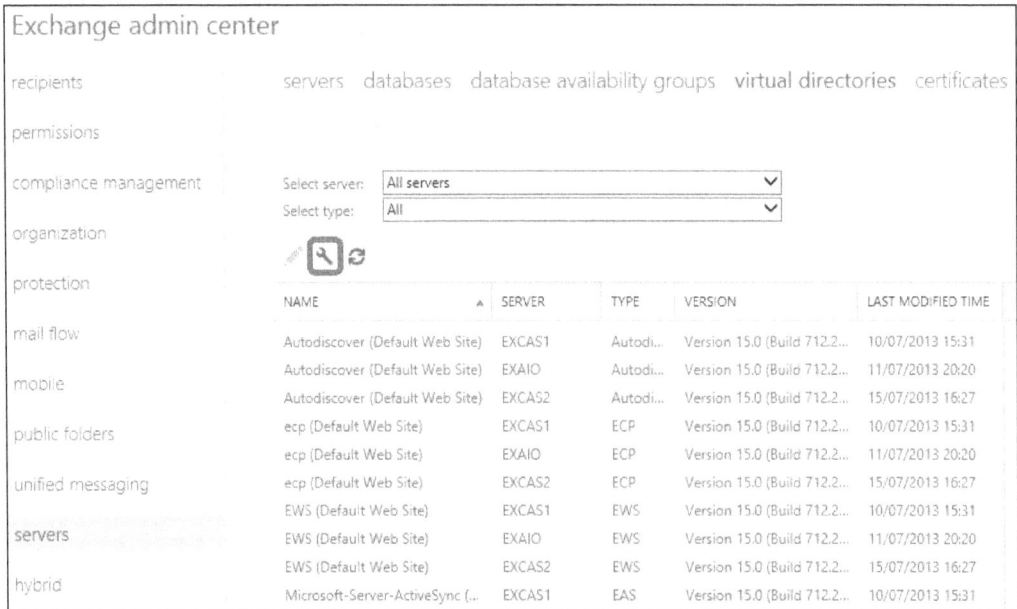

Exchange admin center

recipients	servers databases database availability groups **virtual directories** certificates
permissions	
compliance management	Select server: All servers ▾
	Select type: All ▾
organization	
protection	

NAME	SERVER	TYPE	VERSION	LAST MODIFIED TIME
Autodiscover (Default Web Site)	EXCAS1	Autodi...	Version 15.0 (Build 712.2...	10/07/2013 15:31
Autodiscover (Default Web Site)	EXAIO	Autodi...	Version 15.0 (Build 712.2...	11/07/2013 20:20
Autodiscover (Default Web Site)	EXCAS2	Autodi...	Version 15.0 (Build 712.2...	15/07/2013 16:27
ecp (Default Web Site)	EXCAS1	ECP	Version 15.0 (Build 712.2...	10/07/2013 15:31
ecp (Default Web Site)	EXAIO	ECP	Version 15.0 (Build 712.2...	11/07/2013 20:20
ecp (Default Web Site)	EXCAS2	ECP	Version 15.0 (Build 712.2...	15/07/2013 16:27
EWS (Default Web Site)	EXCAS1	EWS	Version 15.0 (Build 712.2...	10/07/2013 15:31
EWS (Default Web Site)	EXAIO	EWS	Version 15.0 (Build 712.2...	11/07/2013 20:20
EWS (Default Web Site)	EXCAS2	EWS	Version 15.0 (Build 712.2...	15/07/2013 16:27
Microsoft-Server-ActiveSync (...	EXCAS1	EAS	Version 15.0 (Build 712.2...	10/07/2013 15:31

(sidebar continued: mail flow, mobile, public folders, unified messaging, servers, hybrid)

On the **configure external access domain** page, we add all the CASs we want to be configured with this namespace, we enter our primary HTTPS name, and then we click on **save** to implement the change for the OWA, EAC, OAB, EWS, and ActiveSync virtual directories. This ensures that requests for any of these services will go through the load balancer, and as such, are made highly available as seen in the following screenshot:

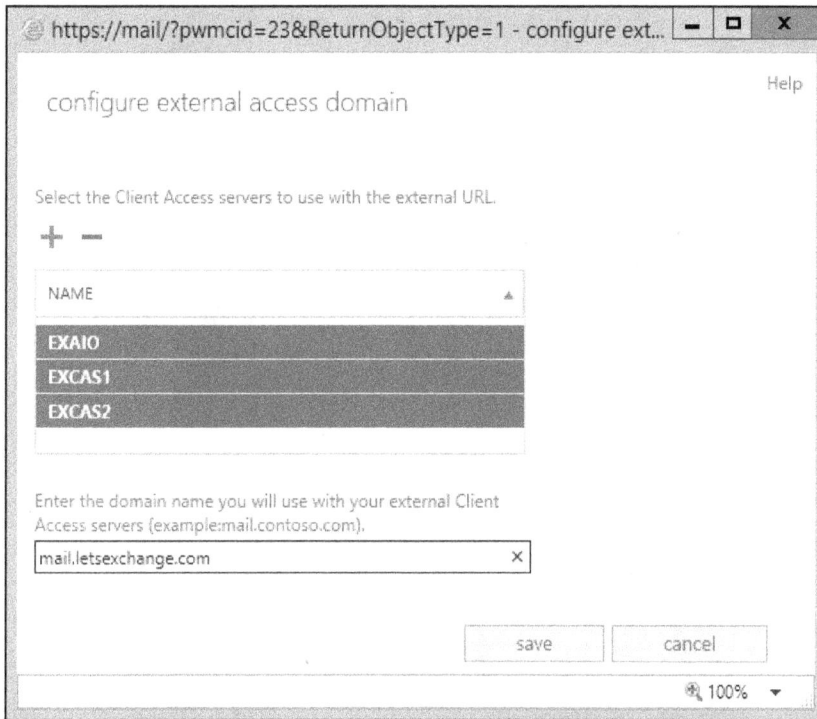

This will automatically configure the `ExternalUrl` parameters for all the virtual directories so that we can start load balancing external requests for these services. If the external URLs are not configured correctly, the service information provided to the clients may be incorrect for external users. They might be able to connect to their mailbox, but they will not be able to use Exchange features such as the Availability service, Automatic Replies, **Offline Address Book (OAB)**, or Unified Messaging.

> In this scenario, I am assuming that all CASs are Internet-facing. If they were not, then the `ExternalURL` parameters would be left at *$null* as these would only be configured in the Internet-facing CASs.

Once all external URLs have been configured correctly, we also need to update the internal URLs. As can be seen from the following screenshot, these have not been updated yet. As such, we cannot load balance internal requests until the internal URLs are updated.

The easiest way to update all of them and minimize any possible mistakes is to use PowerShell. The following code gets a list of all the CASs in the environment (again, assuming all of them are Internet-facing). It then goes through all of the returned servers and updates the `InternalURL` attribute for all the virtual directories to `mail.letsexchange.com` as well:

```
Get-ClientAccessServer | ForEach {

  Set-OwaVirtualDirectory "$($_.Identity)\OWA (Default Web Site)"
-InternalUrl "https://mail.letsexchange.com/owa"


  Set-OabVirtualDirectory "$($_.Identity)\OAB (Default Web Site)"
-InternalUrl "https://mail.letsexchange.com/OAB"


  Set-EcpVirtualDirectory "$($_.Identity)\ECP (Default Web Site)"
-InternalUrl "https://mail.letsexchange.com/ecp"
```

```
  Set-ActiveSyncVirtualDirectory "$($_.Identity)\Microsoft-Server-
ActiveSync (Default Web Site)" -InternalUrl "https://mail.letsexchange.
com/Microsoft-Server-ActiveSync"


  Set-WebServicesVirtualDirectory "$($_.Identity)\EWS (Default Web Site)"
-InternalUrl "https://mail.letsexchange.com/ews/exchange.asmx"


  Set-ClientAccessServer -AutoDiscoverServiceInternalUri "https://
autodiscover.letsexchange.com/autodiscover/autodiscover.xml"
}
```

Finally, we need to configure Outlook Anywhere. Again, this can be done through
the EAC by navigating to **servers | virtual directories**, selecting each CAS one at a
time, and editing its Outlook Anywhere properties to use `mail.letsexchange.com`
instead of the server's FQDN.

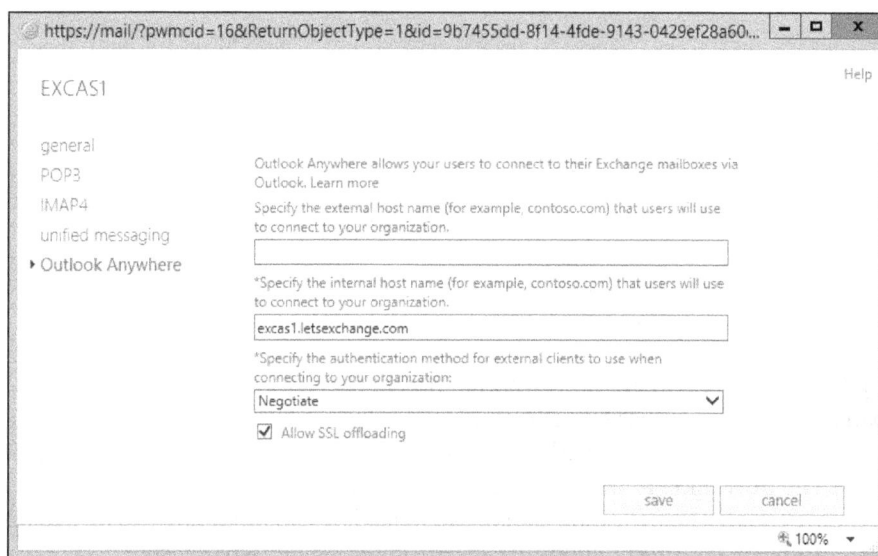

In environments with multiple CASs, the way less prone to errors is to update all
of them at once using PowerShell. In the following example, we configure Outlook
Anywhere URLs for all the CASs as well as settings regarding the use of certificates
and the authentication methods available to clients:

```
Get-OutlookAnywhere | Set-OutlookAnywhere -ExternalHostname
mail.letsexchange.com -ExternalClientsRequireSsl $True -
ExternalClientAuthenticationMethod Negotiate -InternalHostname mail.
letsexchange.com -InternalClientsRequireSsl $False
```

After saving the configuration and running an `iisreset /noforce` command on all the updated CASs, we have a complete configuration using Layer 4 load balancing and a single namespace. Although this method might cause some issues for users in certain scenarios, it is certainly the most cost-effective and easiest way of properly load balancing Exchange 2013.

Layer 4 with multiple namespaces and IP addresses

Although the previous method is easy to set up and inexpensive, causing service interruption to users is what we are trying to avoid. As such, if we tweak the method, we can simulate Layer 7 functionality and still maintain Layer 4 simplicity. We saw that when using Layer 4, load balancers do not know what the endpoint for a connection is. So, by using a different namespace and IP address for each workload, load balancers now know what the endpoint is without having to decrypt and analyze the traffic.

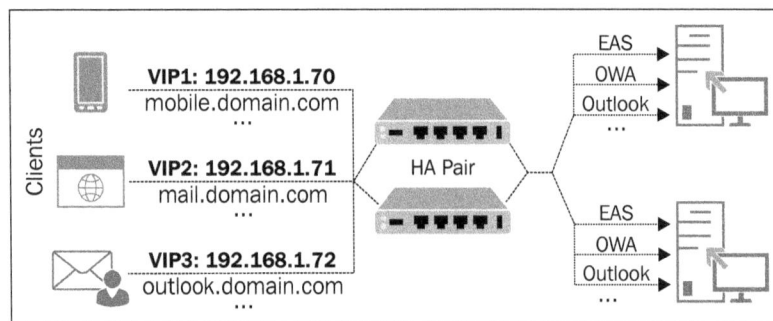

By using this method, we can set individual health checks for all the different workloads, meaning that just as with Layer 7, the failure of a single workload does not impact on other workloads; all of this still with the same level of simplicity as Layer 4. The downside to this method is that it requires multiple IP addresses. While this is perfectly fine for internal connections, it means that different external IP addresses might be required depending on the network infrastructure.

Some readers might be thinking that this approach will complicate everything as users now have to remember multiple URLs. If you think about it, there is only one URL that end users will have to remember: OWA. As long as your environment has Autodiscover configured, all other URLs are automatically configured.

The first step, once again, is making sure all CASs are using the same certificate.

> In this scenario, remember that all the different namespaces need to be included in the certificate.

Next, we configure the necessary DNS entries for each service as follows:

mobile	Host (A)	192.168.1.70
mail	Host (A)	192.168.1.71
outlook	Host (A)	192.168.1.72
webservices	Host (A)	192.168.1.73
oab	Host (A)	192.167.1.74
eac	Host (A)	192.168.1.75
autodiscover	Host (A)	192.168.1.76

We then configure the load balancers with all the preceding VIPs, each monitoring the following URLs for their respective service:

DNS Record	Service	Health Check URL
mobile	Exchange ActiveSync	/Microsoft-Server-ActiveSync
mail	Outlook Web App	/owa/auth/logon.aspx
outlook	Outlook Anywhere	/rpc/rpcproxy.dll
webservices	Exchange Web Services	/EWS/Exchange.asmx
oab	Offline Address Book	/OAB
autodiscover	Autodiscover	/AutoDiscover/AutoDiscover.xml

Microsoft is currently working with a few load balancer vendors to try to make these devices capable of using the Exchange health status produced by the Managed Availability service, thus relying on the Exchange built-in monitoring mechanisms. However, there is little information currently available.

As an alternative, some load balancers support the use of `https://<FQDN>/` `<protocol>/HealthCheck.htm` web pages for health checks. These are presented in Exchange 2013 by Managed Availability and contain a status code regarding the health of their respective service. These URLs are specific for each protocol and do not have to be manually created by the administrator. Some examples are as follows:

- `https://autodiscover.domain.com/Autodiscover/HealthCheck.htm`
- `https://mail.domain.com/EWS/HealthCheck.htm`
- `https://cas1.domain.com/OWA/HealthCheck.htm`

> The `healthcheck.htm file` is simply a "virtual file" that exists for each of the virtual directories and that is generated as soon as a user or application polls for it. You will not find it in any of the virtual directories by browsing them.

Similar to the process employed in the first method, we now need to configure each service's external and internal URLs. To do this through the EAC, navigate to **servers | virtual directories**. Select all virtual directories for a particular service and use the bulk edit options to update the **External URL** for each service one by one as shown in the following screenshot:

Alternatively, use PowerShell. The following code updates all the `InternalUrl` attributes for all the virtual directories just like in the first method (you can also update the external URLs at the same time):

```
Get-ClientAccessServer | ForEach {

  Set-OwaVirtualDirectory "$($_.Identity)\OWA (Default Web Site)"
-InternalUrl "https://mail.letsexchange.com/owa"


  Set-OabVirtualDirectory "$($_.Identity)\OAB (Default Web Site)"
-InternalUrl "https://oab.letsexchange.com/OAB"


  Set-EcpVirtualDirectory "$($_.Identity)\ECP (Default Web Site)"
-InternalUrl "https://eac.letsexchange.com/ecp"


  Set-ActiveSyncVirtualDirectory "$($_.Identity)\Microsoft-Server-
ActiveSync (Default Web Site)" -InternalUrl "https://mobile.letsexchange.
com/Microsoft-Server-ActiveSync"


  Set-WebServicesVirtualDirectory "$($_.Identity)\EWS (Default Web Site)"
-InternalUrl "https://webservices.letsexchange.com/ews/exchange.asmx"


  Set-ClientAccessServer -AutoDiscoverServiceInternalUri "https://
autodiscover.letsexchange.com/autodiscover/autodiscover.xml"

}
```

After saving the configuration, along with running an `iisreset /noforce` command on all the updated CASs, we have a complete configuration using Layer 4 load balancing and multiple namespaces and IP addresses. With the exceptions of requiring multiple IP addresses and a bit more configuration, this method is far more effective than the previous one as it allows the load balancers to monitor each service individually without the complexity of Layer 7.

Layer 7 with a single namespace and IP address

As already discussed, Layer 7 load balancing is able to decrypt traffic and analyze it in order to take the correct actions based on the destination or type of the traffic. This allows load balancers to differentiate between different Exchange workloads and determine what the destination URL is, while still using a single IP address for the common namespace.

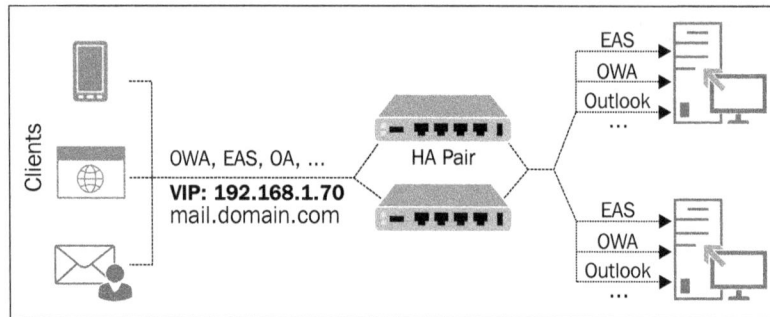

The main advantage of this method is that services have their own set of health criteria, meaning that if OWA fails on a particular server, other workloads on that server will not be affected. Whereas if OWA is down, other protocols continue to be healthy and load balancers continue to forward packets to that server for the other workloads.

Although Layer 4 is all that is necessary for Exchange 2013, Layer 7 is by far the best way to achieve the highest possible level of availability for the CAS role as it still offers some clear benefits over Layer 4. However, it comes with a cost in terms of hardware and by often requiring someone highly technical, as the configuration of some load balancers is considerably more complex.

Selecting the correct method

The question now is which method should I choose? Again, this depends on two main factors: the organization's requirements and available budget. For all the reasons already emphasized, a Layer 7 load balancer is still the best option as it will guarantee the highest level of availability when compared to all other options. However, an implementation of Layer 4 with multiple VIPs provides an excellent load balancing solution for most **Small and Medium Enterprises (SME)**.

Another key factor to keep in mind is the difference in the health checks each load balancer performs. For example, some load balancers will only perform a simple HTTP GET method to /rpc/rpcproxy.dll when trying to determine the availability of the Outlook Anywhere service, while others will actually try to authenticate against rpcproxy.dll (using a username/password defined by the administrator), and only if the authentication fails is the service marked as being down.

The following table summarizes the key differences between each method, together with their advantages and disadvantages:

Method	Advantages	Disadvantages
Windows NLB	• Free • Per-server availability	• No per-protocol availability • Cannot be used on servers where DAGs are also used • Limited scalability • CPU overhead on hosts
DNS Round Robin	• Free	• Manual intervention required • Failovers not always seamless • Dependent on client-side features/logic (timeout) • No health checks
Layer 4: Single VIP	• Easy to configure • Less resource intensive • Single IP/URL • Inexpensive	• No per-protocol availability • No granular health checks
Layer 4: Multiple VIPs	• Relatively easy to set up • Less resource intensive • Per-protocol availability • Granular health checks • Usually provides additional statistics/logging	• Multiple IPs/URLs • Certificate with more names • Can become more expensive due to IP and certificate requirements

Method	Advantages	Disadvantages
Layer 7: Single VIP	• Single IP/URL • Per-protocol availability • Granular health checks • Usually provides additional statistics/logging	• More difficult to configure • More resource intensive • More expensive

The Autodiscover service

In the last few versions of Exchange, the Autodiscover service has been available. This service greatly simplifies deployments by automatically configuring user profile settings for clients running Outlook as well as supported mobile phones.

With earlier versions of Outlook (Outlook 2003 or earlier versions) and Exchange (Exchange 2003 SP2 or earlier versions), administrators had to manually configure user profiles to access Exchange. If the messaging environment was changed, more work was required on these profiles, or Outlook would stop functioning properly.

In order to achieve a highly available scenario, Autodiscover is a crucial component. Before detailing how it should be configured, we need to first understand how Autodiscover works.

Using Autodiscover, Outlook locates the connection point made up of the user's mailbox GUID, plus the @ sign, plus the domain of the user's primary SMTP address. The following information is also returned to the client:

- Display name of the user
- Internal and external connection settings
- The URLs for various Exchange features such as free/busy information, OAB, and Unified Messaging
- Server settings for Outlook Anywhere

Autodiscover handles requests from Outlook 2007 (and later versions) clients as well as from supported mobile devices when a user's account is configured or updated, when Outlook periodically checks for changes to the Web Services URLs, and when network connection changes occur in the messaging environment.

When a 2013 CAS is installed, a virtual directory called Autodiscover gets created in IIS under the default website, which handles Autodiscover requests from Outlook and mobile devices. Additionally, an AD object named **Service Connection Point** (**SCP**) is created on the server where the CAS role is installed (if multiple CASs are deployed, an SCP record is generated for each CAS). This object has the authoritative list of Autodiscover service URLs for the entire forest and can be updated through the `Set-ClientAccessServer` cmdlet. By default, the Autodiscover URL is set to the server FQDN (we will be changing this to a generic name to be used with a load balancer):

```
Machine: EXCAS1.letsexchange.com                        _  □  x

[PS] C:\>Get-ClientAccessServer EXCAS1 | FL AutoDiscover*

AutoDiscoverServiceCN           : EXCAS1
AutoDiscoverServiceClassName    : ms-Exchange-AutoDiscover-Service
AutoDiscoverServiceInternalUri  : https://excas1.letsexchange.com/
                                  Autodiscover/Autodiscover.xml
AutoDiscoverServiceGuid         : 77378f46-2c66-4aa9-a6a6-3e7a48b1
                                  9596
AutoDiscoverSiteScope           : {Default-First-Site-Name}


[PS] C:\>
```

SCP objects can be found in the directory at the following path:

```
CN=<exchange_server>,CN=Autodiscover,CN=Protocols,CN=<exchange_
server>,CN=Servers,CN=Exchange Administrative Group (FYDIBOHF23SPDLT),CN=
Administrative Groups,CN=<organization_name>,CN=Microsoft Exchange,CN=Ser
vices,CN=Configuration,DC=<domain>,DC=<com>
```

Before running `Set-ClientAccessServer`, ensure that the **Authenticated Users** group is granted **Read** permissions to the SCP object; otherwise, users will not be able to search for and read the SCP's details as can be seen in the following screenshot:

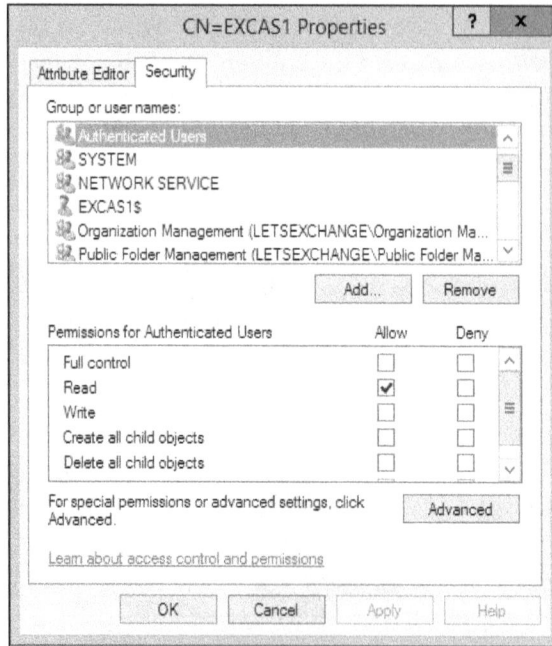

When a client that is domain-joined connects to AD, it authenticates to AD and locates the Autodiscover SCP objects. Once the client acquires this information, it connects to the first CAS in the list and obtains an XML file containing the profile information needed in order to connect to the user's mailbox as well as Exchange features as follows:

1. Outlook performs an **LDAP (Lightweight Directory Access Protocol)** query against AD looking for all available SCP objects.

2. Based on the client's AD site, Outlook sorts the results and one of the following two lists is generated:

   ° An in-site list with SCP records that contain the `AutodiscoverSiteScope` information seen in the first screenshot under the *Autodiscover service* section. This parameter (set using the `Set-ClientAccessServer` cmdlet) stipulates which site the Autodiscover service is authoritative to. The information in this list matches the Outlook client's AD site.

   ° An out-of-site list if there are no in-site records. In environments with remote sites that do not have Exchange servers, the `AutodiscoverSiteScope` parameter can be used on specific CASs to specify multiple sites. This way, Outlook clients will use SCP objects physically closer (this is known as site affinity).

3. Outlook then tries to connect to each Autodiscover URL generated from one of the previous lists. If unable to do so, it will try the predefined URLs `https://<domain.com>/autodiscover/autodiscover.xml` and `https://autodiscover.<domain.com>/autodiscover/autodiscover.xml` using DNS. If unsuccessful, it tries to use the SRV record lookup method (discussed later in this chapter). If all these methods fail, Outlook will not be able to obtain URL settings and Outlook Anywhere configuration.

4. Autodiscover queries AD in order to obtain Exchange services' URLs (for those that have been configured) and connection settings.

5. Autodiscover returns an XML file containing the information from step 4.

6. Outlook uses the suitable connection settings and configuration information to connect to Exchange.

An external or non-domain-joined client will first try to query AD for the SCP object in order to locate the Autodiscover service. As the client is not able to contact AD, it tries to use DNS to locate the Autodiscover service. Here, the client uses the primary SMTP domain address from the e-mail address, such as `letsexchange.com`, and checks DNS using the predefined URLs in step 3:

• `https://letsexchange.com/autodiscover/autodiscover.xml`
• `https://autodiscover.letsexchange.com/autodiscover/autodiscover.xml`

> For clients to be able to use DNS to locate Autodiscover, you need to create a DNS record that maps `autodiscover.domain.com` to the public IP address of the CAS or servers where the Autodiscover service is hosted.

As already mentioned, an Autodiscover SCP object is created for each CAS. These SCP objects contain an attribute called `ServiceBindingInformation` with the FQDN of the CAS in the form `https://excas1.letsexchange.com/autodiscover/autodiscover.xml`, for example, where `excas1.letsexchange.com` is the FQDN for one CAS as seen in the following screenshot:

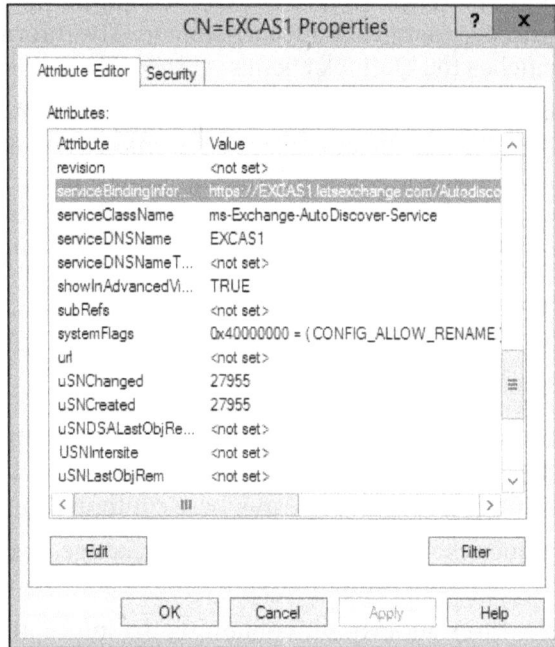

However, a valid SSL certificate is required for the predefined URL method; in this case, the certificate must include `excas1.letsexchange.com`. There are two ways of overcoming this: using a DNS SRV record or by updating the SCPs. Let us now explore how to do this.

In the first method, if Outlook is unable to contact the predefined URLs, it performs an additional check for a DNS SRV record. To use this method, an Autodiscover SRV record has to be created in the external DNS zone matching the domain of the user's SMTP address. For example, if a user has a primary SMTP address of `user@letsexchange.com`, the record must be created in the `letsexchange.com` external DNS zone. If an organization has multiple primary SMTP address domains, a record must be created in each zone:

1. In the external DNS zone(s), remove any CNAME or HOST (A) records associated with the Autodiscover service.

2. Create a new SRV record using the following parameters:

```
Service: _autodiscover
Protocol: _tcp
Port Number: 443
Host: mail.letsexchange.com
```

> In this example, `mail.letsexchange.com` is a name valid for the certificate used. Typically, this is the same DNS name used for OWA, Outlook Anywhere, and other services.

In this scenario, after failing to check the predefined URLs, Autodiscover uses DNS SRV lookup for `_autodiscover._tcp.letsexchange.com`, and then `mail.letsexchange.com` is returned. Outlook then continues with Autodiscover and a POST request is posted to `https://mail.letsexchange.com/autodiscover/autodiscover.xml`.

The second method is by updating the SCPs. To guarantee that Autodiscover is always available to users, load balancers should be configured with a VIP for the Autodiscover URL. By doing so, we guarantee that when clients try to resolve `autodiscover.domain.com`, they will never try to connect to a CAS that is not available. In order to achieve this, we need to update the Autodiscover SCPs so that they do not return servers' FQDNs but a generic name instead, which is as follows:

```
Get-ClientAccessServer | Set-ClientAccessServer
-AutoDiscoverServiceInternalUri "https://autodiscover.<domain.com>/
autodiscover/autodiscover.xml"
```

If you have worked extensively with Exchange and Autodiscover before, you might be wondering, "What about the internal and external URLs for the Autodiscover virtual directory? Surely these should also be configured and load balanced?" Actually, these URLs are not used for anything—this is why you do not see them pointing to the server's FQDN on a default installation as shown in the following screenshot:

As discussed previously, the `Set-ClientAccessServer` cmdlet is only used with the `AutoDiscoverServiceInternalUri` parameter to define the hostname that should be used by clients to look up Autodiscover information (for internal domain-joined clients) as well as DNS or SRV records for external clients.

So why are these parameters available for the Autodiscover virtual directory if they are not used? The reason is very simple: in the schema that defines Exchange virtual directory objects, `InternalURL` and `ExternalURL` are mandatory, so every object of this class must have these two attributes. While in previous versions of Exchange you could actually configure these attributes, in Exchange 2013 you cannot. If you try using the `Set-AutodiscoverVirtualDirectory` cmdlet to set them, you will receive an error saying those parameters do not exist.

After all these changes, we now need to make sure Autodiscover is actually working as expected. To do this, there are a few methods. For external tests, we can use the **Exchange Remote Connectivity Analyzer** website or the **Test E-Mail AutoConfiguration** feature of Outlook. For internal tests, we can use the latter and the `Test-OutlookWebServices` cmdlet. This cmdlet is typically the first test performed, as it provides detailed information both in successful and failed tests when used with the `Format-List` cmdlet as follows:

```
[=]                 Machine: EXCAS1.letsexchange.com          [-] [□] [X]
[PS] C:\>$cred = Get-Credential

cmdlet Get-Credential at command pipeline position 1
Supply values for the following parameters:
Credential
[PS] C:\>Test-OutlookWebServices Nuno -MailboxCredential $cred | F
T ServiceEndpoint, Scenario, Result -AutoSize

ServiceEndpoint                                   Scenario    Result
---------------                                   --------    ------
autodiscover.letsexchange.com AutoDiscoverOutlookProvider Success
mail.letsexchange.com              ExchangeWebServices Success
mail.letsexchange.com              AvailabilityService Success
mail.letsexchange.com              OfflineAddressBook Success


[PS] C:\>_
```

In the previous screenshot, we can see that the URLs provided by Autodiscover for various Exchange features are all using the same namespace as we configured earlier.

You will notice that the first scenario mentions `AutoDiscoverOutlookProvider`. Outlook providers are components that allow Autodiscover to function completely and are specifically related to the type of client that is trying to connect and be configured. When the CAS role is installed, by default, three providers are created and used to configure settings individually for internal Outlook clients (**EXCH**), Outlook Anywhere (**EXPR**), and OWA (**WEB**). When creating or refreshing an Outlook profile, a request is placed to the Autodiscover service that determines which provider needs to handle the request. While in Exchange 2007 and 2010 there was only one namespace we could configure, in Exchange 2013, we have both an internal and an external hostname for Outlook Anywhere: one for users connected to the corporate domain and another for external users. Due to this change, a new provider named **ExHTTP** was introduced. However, ExHTTP is not an actual provider, but a calculated set of values from the EXCH and EXPR settings that Outlook will process in order—internal first and external second.

At this stage, we just need to focus on the `CertPrincipalName` property of EXPR. This property specifies the SSL certificate principal name required when connecting externally using SSL. When this property is blank (which it is by default), Autodiscover will replace it with the server FQDN that the client is connecting to. When everything is configured to use a common namespace, such as `mail.domain.com`, and this hostname is the certificate's principal name, then no configuration is needed and everything works fine. However, if for example a wildcard certificate `*.domain.com` is used, then the value of `CertPrincipalName` will never match the certificate's principal name, which will cause issues to external Outlook clients. In this scenario, we need to run the following cmdlet to manually populate this property with the correct value:

```
Set-OutlookProvider EXPR -CertPrincipalName msstd:*.domain.com
```

> This is particularly important when the Outlook option **Only connect to proxy servers that have this principal name in their certificate** is selected.

Since the initial Autodiscover test was successful, Outlook itself should be able to locate the Autodiscover endpoint. Using the **Test E-Mail AutoConfiguration** feature, in the following screenshot, we can see that the URL `https://autodiscover.letsexchange.com/Autodiscover/Autodiscover.xml` was located by SCP and contacted successfully:

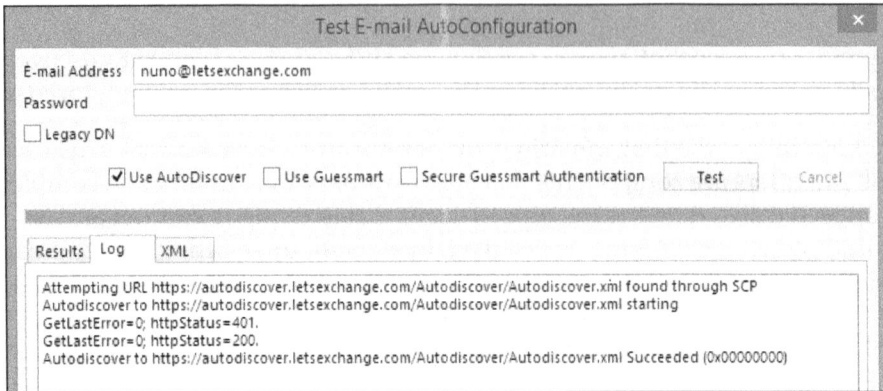

In the following screenshot, we can see all the details returned by Autodiscover, including all the services using the same namespace (**mail.letsexchange.com**) as previously configured in the load balancing section:

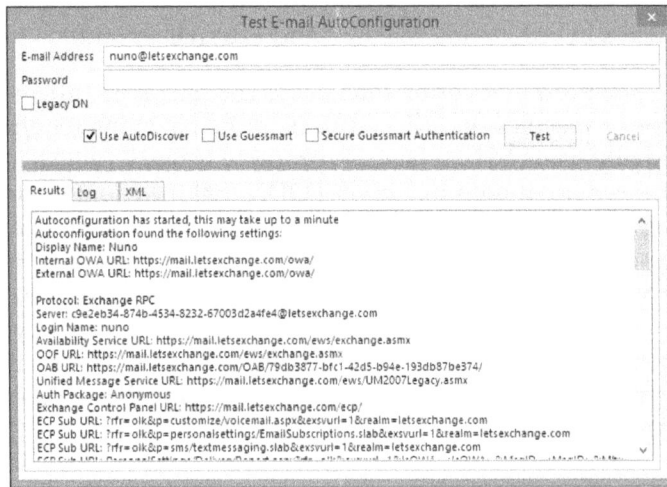

Explaining digital certificates for Exchange

A digital certificate (known in cryptography as a public key certificate) is an electronic document issued by a **Certification Authority** (**CA**) used to establish a user's or server's credentials when doing electronic transactions. It contains certain details such as a name, a serial number, expiration dates, a copy of the certificate holder's public key (used to encrypt messages and digital signatures), and the digital signature of the CA so that a recipient can verify that the certificate is real. Digital certificates provide a means of proving an identity just like a driver's license or a passport. The common use of a digital certificate is to verify that a user sending a message is who he/she claims to be and to provide the receiver with the means to encode a reply.

Secure Sockets Layer (**SSL**), and its successor **Transport Layer Security** (**TLS**), are the most common methods used to secure communications between servers and clients by the use of digital certificates, and Exchange makes extensive use of these.

When Exchange is installed, self-signed certificates installed on CAS and Mailbox servers are used so that all network communications are encrypted. "Self-signed" means that these certificates are only created and signed by the Exchange servers themselves. Because they are not signed by a largely trusted CA such as VeriSign or Thawte, they are only trusted by Exchange servers in the same organization and no other software. These certificates are enabled by default for all Exchange services and have a **Subject Alternative Name** (**SAN**) corresponding to the server name of where they are installed this can be seen in the following screenshot:

The self-signed certificate on Mailbox servers is used to automatically encrypt communications between the CAS and the Mailbox server out of the box. Because these certificates are trusted by CASs, a third-party certificate is not necessary on Mailbox servers. On the other hand, the self-signed certificate on CASs allows client protocols such as ActiveSync or OWA to use SSL for their communications. Many people claim that Outlook Anywhere will not work with a self-signed certificate on the CAS, but it will—it is just not supported. Even though other Exchange servers will automatically trust these certificates, if it's in the same organization, clients such as web browsers or mobile devices will not. When a client uses SSL to connect to a server and is presented with the server's self-signed certificate, it gets prompted to verify if a trusted authority issued the certificate. Only by confirming the trust can the SSL communication continue. As such, when using self-signed certificates, they should be copied to the client's trusted root certificate store to avoid this prompt.

For these reasons, CAS self-signed certificates are only intended to be temporary and should be replaced with ones that clients automatically trust, such as one from a public CA. If an organization has its own internal **Public Key Infrastructure (PKI)**, certificates issued by the PKI can be used if all clients trust this entity.

> To reiterate, self-signed certificates installed by default on the Mailbox servers do not need to be replaced with a trusted third-party certificate. The CASs automatically trust these certificates and no configuration is needed.

By default, the following services are all provided by a single website in IIS. Because a website can only have one certificate associated with it, all of these services use the same certificate on a given CAS. This means that all the names/URLs that clients use to access these services must be in the certificate if different namespaces such as the following are used:

- Outlook Web App
- Exchange Administration Center
- Exchange Web Services
- Exchange ActiveSync
- Outlook Anywhere
- Autodiscover
- Offline Address Book

The exceptions are the POP, IMAP, and SMTP services, which can use separate certificates. To simplify administration, it is recommended to use a single certificate for all these services including POP and IMAP. Each Receive Connector can also use a different certificate to secure the SMTP traffic with TLS. As with other services, contemplate using a single certificate that includes all names for which you have to support the TLS traffic.

> Many companies use an invalid (non-public/non-routable) namespace for their internal domain name, such as `letsexchange.local`, or a public domain name that they do not actually own and cannot use externally. The problem is that many CAs that provide SSL certificates are beginning to reject requests for these types of Subject Alternate Names. Since the beginning of 2014, CAs do not issue a `<domain>.local` certificate, as many have started to reject these since 2013. As a result, organizations will not be able to get a valid SSL certificate that allows `<domain>.local` as a SAN, causing possible issues for their Exchange deployment if measures are not taken beforehand.

The CA/Browser Forum, a collaborative effort between Certificate Authorities (companies such as DigiCert or Verisign that issue certificates) and Web Browsers (companies such as Google or Microsoft), has introduced new requirements for certificate issuance. As part of these new requirements, CAs must immediately begin to phase out the issuance of certificates issued to either the internal server names or reserved IP addresses and revoke any certificates containing internal names by October 2016. In addition, these requirements prevent CAs from issuing internal name certificates that expire after November 1, 2015. After 2015, it will be impossible to obtain a publicly trusted certificate for any hostname that cannot be externally verified.

For organizations that already have Exchange deployed in a `.local` domain, there are several alternatives: renaming the AD domain is an option, although not recommended; migrating to a new AD domain; using an internal PKI together with a certificate from a public CA; or probably the easiest option would be using PinPoint DNS Zones that are very similar to Split DNS but are easier to set up and greatly simplify the administrative effort needed to maintain records.

> Although not related to high availability, note that SSL Offloading (also known as SSL Acceleration) is not supported in Exchange 2013 at the time of writing this book. SSL Bridging (also known as Reverse SSL), on the other hand, is fully supported.

Listing best practices

There is no doubt that digital certificates play a major role in Exchange, and a proper configuration will save a lot of headaches. Their configuration will vary based on specific organizational needs, but there are some best practices that you should always follow, or at least, be aware of. They are as follows:

- Use a trusted third-party CA so that clients do not receive errors regarding untrusted certificates and to simplify administration as most clients will trust their root certificates out of the box. Nevertheless, you should always ensure that the CA you chose is trusted by your clients and that it also provides Unified Communications certificates for use with Exchange.

- Use SAN certificates. Subject to how Exchange service names are configured, Exchange might require a certificate that represents multiple domain names. Even though a wildcard certificate, such as `*.letsexchange.com`, can resolve this problem, not everyone is comfortable with the security implications of certificates that can be used for any subdomain. As a more secure alternative, list all the required domains as SANs in the certificate.

- Use the Exchange certificate wizard to help create the certificate request and ensure that all the required names for the certificate are requested. Some CAs also offer a period during which you can reissue a certificate with additional names at no extra cost.

- Use as few names as possible. Thanks to the new Exchange architecture, this is particularly true in a multi-site environment, as we will see in *Chapter 4, Achieving Site Resilience*. This is usually a topic that causes the most confusion around administrators, and is the reason why sometimes certificates are so expensive—they have more SANs than necessary. You do not need to include individual server hostnames in your certificate. The names that must be part of the certificate are the ones used by clients to connect to Exchange, such as `mail.<domain>.com` (which can be anything you want and can cover most connections to Exchange, including Outlook, OWA, OAB, POP3, IMAP4, EWS, SMTP, EAC, and ActiveSync), `autodiscover.<domain>.com` (which should always be present in this format), and `legacy.<domain>.com` (which is only required if you are transitioning from Exchange 2007 to 2013).

- Use as few certificates as possible. As discussed earlier, you should always use the same certificate on all CASs. This is especially important in a site resilience scenario, as we will see in *Chapter 4, Achieving Site Resilience*.

Summary

Achieving high availability for Client Access servers is a two-step process. First, you need to deploy multiple CASs, and second, you need to use a load balancing solution that best meets your organization's needs and requirements. This will significantly decrease, or even fully prevent, downtime and avoid single point of failures for this role.

With all the architectural changes made to Exchange 2013, Layer 4 load balancing is now a viable solution, and one that is more than adequate for most organizations. However, for some specific scenarios, Layer 7 might still be required due to its capabilities such as to analyze traffic as it passes through the load balancer.

Finally, it is crucial that certificates and Exchange services such as Autodiscover are correctly configured to take full advantage of the load balancer capabilities and Exchange availability features.

In the next chapter, we will explore high availability for the Mailbox server role, including all the changes and improvements introduced by Exchange 2013 over the earlier versions.

3
High Availability with the Mailbox Server

The Mailbox server role, similar to the Client Access Server (CAS) role, has undergone some great changes in Exchange 2013. While in Exchange 2010 this role basically provided for message storage, in 2013 it also includes components previously found in separate roles such as Transport service, Client Access protocols, and Unified Messaging components. Mailbox servers now host every component and protocol that renders, processes, and stores user data.

As mentioned in *Chapter 1, Getting Started*, Exchange 2013 is made up of two foundational blocks: Client Access array and Database Availability Group (DAG), each providing an element of fault tolerance and high availability, decoupled from each other.

In this chapter, we will explore how to achieve high availability with the Mailbox server in Exchange 2013. Although the way this is achieved is still through the deployment of one or more DAGs, this technology has slightly improved compared to Exchange 2010.

Before we delve into DAGs, let us first go through some other improvements and new features of Exchange 2013 that are relevant to availability.

Reducing input/output operations per second

Although not directly related to high availability, the reduction in **I/O operations per second (IOPS)** introduced in Exchange 2013 influences the levels of availability provided by an Exchange deployment.

Passive database copies in Exchange 2010 had a checkpoint depth of only 5 MB to ensure a fast failover (a log of checkpoint depth is used to guarantee that log/database cache changes are written faster to the database). Additionally, passive copies performed pre-reading of data aggressively to keep up with the 5 MB checkpoint depth. This caused the IOPS of passive database copies to be the same as the IOPS of active database copies. On the other hand, Exchange 2013 is capable of providing a fast failover, though it uses a high checkpoint depth of 100 MB on passive database copies. As such, Microsoft was able to de-tune passive database copies such that they are not so aggressive. As a result of both these changes, the IOPS of passive database copies are now about 50 percent of the active database copies.

This change also has an impact on availability. In Exchange 2010, when performing a failover, the database cache would get flushed as the database transitioned from a passive to an active copy. However, the **Extensible Storage Engine** (ESE) log was rewritten in Exchange 2013, so the cache is persistent throughout this transition. Because the cache no longer needs to be flushed (as it needs to be during transition), a faster failover is achieved.

Another change is in regard to background database maintenance. While in Exchange 2010, background database maintenance was performed at approximately 5 MB per second per copy; this has now been throttled down to 1 MB per second per copy, providing a 50 percent IOPS reduction over Exchange 2010.

Automatically recovering after storage failures

Exchange 2013 further improves the bug check behavior introduced in Exchange 2010 by including features that allow for self-recovery when certain failures happen. It now checks for excessive memory use by the Replication service and long I/O times, among other checks.

As an example, because the Crimson channel is a crucial component for normal operations, the Replication service checks every 30 seconds if it can be accessed. If the Crimson channel is not available, maybe due to a failure with the event channel for example, the Replication service tries to recover the server by rebooting it, which triggers a failover.

> Windows Server 2012 has two categories of event logs: the traditional Windows logs that include the usual Application, Security, and System event logs, and Applications and Services. Applications and Services logs are a new category of event logs used to store events from a single component or application, such as Exchange in this case. This new category is referred to as an application's **Crimson channel**.

In Exchange 2010, the following recovery mechanisms were included to provide enhanced resilience:

Name	Check	Action	Threshold
Database hung I/O detection	Outstanding I/Os	A failure item is generated in the Crimson channel so the server gets restarted	4 minutes
Crimson channel heartbeat	Guarantees that failure items can both be read from and written to the Crimson channel	The replication service heartbeats the Crimson channel and restarts the server if the heartbeat fails	30 seconds
System disk heartbeat	Checks the system disk state	Sends unbuffered I/O regularly to the system disk; server is restarted if heartbeat times out	2 minutes

Exchange 2013 includes new important checks for other events, further enhancing resilience and high availability:

Name	Check	Action	Threshold
System bad state	Threads cannot be scheduled	Server is restarted	302 seconds
Long I/O times	Measures I/O latency	Server is restarted	41 seconds
Memory use by the replication service	Measures the `MSExchangeRepl.exe` working set	• Event 4395 is logged in the Crimson channel with a request to terminate service • `MSExchangeRepl.exe` is terminated • If termination fails, server is restarted	4 GB
Bus reset (System Event 129)	Checks System Event log for event 129	Server is restarted	When event occurs

Managed Store

The Exchange Store service in Exchange 2013 has been rewritten in such a way that each database now runs under its own process, thus preventing store issues to affect all databases in the server. **Managed Store** is the new name for the rewritten Information Store process (`store.exe`). It is now written in C#, designed to enable a more granular management of resources (additional I/O reduction, for example) and is even more integrated with the Exchange Replication service (`MSExchangeRepl.exe`), in order to provide a higher level of availability.

The database engine continues to be ESE, but the mailbox database schema itself has changed in order to provide many optimizations.

The Managed Store is composed of two processes. The first one is the **Store Worker Process** (`Microsoft.Exchange.Store.Worker.exe`) that is similar to the old `store.exe` process. The difference is, as already mentioned, that there is one Store Worker Process for each database. This means that if one of these processes fails, only the database it is responsible for will be affected, while all the other databases will remain operational.

The second one is the **Store Service Process** (`Microsoft.Exchange.Store.Service.exe`) that controls all store worker processes. For example, when a database is mounted, the store service process will start a new store worker process for that particular database. On the other hand, when a database is dismounted, it will terminate the store worker process responsible for that database.

Managed Store is now integrated with the FAST search engine (the same used in SharePoint 2013), instead of the Exchange 2010 multi-mailbox search infrastructure provided by MS-Search. This new search engine provides consistent and more robust indexing and searching mechanisms across Microsoft servers.

In Exchange 2010, a single process made memory management easier. Exchange 2013 has a dedicated worker process for each database, and it is now possible to have both active and passive databases not just on the same server but also on the same volume (a feature named multiple databases per volume). Therefore, the memory cache management had to change and become more intelligent about the way memory is allocated to cache management. It first looks at the number of databases on the server, adds a property called "maximum active databases", looks at the number of active and passive databases, and then uses these values to calculate the amount of memory. Because the cache target is calculated at service startup and not dynamically reconfigured on the fly, any substantial database changes, such as adding or removing databases, will require a restart of the services to ensure that the cache is reflective of the actual number of active/passive databases. Therefore, the following message is presented when, for example, a new database is added:

warning

Please restart the Microsoft Exchange Information Store
service on server EXAIO after adding new mailbox databases.

ok

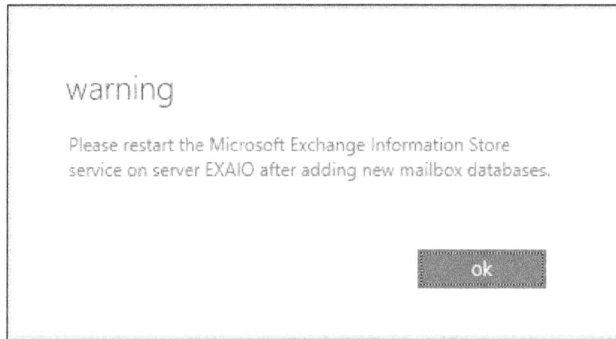

Automatic Reseed

Although DAGs are probably the best improvement made to Exchange in terms
of availability, not every organization can afford to deploy multiple servers to
accommodate database copies. Most of the time, the issue is the extra storage
required and not so much the servers themselves. For these organizations, **Automatic
Reseed** in Exchange 2013, or simply **AutoReseed**, might be a good alternative.

When using DAGs, if the disk hosting an active database copy fails, Exchange fails
over that database to another server. Then, an administrator typically replaces the
failed disk and reseeds the database back to the server where the failure occurred.
Of course, it is assumed that there is no resilience at the storage level, by using either
enterprise-level storage or **Redundant Array of Independent Disks (RAID)**, which
automatically overcomes this particular scenario.

The sole purpose of AutoReseed is to avoid this situation by automatically restoring
database redundancy through the use of spare disks specifically provisioned for
AutoReseed. This becomes important especially now that Exchange is further
optimized for large disks by supporting multiple databases per volume. AutoReseed
involves the use of mount points to use volumes for the database(s) and to perform a
reseed in case of a failure. In most scenarios, the following steps can be performed:

1. Mount the volumes intended for databases, as well as spare volumes used
   for reseed, under one mount point, for example `C:\ExchangeVolumes`.

2. Mount the databases' root directories as another mount point, for example
   `C:\ExchangeDatabases`. Now, create two separate directories for each
   database: one for log files and another for the database itself.

3. Configure the following DAG properties for AutoReseed:
   `AutoDagVolumesRootFolderPath`, `AutoDagDatabasesRootFolderPath`,
   and `AutoDagDatabaseCopiesPerVolume`.

4. Create the database(s).

The process flow of AutoReseed is as follows:

1. The replication service checks periodically for database copies in a FailedAndSuspended state.

2. If a database copy is in the FailedAndSuspended state for 15 consecutive minutes, Exchange tries to resume the database copy up to three times, waiting five minutes between each attempt. If the resume actions do not bring the database copy to a healthy state, the workflow continues.

3. AutoReseed performs a variety of pre-requisite checks, such as verifying if there are any spare drives available if the database and logs are configured on the same volume and checking that nothing might prevent Exchange from performing a database reseed.

4. If all the preceding checks pass successfully, the Replication service tries to allocate and remap a spare volume up to five times, waiting one hour between each attempt.

5. AutoReseed now performs an InPlaceSeed check using the SafeDeleteExistingFiles seeding switch up to five times, waiting one hour between each attempt.

6. Once the reseed operation is over, the Replication service verifies if the new seeded copy is healthy.

> Notice that in step 4, when AutoReseed remaps a spare drive from a Windows and Exchange perspective, the affected database is still located in the same folder path as before (remember that mount points are being used). For this reason, Exchange will simply start reseeding the database back to its original location.

All that the administrators now need to do is simply replace the failed disk and reconfigure it as a spare for AutoReseed.

Let us consider a basic scenario with one database:

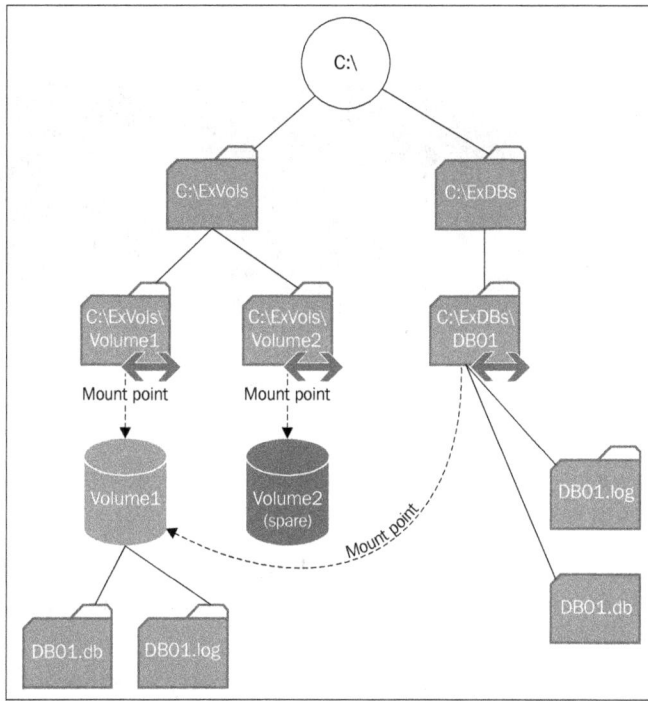

There are two volumes for this scenario:

- **Volume1** hosts database DB01
- **Volume2** is the spare drive

> It is perfectly normal to use several volumes as well as multiple databases per volume. AutoReseed limits were increased from four to eight databases per volume in CU1.

For this demonstration, we have one DAG with two members: servers **EXMBX1** and **EXMBX2** (without databases):

```
                    Machine: EXMBX1.letsexchange.com         [ - ] [ □ ] [ X ]

[PS] C:\>
[PS] C:\>Get-DatabaseAvailabilityGroup -Status

Name                    Member Servers              Operational Servers
_____                _____             _____
DAG1                    {EXMBX2, EXMBX1}            {EXMBX1, EXMBX2}


[PS] C:\>
```

Next, we configure server **EXMBX1** with two new disks named Volume1 (E:) and Volume2 (F:).

As mentioned previously, to configure AutoReseed we need to first configure three new DAG properties introduced in Exchange 2013:

- The AutoDagVolumesRootFolderPath property specifies which mount point will contain the volumes for databases and spares. The default is `C:\ExchangeVolumes`.

- The AutoDagDatabasesRootFolderPath property specifies which mount point will contain the databases. The default is `C:\ExchangeDatabases`.

- The AutoDagDatabaseCopiesPerVolume property specifies how many database copies we will be using per volume.

> Not all of a particular DAG's databases need to be located in the folders. However, AutoReseed only works with databases that are configured in these folders.

To configure these properties, the `Set-DatabaseAvailabilityGroup` cmdlet is used:

```
                    Machine: EXMBX1.letsexchange.com         [ - ] [ □ ] [ X ]

[PS] C:\>
[PS] C:\>Set-DatabaseAvailabilityGroup DAG1 -AutoDagDatabasesRoot
FolderPath "C:\ExDBs" -AutoDagVolumesRootFolderPath "C:\ExVols" -
AutoDagDatabaseCopiesPerVolume 1
[PS] C:\>
[PS] C:\>
```

Configuring folders for databases and volumes

In this step, we will create the root folders that will hold the databases and volumes:

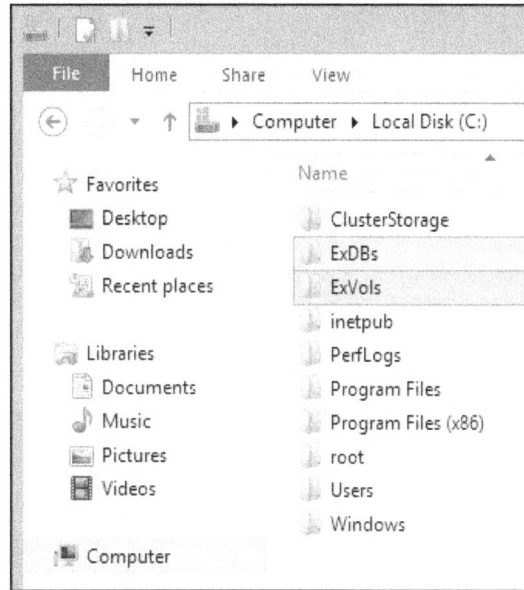

Mounting volume folders

Now we will mount each volume in a mounted folder under `C:\ExVols`. In this case, because only two volumes are being used, we need to create two folders with the names `Volume1` and `Volume2`, as shown in the following screenshot:

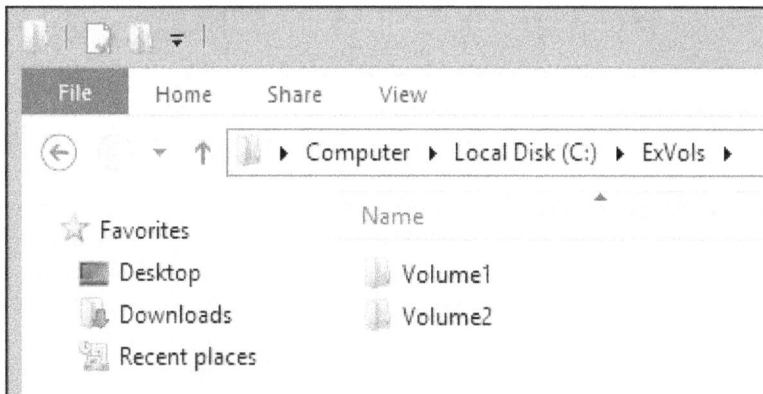

In order to mount the volumes into these two folders, perform the following steps:

1. Open the Windows Disk Management service (`diskmgmt.msc`) using the **Run** command (Windows key + *R*).

2. We start with **Volume1** by right-clicking on the volume and selecting **Change Drive Letter and Paths...**, as shown in the following screenshot:

3. Click on **Add...**, as shown in the following screenshot:

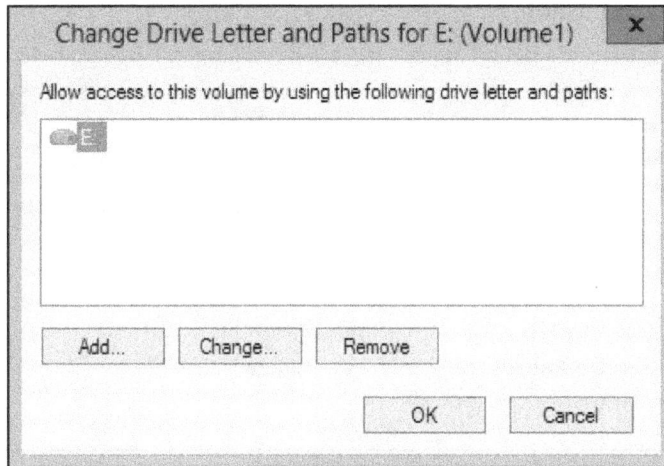

4. Click on **Browse...** and then navigate to the **Volume1** location, as shown in the following screenshot. Click on **OK** twice.

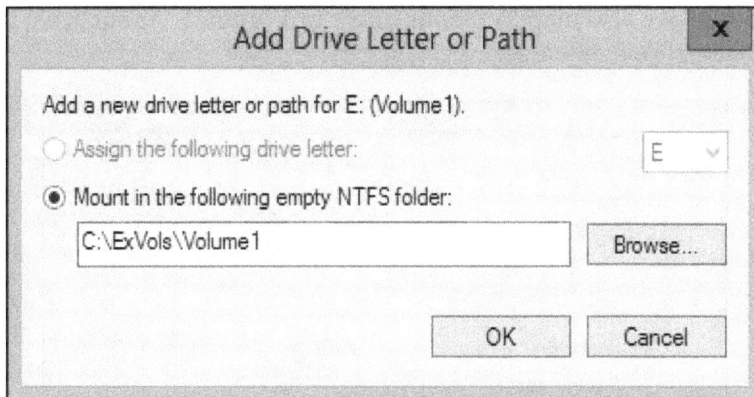

After doing the same for **Volume2**, both folders should be displayed with different icons, showing they are now configured as mount points, as shown in the following screenshot:

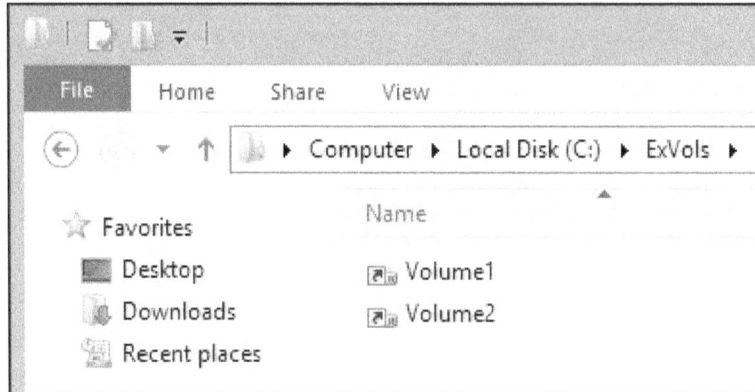

Mounting database folders

Now we need to configure the database folder. Since we are only dealing with a single database, we also map `C:\ExDBs\DB01` to **Volume1**. As such, we first create the folder `C:\ExDBs\DB01`:

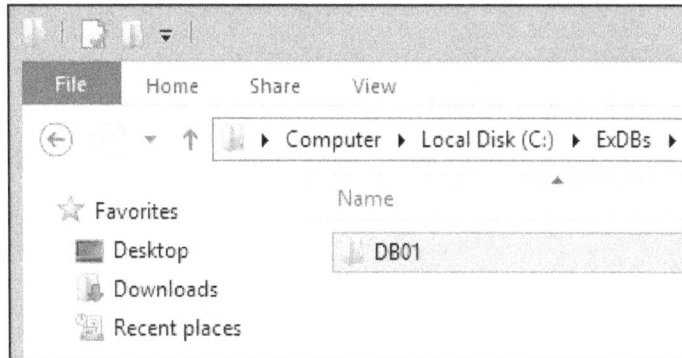

This time, instead of mapping the folder to **Volume1** using Windows Disk Management, let's use the `MountVol.exe` tool. Running `mountvol` from a command prompt lists all the volumes available to mount, as shown in the following screenshot:

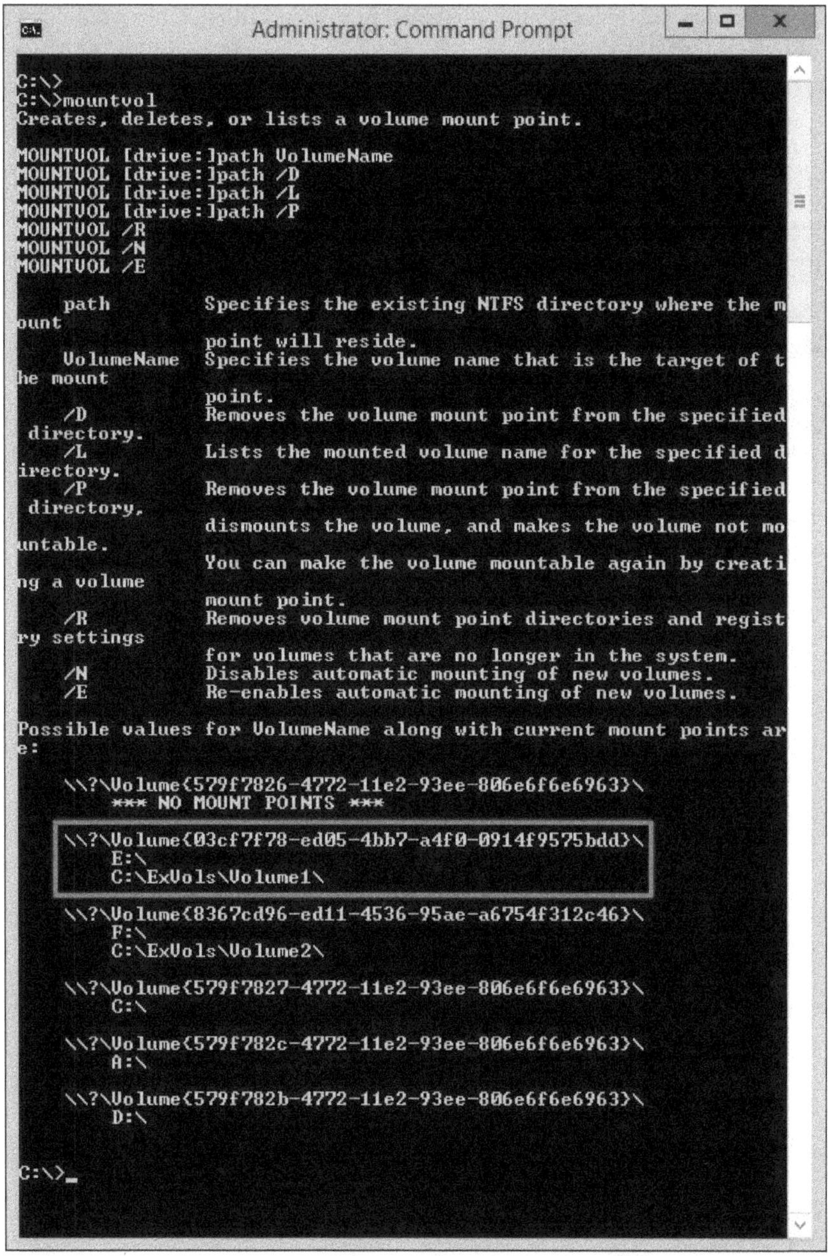
Administrator: Command Prompt
C:\>
C:\>mountvol
Creates, deletes, or lists a volume mount point.
MOUNTVOL [drive:]path VolumeName
MOUNTVOL [drive:]path /D
MOUNTVOL [drive:]path /L
MOUNTVOL [drive:]path /P
MOUNTVOL /R
MOUNTVOL /N
MOUNTVOL /E
path Specifies the existing NTFS directory where the mount
point will reside.
VolumeName Specifies the volume name that is the target of the mount
point.
/D Removes the volume mount point from the specified directory.
/L Lists the mounted volume name for the specified directory.
/P Removes the volume mount point from the specified directory,
dismounts the volume, and makes the volume not mountable.
You can make the volume mountable again by creating a volume
mount point.
/R Removes volume mount point directories and registry settings
for volumes that are no longer in the system.
/N Disables automatic mounting of new volumes.
/E Re-enables automatic mounting of new volumes.
Possible values for VolumeName along with current mount points are:
\\?\Volume{579f7826-4772-11e2-93ee-806e6f6e6963}\
*** NO MOUNT POINTS ***
\\?\Volume{03cf7f78-ed05-4bb7-a4f0-0914f9575bdd}\
E:\
C:\ExVols\Volume1\
\\?\Volume{8367cd96-ed11-4536-95ae-a6754f312c46}\
F:\
C:\ExVols\Volume2\
\\?\Volume{579f7827-4772-11e2-93ee-806e6f6e6963}\
C:\
\\?\Volume{579f782c-4772-11e2-93ee-806e6f6e6963}\
A:\
\\?\Volume{579f782b-4772-11e2-93ee-806e6f6e6963}\
D:\
C:\>

For this scenario, we know the volume we are interested in is \\?\Volume{03cf7f78-ed05-4bb7-a4f0-0914f9575bdd}\ as the folder Volume1 is mounted to it. To mount C:\ExDBs\DB01 to this volume as well, we need to run the command shown in the following screenshot:

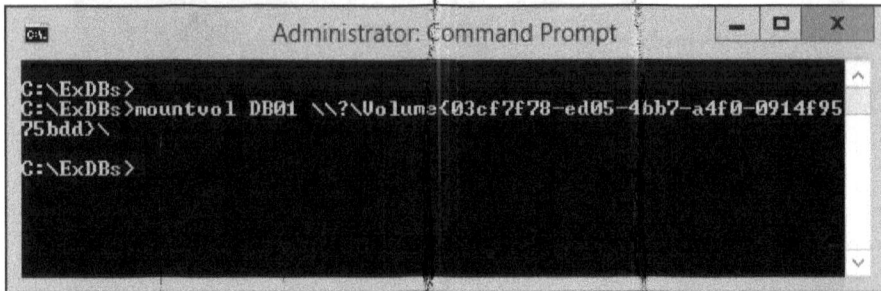

The folder icon of C:\ExDBs\DB01 should now have changed to reflect that it is now configured as a mount point, as shown in the following screenshot:

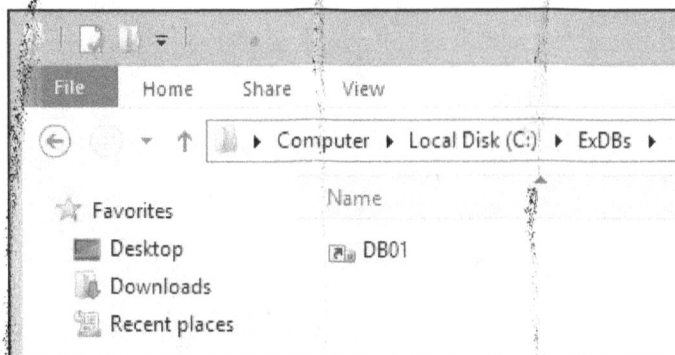

If we list the mounted volume names for this folder, we see that **DB01** is mounted to **Volume1**, as shown in the following screenshot:

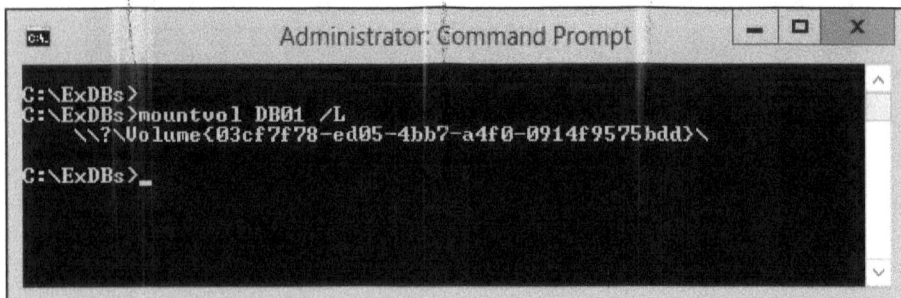

Running `mountvol` again should show that **Volume1** is also mounted to this folder, as highlighted in the following screenshot:

```
Possible values for VolumeName along with current mount points ar
e:

    \\?\Volume{579f7826-4772-11e2-93ee-806e6f6e6963}\
        *** NO MOUNT POINTS ***

    \\?\Volume{03cf7f78-ed05-4bb7-a4f0-0914f9575bdd}\
        E:\
        C:\ExVols\Volume1\
        C:\ExDBs\DB01\

    \\?\Volume{8367cd96-ed11-4536-95ae-a6754f312c46}\
        F:\
        C:\ExVols\Volume2\

    \\?\Volume{579f7827-4772-11e2-93ee-806e6f6e6963}\
        C:\

    \\?\Volume{579f782c-4772-11e2-93ee-806e6f6e6963}\
        A:\

    \\?\Volume{579f782b-4772-11e2-93ee-806e6f6e6963}\
        D:\

C:\ExDBs>
```

Creating a database directory structure

Now we need to create the directories to be used to keep the database files: one for the log files and another for the database itself. When configuring more than one database per volume, the folders are all created here; two folders per database. We can create both of these folders by navigating either to C:\ExDBs\DB01 or to **Volume1** (E:\ in this case) since both point to the same volume, as seen in the following screenshot:

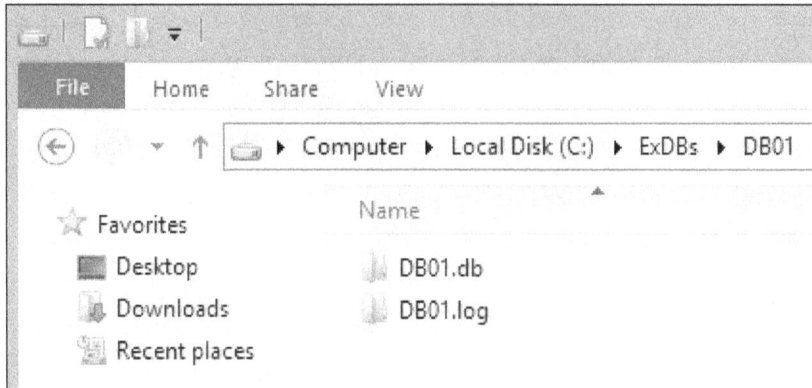

Creating a mailbox database

Finally, we create the database and configure it to use the appropriate folders with the help of commands, as shown in the following screenshot:

After the database is mounted, we add a copy on the server **EXMBX2** and make sure it is healthy by running the appropriate commands, as shown in the following screenshot:

Checking the database creation

As the data is actually stored in **Volume1**, the `C:\ExDBs folder` in **EXMBX1** should not take up any space, as seen in the following screenshot:

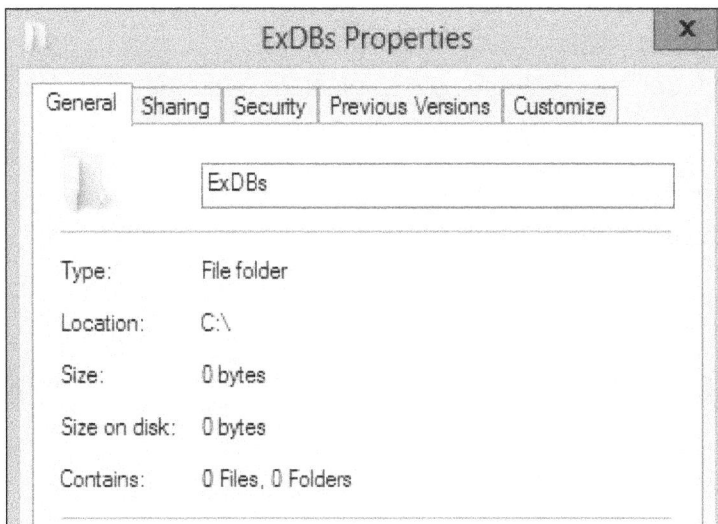

On the other hand, if we check the same folder on **EXMBX2**, it will be quite different as we did not configure AutoReseed on EXMBX2. As such, Exchange keeps all the files in the actual folder, `C:\ExDBs`. This is absolutely fine, but it means that a drive failure on EXMBX2 affecting the folder might affect the database. The properties of the `ExDBs` folder are shown in the following screenshot:

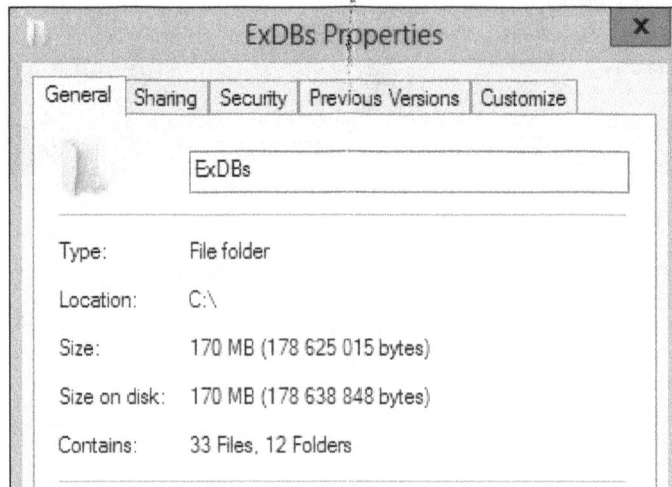

Testing AutoReseed

To check if AutoReseed is working as expected, we take **Volume1** offline, hopefully making Exchange automatically failover DB01 to EXMBX2 and making AutoReseed start reseeding DB01 into the spare volume configured in EXMBX1.

In order to take the disk offline, we can use Windows Disk Management. Simply right-click on **Disk 1** and select **Offline**. The result is shown in the following screenshot:

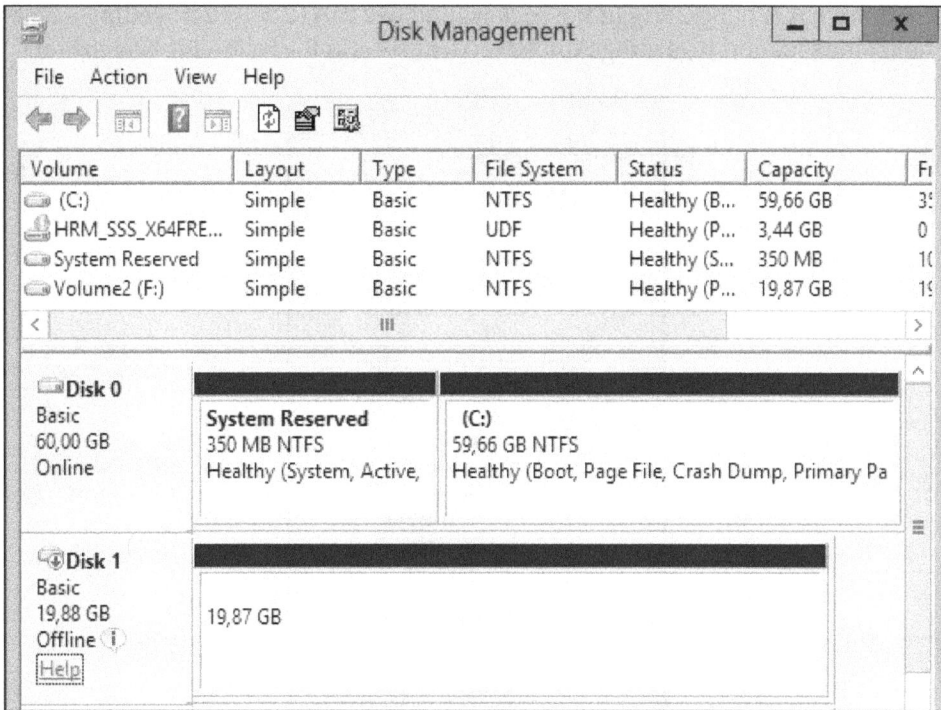

At this stage, Exchange should immediately failover DB01 to EXMBX2. This can be verified by entering a command, as shown in the following screenshot:

To monitor what is happening in the background, we can look in the Seeding event log that holds information regarding AutoReseed, as seen in the following screenshot:

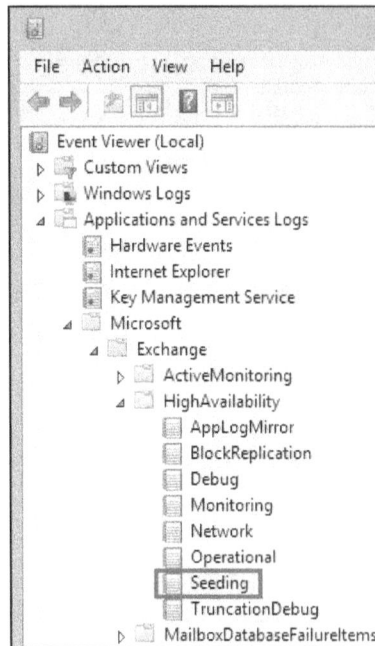

After AutoReseed detects the failed disk, an event showing the reseed starts, as seen in the following screenshot:

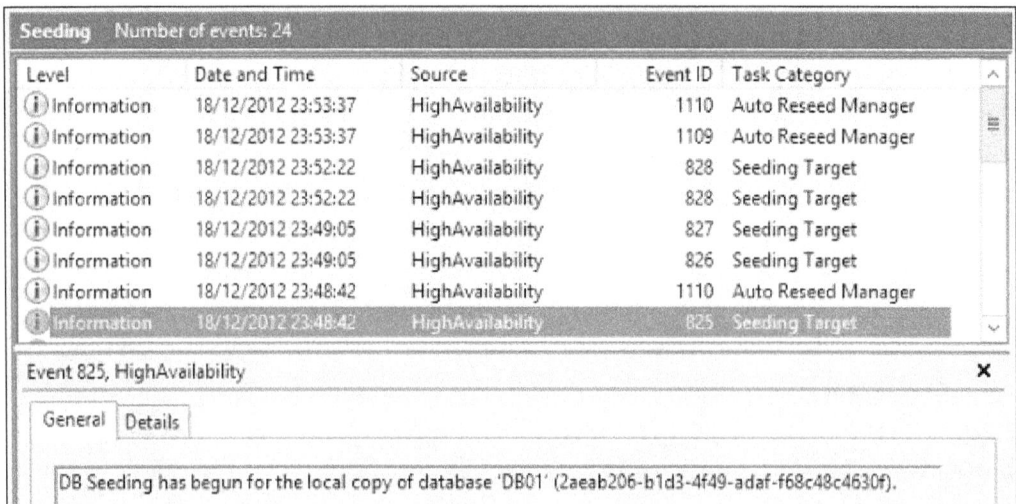

As soon as the reseed completes, another event starts and a message showing that the seeding has been completed is displayed, as seen in the following screenshot:

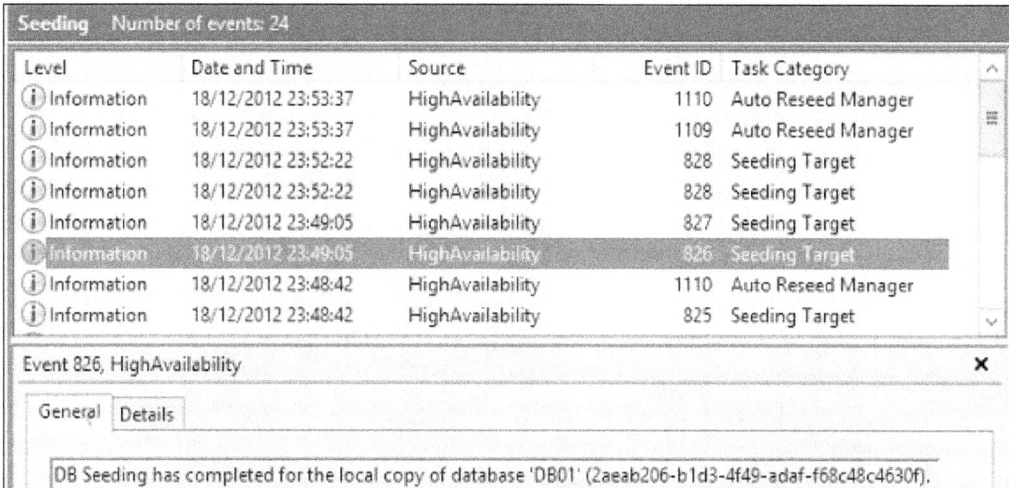

Seeding	Number of events: 24				
Level	Date and Time	Source	Event ID	Task Category	
ⓘ Information	18/12/2012 23:53:37	HighAvailability	1110	Auto Reseed Manager	∧
ⓘ Information	18/12/2012 23:53:37	HighAvailability	1109	Auto Reseed Manager	≡
ⓘ Information	18/12/2012 23:52:22	HighAvailability	828	Seeding Target	
ⓘ Information	18/12/2012 23:52:22	HighAvailability	828	Seeding Target	
ⓘ Information	18/12/2012 23:49:05	HighAvailability	827	Seeding Target	
ⓘ Information	18/12/2012 23:49:05	HighAvailability	826	Seeding Target	
ⓘ Information	18/12/2012 23:48:42	HighAvailability	1110	Auto Reseed Manager	
ⓘ Information	18/12/2012 23:48:42	HighAvailability	825	Seeding Target	∨

Event 826, HighAvailability   ✕

General | Details

DB Seeding has completed for the local copy of database 'DB01' (2aeab206-b1d3-4f49-adaf-f68c48c4630f).

A final event displaying the successful creation of a healthy copy is seen in the following screenshot:

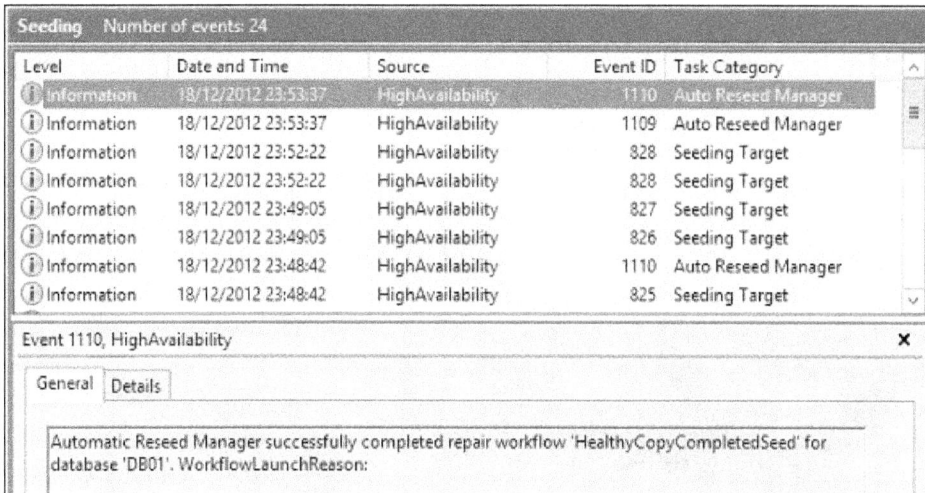

Seeding	Number of events: 24				
Level	Date and Time	Source	Event ID	Task Category	
ⓘ Information	18/12/2012 23:53:37	HighAvailability	1110	Auto Reseed Manager	∧
ⓘ Information	18/12/2012 23:53:37	HighAvailability	1109	Auto Reseed Manager	≡
ⓘ Information	18/12/2012 23:52:22	HighAvailability	828	Seeding Target	
ⓘ Information	18/12/2012 23:52:22	HighAvailability	828	Seeding Target	
ⓘ Information	18/12/2012 23:49:05	HighAvailability	827	Seeding Target	
ⓘ Information	18/12/2012 23:49:05	HighAvailability	826	Seeding Target	
ⓘ Information	18/12/2012 23:48:42	HighAvailability	1110	Auto Reseed Manager	
ⓘ Information	18/12/2012 23:48:42	HighAvailability	825	Seeding Target	∨

Event 1110, HighAvailability   ✕

General | Details

Automatic Reseed Manager successfully completed repair workflow 'HealthyCopyCompletedSeed' for database 'DB01'. WorkflowLaunchReason:

As mentioned previously, Exchange will try to allocate and remap a spare drive. At this stage, if we check where `C:\ExDBs\DB01` is mapped to, we should see that it is no longer **Volume1** but **Volume2**, as highlighted in the following screenshot:

```
                    Administrator: Command Prompt              _ □ X

Possible values for VolumeName along with current mount points ar
e:

    \\?\Volume{579f7826-4772-11e2-93ee-806e6f6e6963}\
        *** NO MOUNT POINTS ***

    \\?\Volume{8367cd96-ed11-4536-95ae-a6754f312c46}\
        F:\
        C:\ExVols\Volume2\
        C:\ExDBs\DB01\

    \\?\Volume{579f7827-4772-11e2-93ee-806e6f6e6963}\
        C:\

    \\?\Volume{579f782c-4772-11e2-93ee-806e6f6e6963}\
        A:\

    \\?\Volume{579f782b-4772-11e2-93ee-806e6f6e6963}\
        D:\

C:\ExDBs>
C:\ExDBs>mountvol DB01 /L
    \\?\Volume{8367cd96-ed11-4536-95ae-a6754f312c46}\

C:\ExDBs>_
```

As AutoReseed remaps the drive from a Windows and Exchange perspective, database `DB01` is located in the exact same place as before (remember we are using mount points). As such, Exchange starts reseeding the database to its "original" location after a few seconds, which should take the database copy to a healthy state again:

```
                    Machine: EXMBX1.letsexchange.com            _ □ X

[PS] C:\>
[PS] C:\>Get-MailboxDatabaseCopyStatus DB01 | FT -AutoSize

Name           Status            CopyQueueLength ReplayQueueLength
----           ------            --------------- -----------------
DB01\EXMBX1 FailedAndSuspended 9                 0
DB01\EXMBX2 Mounted            0                 0


[PS] C:\>Get-MailboxDatabaseCopyStatus DB01 | FT -AutoSize

Name        Status  CopyQueueLength ReplayQueueLength LastInspec
                                                      tedLogTime
----        ------  --------------- ----------------- ----------
DB01\EXMBX1 Healthy 0               0                 18/12/2...
DB01\EXMBX2 Mounted 0               0

[PS] C:\>
```

In the following screenshot, we can see the database files are automatically reseeded by Exchange:

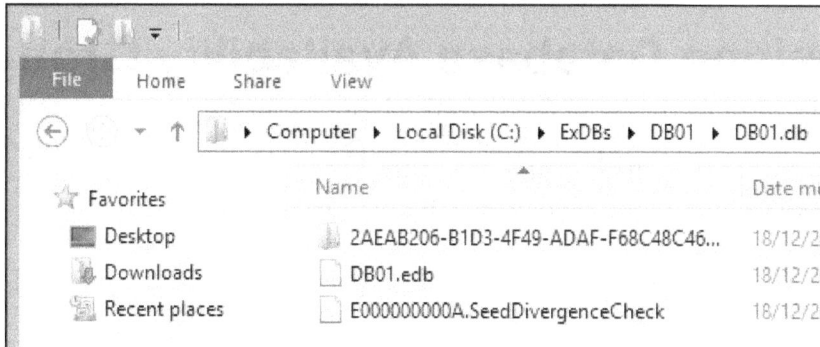

During the entire process, user experience is identical to any failover or switchover; users will momentarily be disconnected from their mailbox, but will also get connected again straight away.

The following diagram shows how everything looks at this stage for this scenario:

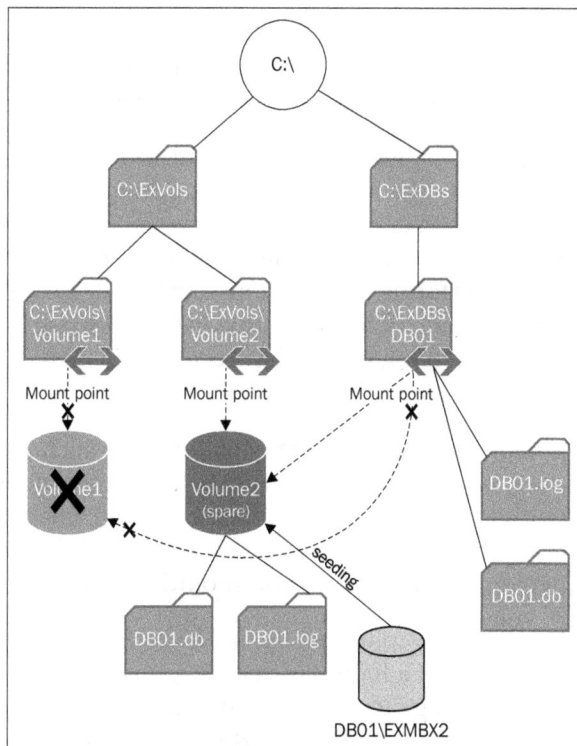

All that needs to be done is to replace the failed disk and configure it as a spare for AutoReseed.

Revisiting Database Availability Groups

Despite the obvious change in configuring a DAG through the Exchange Admin Center versus using the old Exchange Management Console, configuring a DAG in Exchange 2013 is virtually the same as in 2010. However, some improvements have been introduced to this technology, which is worth covering here.

> Note that both Exchange 2013 Standard and Enterprise features can be used for DAGs and that a DAG can contain a mix of both. However, each DAG member must be running the exact same operating system, either Windows Server 2008 R2 or Windows Server 2012.

Best copy selection changes

A critical component of any DAG is **Active Manager**, part of the Microsoft Exchange Replication service, which runs on all Mailbox servers and is responsible for managing DAGs and database copies. While there is only the Standalone Active Manager role for non-DAG members, there are two roles, namely the **Primary Active Manager** (**PAM**) and the **Standby Active Manager** (**SAM**) for DAG members.

PAM decides which database copies should be active and which should be passive, is responsible for collecting change notifications regarding the topology, and takes the necessary actions during server failures. The server holding the PAM role is always the DAG member which owns the cluster quorum resource (default cluster group) at that time. It also performs the functions, such as detecting local failures of databases and Information Store, of the SAM role. If the PAM server fails, its role is automatically moved to a surviving server that becomes the new PAM server and owns the cluster quorum resource.

SAM provides information to other Exchange components, such as the Transport or Client Access services, regarding which server is hosting the active copy of a database. It also detects local failures of databases and Information Store. If a database is replicated and is affected by a failure, it asks the PAM to initiate a failover (it does not decide where the database should be failed over to).

The Replication service regularly monitors the health of ESE for any I/O problems as well all mounted databases. If a failure is detected, it notifies the Active Manager that determines the database copy to be mounted, what is required to mount it, tracks the new database active copy, and provides this information to the CAS.

Whenever the active copy of a replicated database fails, Active Manager tries to select the best passive copy of the failed database to be activated. This process was called **Best Copy Selection (BCS)** in Exchange 2010, but it is now called **Best Copy and Server Selection (BCSS)** and takes the following steps:

1. A failure is detected or a targetless switchover is initiated.

2. PAM runs the Best Copy and Server Selection algorithm.

3. The **Attempt Copy Last Logs (ACLL)** process attempts to copy any possible missing log files from the server previously hosting the active database copy.

4. After the ACLL process finishes, the copy queue length of the database about to be activated is compared to the AutoDatabaseMountDial value of the servers hosting the copies of the database. One of the following steps is taken depending on the value of the missing logs:

    ° If there are same or less number of missing logs than the value of AutoDatabaseMountDial, step 5 occurs

    ° If there are more missing logs than the value of AutoDatabaseMountDial, Active Manager tries to activate the next best copy available (if any)

5. PAM requests the Managed Store to mount the database and either of the following two events happen:

    ° The database gets mounted and is made available to users

    ° The database does not get mounted and PAM goes through steps 3 and 4 for the next best copy (as long as there is one available)

> PAM knows how many active databases there are per server, so that during the BCSS process it ensures that the value of MaximumActiveDatabases, if configured, is honored. This change allows the servers already hosting the maximum amount of active databases to be excluded by Active Manager when determining potential candidates for activation.

The old BCS process assessed several database copy aspects in order to determine the best copy to be activated. This included database status, replay and copy queue length, and content index status. Active Manager in Exchange 2013 goes through the same BCS checks, but it also includes four new health checks to evaluate protocol health (something that Exchange 2010 did not do) in the following order:

1. **All Healthy**: This determines if all the server's monitoring components are in a healthy state.

2. **Up to Normal Healthy**: This determines if all the server's monitoring components, with a priority of normal, are in a healthy state.

3. **All Better than Source**: This determines if any of the server's monitoring components is in a better state than the server hosting the affected copy.

4. **Same as Source**: This determines if any of the server's monitoring components is in the same state as the server hosting the affected copy.

In case BCSS is invoked because of a failed component, such as OWA, an extra requirement is set: the health of the component (OWA) on the target server has to be better than its health on the server where the failover occurred.

Besides failure of protocols, when it comes to database failures, Active Manager still goes through the same checks as in Exchange 2010. It starts the best copy selection process by listing the potential database copy candidates for activation, ignoring any that are unreachable or blocked from activation. The list is then sorted based on each database's AutoDatabaseMountDial property. Next, it goes through the list and excludes any that are not in a Healthy, DisconnectedAndHealthy, DisconnectedAndResynchronizing, or SeedingSource state, and evaluates their activation potential by using the same criteria as Exchange 2010: database copy status, copy/replay queue length, and content index status. If no database copies meeting the criteria can be found, Active Manager is unable to activate a database copy automatically.

The DAG Management Service

Exchange 2013 Release To Manufacturing (RTM) Cumulative Update 2 introduced a new service for DAG members named **Microsoft Exchange DAG Management Service** (`MSExchangeDAGMgmt`). This service has DAG monitoring features that were part of the Replication service and it is used to track failovers, provide information on health status and logging events, and leaves the Replication service to deal with replicating transactions between mailbox servers within the DAG. Although logging is now part of this new service, events remain to be written to the Application Event Log using the same Crimson channel and still using `MSExchangeRepl` as the source.

The DAG network auto-configuration

The first DAG networks in Exchange 2010 were created based on the subnets the Cluster service found. In deployments with multiple networks and where interfaces for a specific network (such as a MAPI network) were on the same subnet, there was not much additional configuration needed. On the other hand, in a deployment where interfaces for a specific network were on multiple subnets, an additional task known as **collapsing DAG networks** had to be performed. In Exchange 2013, this is no longer required as it still uses the same detection methods to distinguish between Replication and MAPI networks, but it now collapses DAG networks automatically.

DAG network properties can only be viewed in the Exchange Admin Center (EAC) after configuring the DAG for manual network configuration by enabling the **Configure database availability group networks manually** option, as seen in the following screenshot:

Alternatively, the `Set-DatabaseAvailabilityGroup` cmdlet can be used to set the `ManualDagNetworkConfiguration` parameter to `$True`.

Using either method to enable manual DAG network configuration allows administrators to perform the following functions:

- Add or remove DAG networks
- Exclude iSCSI or other networks (for example, a dedicated network for backups)
- Disable replication on the MAPI network (optional)

Although this auto configuration is useful, similar to Exchange 2010, it is still very important to ensure each NIC is configured based on the use it is intended for (MAPI or Replication). For example, while the MAPI network is DNS-registered, the Replication network is not; in a multi-subnet environment, the MAPI network has a default gateway while the Replication network does not; and so on. If these configuration settings are correct, then it becomes much easier to manage DAG networks as Exchange will do its part of the job.

> Custom configuration is not a foolproof feature and you should always ensure your DAG networks are configured according to Microsoft's best practices.

Single copy alert enhancements

I am sure there is no need to say that ensuring servers are operating in a reliable way and mailbox database copies remain healthy are the main tasks of daily Exchange messaging operations. In any Exchange deployment, hardware, Exchange services, and Windows operating systems must be actively monitored. When trying to achieve an Exchange 2013 resilient environment, it is crucial to monitor the status and health of DAGs and their database copies. This is particularly critical when there is only one database copy left healthy in environments that do not use a resilient storage system. In a RAID 10 configuration, for example, an active mailbox database copy is not affected by a single disk failure. However, in a RAID 0 or JBOD configuration, a failure of a single disk will force a database failover.

In Exchange 2010, the `CheckDatabaseRedundancy.ps1` script monitored the redundancy of replicated databases by checking if there were at least two healthy copies configured and alerting through event logs when only a single healthy copy existed. However, administrators had to manually run the script, create a scheduled task to run it regularly, or invoke it using a monitoring solution such as Microsoft System Center Operations Manager (SCOM), further covered in *Chapter 8, Monitoring Exchange*. Since knowing when a database is down to a single healthy copy is crucial, this script was replaced in Exchange 2013 with a native and integrated functional part of Managed Availability. Exchange 2013 continues to alert through event log notifications, but it now uses Event ID 4138 (red alert) and 4139 (green alert).

Furthermore, this functionality has been improved in order to reduce the alert noise level that could be generated when multiple databases on the same server went into a single copy condition. While in Exchange 2010, an alert was generated on a per-database level; now these are generated only on a per-server basis. This means that an outage affecting an entire server causing several databases to go into a single copy condition will only generate one alert per server.

Lagged copy enhancements

While database copies and features such as In-Place Hold can provide protection against failures that would normally cause data loss, they cannot protect against data loss due to logical corruption. This is what lagged copies were designed to avoid.

Replay lag time is a property of database copies that specifies how long to delay replaying the logs for the database copy. Log truncation, which works the same as it did in Exchange 2010, specifies how long the Replication service waits before truncating the log files replayed into the database passive copy.

Exchange 2013 has introduced two lagged copies enhancements: log files automatic play down and integration with Safety Net.

Safety Net, explored in depth in *Chapter 5, Transport High Availability*, is a transport feature that stores copies of delivered e-mails for a period of time so they can be re-delivered in case of any problems that affect the active database copy. By integrating lagged copies with Safety Net, it becomes much easier to activate a lagged database copy. Consider an example of a lagged copy that has a three day replay lag, in which case Safety Net should be configured to retain e-mails for three days (`Set-TransportConfig -SafetyNetHoldTime 3`). If the lagged copy needs to be activated, one can suspend replication to it and copy it (so the original lagged copy is not lost). Then, all the log files can be discarded with the exception of those in the required time range. The copy is then mounted, and an automatic request is sent to Safety Net to redeliver the last three days' worth of e-mails. This way, administrators do not need to determine when corruption started as Exchange will automatically redeliver the last three days' of e-mails minus the e-mails usually lost in a lossy failover.

The second improvement is that lagged copies can automatically start replaying log files if:

- The threshold for low disk space is reached
- The lagged copy itself has become physically corrupt
- There are fewer than three available healthy copies for more than 24 hours

This behavior, however, is disabled by default. To enable it, run the following cmdlet:

```
Set-DatabaseAvailabilityGroup <DAG_Name> -ReplayLagManagerEnabled $True
```

After enabling automatic replay, you can further customize it. For example, you can change the low disk space threshold by means of a registry entry:

```
HKLM\Software\Microsoft\ExchangeServer\v15\Replay\Parameters\
ReplayLagPlayDownPercentDiskFreeSpace
```

We can also change the default value of three available healthy copies by changing the following registry entry:

```
HKLM\Software\Microsoft\ExchangeServer\v15\Replay\Parameters\
ReplayLagManagerNumAvailableCopies
```

Dynamic Quorum

When adding a DAG's first server, a failover cluster is created automatically and exclusively for the DAG. Although Exchange is not a clustered application, DAGs use certain clustering features, such as cluster networks, cluster heartbeat, and cluster database to store database state changes. When more servers are added to the same DAG, they join the underlying cluster. The quorum model of the cluster is adjusted automatically and the server is added to the AD DAG object.

A failover cluster uses a quorum: a consensus of voters, in order to guarantee that only one group of members (either a majority of members or all members) is operating at one time. This is, by far, not a new concept as Exchange has been using failover clustering and quorums for a very long time. At the same time, the term *quorum* is also used to describe the data representing the configuration shared among all cluster members. All DAGs require their failover cluster to retain quorum. If the quorum is lost, all DAG operations are terminated and all databases in the DAG are dismounted.

Quorum is important for the following two reasons:

- To ensure consistency so that each member has an identical view of the cluster as the other members
- To avoid segregation (like split brain) by acting as a tiebreaker

Majority Node Set clustering

Majority Node Set is a Windows clustering model used since the early versions of Exchange. This model requires 50 percent of the voters (servers and/or one file share witness) to be up and running.

DAGs that have an even number of members use a quorum mode known as **Node and File Share Majority** that uses a witness server to act as a tiebreaker. Each DAG member gets a vote and the witness server is used to give one member a weighted vote. The system disk of each DAG member stores the cluster quorum data and a particular file (`witness.log`) on the witness server (thus the name *File Share*) is used to track which member has the most up-to-date copy of the data as the witness server does not keep a copy of the cluster quorum data.

When using this mode, a majority of the voters have to be operational and be able to communicate between themselves in order to maintain quorum. If this majority is unable to communicate, the DAG's cluster loses quorum and administrator intervention is required for the DAG to become operational again. When the witness server is required for quorum, any member that is able to communicate with it can place a Server Message Block lock on the `witness.log` file. The one who is able to lock the witness server (locking node) holds an additional vote. The servers in contact with this node are in the majority and, as such, retain quorum. Any member that is unable to contact the locking node, on the other hand, is in the minority and therefore loses quorum.

Let's consider a four-member DAG. As this is a DAG with an even number of members, a witness server is required in order to provide one of the members with a fifth vote. If quorum is to be maintained, at least three voters need to be able to communicate with each other. A maximum of two voters can be offline at any time without causing any disruption. However, if three or more are offline, the DAG will lose quorum and databases will be taken offline. A four-member DAG setup can be seen in the following diagram:

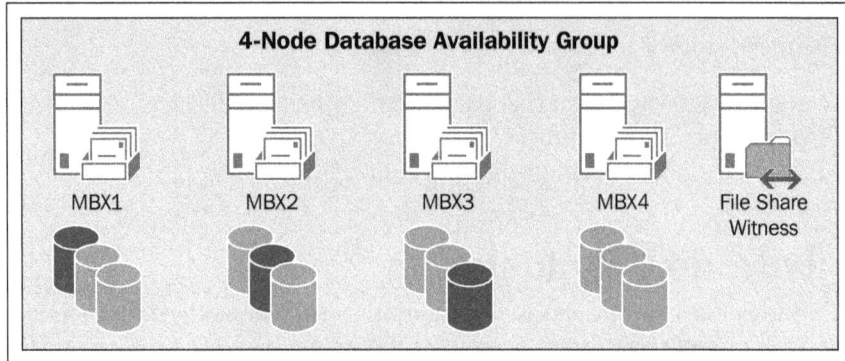

4-Node Database Availability Group

MBX1   MBX2   MBX3   MBX4   File Share Witness

The formula that helps administrators to calculate how many nodes in a cluster have to be available before the cluster is brought offline is $(n/2) + 1$, where n is the total number of DAG members (note that $n/2$ is always rounded down). So, in our four-member DAG setup, we have $(5/2) + 1 = 2+1 = 3$ nodes.

With regard to DAGs with an odd number of members, the quorum mode used is known as **Node Majority**. Here, each member gets a vote as before and their local system disk is still used to keep the cluster quorum data. If the DAG configuration changes, the change is propagated to each member and written to disk — this change will only be considered committed, and made persistent, when it is saved to half of the members (rounding down) plus one. Consider a three-member DAG setup. In this setup, the change has to be saved to one plus one members, or two members in total. In this scenario, and using the formula we discussed earlier, only one server can be down at a time. If a second server is also offline, the entire cluster will be brought offline. A three-member DAG setup can be seen in the following diagram:

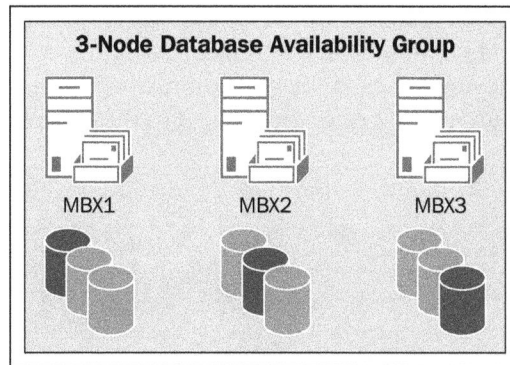

Windows Server 2012

Windows Server 2012 introduced a new model called **Failover Clustering Dynamic Quorum** that we can use with Exchange. When using **Dynamic Quorum**, the cluster dynamically manages the assignment of votes based on the state of each individual node. When a node crashes or is turned off, it loses its quorum vote, only to regain it when it successfully rejoins the cluster. By dynamically changing the assignment of votes, the cluster is able to decrease or increase the number of required quorum votes to keep the cluster running. This way, the cluster is capable of maintaining availability throughout sequential node failures or shutdowns.

With Dynamic Quorum, the quorum majority is calculated based on the number of active cluster members at any time. This is the critical difference when compared to pre-Windows Server 2012 clusters, where the majority of the quorum was fixed based on the initial cluster configuration.

> The advantage Dynamic Quorum brings is that it is now possible for a cluster to run even if the number of nodes remaining in the cluster is less than 50 percent. By dynamically adjusting the requirement for a quorum majority, the cluster is able to withstand sequential node shutdowns down to a single node and still keep running. However, this does not allow the cluster to withstand a simultaneous failure of multiple members, as in order to continue running, the cluster needs to have a quorum majority when the node fails.

The dynamic vote of a node assigned by the cluster can be viewed using the `Get-ClusterNode` cmdlet and by looking at the `DynamicWeight` property of the node. A **0** value shows that the node does not have a quorum vote, and **1** shows that the node does have a quorum vote. This can be viewed in the following screenshot:

It is possible to change the quorum configuration through the Failover Cluster Manager. To do so, select the cluster, click on **More Actions** under **Actions**, and then click on **Configure Cluster Quorum Settings...**, as shown in the following screenshot:

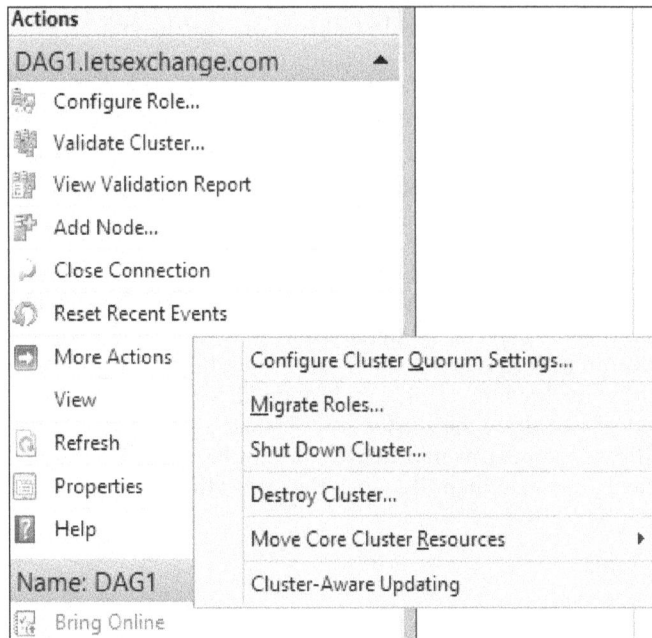

Alternatively, you can also use the Shell to check if Dynamic Quorum is being used, by running the cmdlet shown in the following screenshot:

To enable or disable Dynamic Quorum through the Shell, simply set the DynamicQuorum property to 1 (enabled) or to 0 (disabled) by running:

```
(Get-Cluster "cluster_name").DynamicQuorum=0
```

Let us consider a three-node DAG: three mailbox databases (DB02, DB03, and DB04) with database copies across all three members. As previously discussed, no witness server is required because this is a DAG with an odd number of members. At this stage, all servers are operational and all database copies are mounted on server **EXMBX1** with their respective copies healthy:

Using the Shell, we can check the properties for each of the members of the cluster, including their dynamic weight. As you can see in the following screenshot showing the `DynamicWeight` property, each node has **1** vote at this stage:

Now, let's shut down one of the DAG members. To make this test more interesting, let's shut down the member that is currently hosting all active copies of the three databases on the **EXMBX1** server:

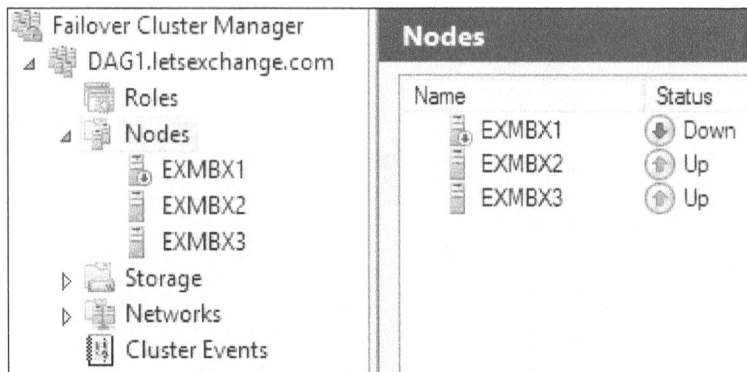

As expected, all databases are failed over to one of the remaining servers, in this case server **EXMBX2**:

```
Machine: EXMBX2.letsexchange.com                    _  □  x

[PS] C:\>
[PS] C:\>Get-MailboxDatabase -Server EXMBX2 | Get-MailboxDatabaseC
opyStatus | Select Name, Status, ContentIndexState

Name                            Status          ContentIndexState
----                            ------          -----------------
DB02\EXMBX1                     ServiceDown             Unknown
DB02\EXMBX2                       Mounted             Healthy
DB02\EXMBX3                       Healthy             Healthy
DB03\EXMBX1                     ServiceDown             Unknown
DB03\EXMBX2                       Mounted             Healthy
DB03\EXMBX3                       Healthy             Healthy
DB04\EXMBX1                     ServiceDown             Unknown
DB04\EXMBX2                       Mounted             Healthy
DB04\EXMBX3                       Healthy             Healthy


[PS] C:\>_
```

So far, this is the exact behavior one would expect from previous versions of Exchange and Windows Server. The difference with Dynamic Quorum is that it now removes the vote from the node with the lowest ID, with only one node keeping a vote. This is because there cannot be any majority with only two nodes left in a cluster, as the majority of two is two. As such, to prevent the cluster from going offline, one of the votes is removed, thus only requiring one vote to maintain the cluster:

```
Machine: EXMBX2.letsexchange.com                    _  □  x

[PS] C:\>
[PS] C:\>Get-ClusterNode | FT Name, DynamicWeight, NodeWeight, ID,
 State -AutoSize

Name     DynamicWeight NodeWeight Id State
----     ------------- ---------- -- -----
EXMBX1               0          1 1  Down
EXMBX2               0          1 2  Up
EXMBX3               1          1 3  Up


[PS] C:\>_
```

If this was a pre-Windows Server 2012 cluster, quorum would still be maintained and the DAG would continue to operate without any issues. The difference with Windows Server 2012 is in what happens when we lose another node. In this case, the whole DAG would typically go offline as the remaining node would not be able to achieve a majority. However, this is not the case with Dynamic Quorum.

Let's now shut down **EXMBX2**, which has all the databases mounted. We could also shut down **EXMBX3,** which is the only node with a vote, it would not affect our purpose.

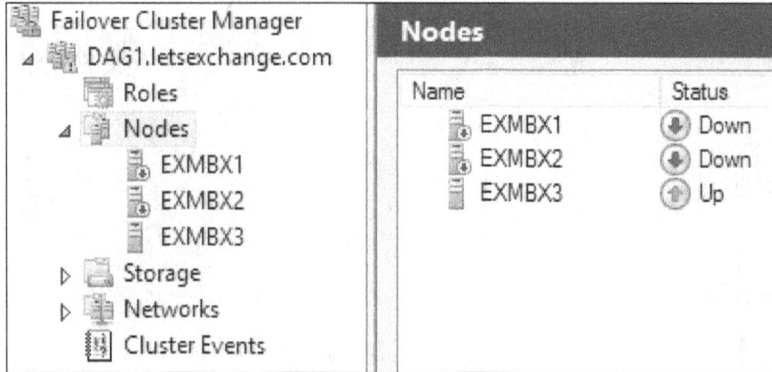

```
Failover Cluster Manager          Nodes
▲ DAG1.letsexchange.com
     Roles                        Name          Status
  ▲ Nodes                          EXMBX1        ⊕ Down
        EXMBX1                      EXMBX2        ⊕ Down
        EXMBX2                      EXMBX3        ⊕ Up
        EXMBX3
  ▷ Storage
  ▷ Networks
     Cluster Events
```

In this case, the vote remains on **EXMBX3** (if we were to shut down **EXMBX3**, the vote would be transferred to **EXMBX2**) and the cluster remains up and running even with just one node remaining!

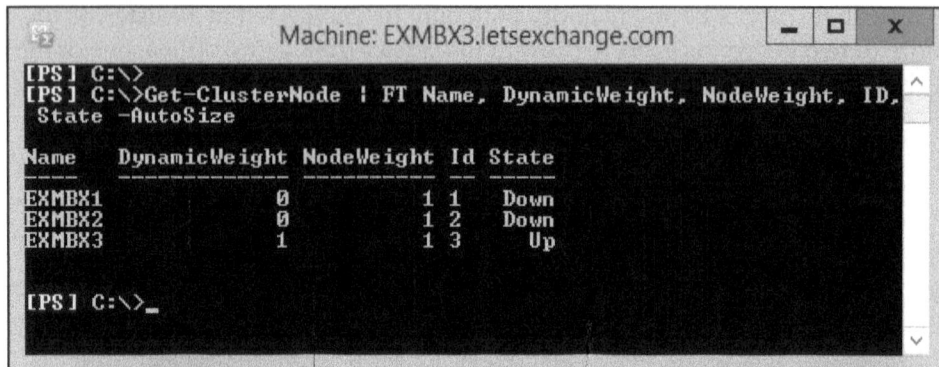

```
Machine: EXMBX3.letsexchange.com                         _ □ X
[PS] C:\>
[PS] C:\>Get-ClusterNode | FT Name, DynamicWeight, NodeWeight, ID,
 State -AutoSize

Name    DynamicWeight NodeWeight Id State
----    ------------- ---------- -- -----
EXMBX1              0          1 1  Down
EXMBX2              0          1 2  Down
EXMBX3              1          1 3  Up

[PS] C:\>_
```

While the DAG would be brought down in such a scenario in previous editions of Windows Server, this is not the case with a dynamic cluster. All databases are successfully failed over to the remaining node and the DAG remains unaffected:

```
                    Machine: EXMBX3.letsexchange.com            _  □  X

[PS] C:\>
[PS] C:\>Get-MailboxDatabase -Server EXMBX3 | Get-MailboxDatabaseC
opyStatus | Select Name, Status, ContentIndexState

Name                                    Status          ContentIndexState
----                                    ------          -----------------
DB02\EXMBX1                           ServiceDown                 Unknown
DB02\EXMBX2                           ServiceDown                 Unknown
DB02\EXMBX3                              Mounted                  Healthy
DB03\EXMBX1                           ServiceDown                 Unknown
DB03\EXMBX2                           ServiceDown                 Unknown
DB03\EXMBX3                              Mounted                  Healthy
DB04\EXMBX1                           ServiceDown                 Unknown
DB04\EXMBX2                           ServiceDown                 Unknown
DB04\EXMBX3                              Mounted                  Healthy


[PS] C:\>
[PS] C:\>Get-DatabaseAvailabilityGroup DAG1 -Status | FL Servers,
OperationalServers


Servers            : {EXMBX3, EXMBX2, EXMBX1}
OperationalServers : {EXMBX3}


[PS] C:\>
```

Remember that Dynamic Quorum only works if the following two conditions are met:

- One node or several nodes fail in a **sequential order**
- The cluster has already achieved quorum

If multiple servers fail at the same time (for example, in a disaster recovery scenario where an entire datacenter with more than one cluster member becomes unavailable), the cluster will not be able to adjust the quorum majority requirement dynamically.

Introducing modern Public Folders

Public Folders (PFs), first introduced in Exchange 4.0, were initially designed as a method of collecting, organizing, and easily sharing information with other users. These days, they are still widely used to share e-mails, contacts, and documents. Users are also able to send e-mails to PFs when these are mail-enabled, allowing PFs to act as a discussion forum or distribution group archive.

Up until Exchange 2013, PFs always had their own dedicated database which could be replicated between servers to achieve resilience and high availability. This also allowed for PFs (or a replica) to be, from a network perspective, closer to users, improving performance and saving bandwidth. One of the biggest headaches with PFs has always been this replication method, with users having to wait several minutes for their PFs to update, among other issues.

PFs take full advantage of the high availability technology of the mailbox store. Specially designed mailboxes are used to store the hierarchy (the structure in which PFs are organized and their properties) as well as the content (the data itself) of PFs. As PFs are now mailboxes, Public Folder Databases no longer exist and high availability is achieved by placing a PF mailbox in the DAG database, therefore a move from the old Multi-Master Replication Model to the new Single-Master Replication Model of DAGs.

To start using PFs in Exchange 2013, the first step is to create a PF mailbox. This is done using the Exchange Admin Centre or the Shell and the `New-Mailbox` cmdlet, but with the `PublicFolder` switch to specify we are creating a PF mailbox and not a normal user mailbox. We can also use the `Database` parameter to specify in which database to create the PF mailbox, but thanks to the Exchange automatic mailbox distribution feature, this is not required.

```
New-Mailbox -Name <PF_Mailbox_Name> -PublicFolder
```

When the first PF mailbox was created, it automatically became the PF **Master Hierarchy Mailbox**, the only one with a writable copy of the hierarchy. Every PF mailbox created after the first one was simply a normal PF mailbox containing a read-only copy of the hierarchy.

When a user creates or deletes a PF (a hierarchy change), this change is redirected to the Master Hierarchy Mailbox and, replicated to all other PF mailboxes to avoid conflicts.

The AD accounts of all PF mailboxes are disabled by default, as one would expect, so that no users can use them to access network services or log in to a workstation. Even assigning users **FullAccess** permissions to the PF mailbox and adding it in Outlook or OWA does not work. Exchange prevents this through an **ErrorExplicitLogonAccessDenied** error in OWA or a **Cannot expand the folder. The set of folders cannot be opened. You do not have permissions to log on** message in Outlook.

Best practices

In order to ensure that Public Folders are always available to users and to minimize their impact on network utilization, there are some concepts and best practices that should be considered:

- Although mailbox databases in Exchange 2013 still have the `PublicFolderDatabase` property, this is not used anymore and there is no database-level setting to specify which PF a database should use. Exchange 2013 provides the ability to specify the PF mailbox on a mailbox-level (using `Set-Mailbox` with the `DefaultPublicFolderMailbox` parameter), but Exchange auto-calculates the per-user hierarchy mailbox by default.

- Mailbox audit logging does not work against PFs.

- Writes against the hierarchy are always performed against the Master Hierarchy Mailbox, the only writeable copy of the hierarchy. If this mailbox is not available, users will be able to view but not write to PFs. Therefore, it is very important to protect this mailbox by creating multiple redundant copies with automatic failover (DAG), just like with regular mailboxes. The same applies for all other PFs if high availability for them is deemed important.

- Each PF mailbox has a copy of the public folder hierarchy.

- PF content is not replicated across multiple PF mailboxes. Therefore, all clients access the same PF mailbox for a given set of content.

- Because of the new architecture of PFs, it is only possible to have a single active copy for each PF mailbox anywhere across the organization. This might not be efficient if the same PF needs to be accessed by users in different locations. However, Microsoft will be addressing this in the future.

Explaining the Offline Address Book

An Offline Address Book, or OAB, is an Address List used by Outlook clients running in Cached Exchange Mode for address book lookups when Outlook has no connectivity to Exchange. It reduces the workload on Exchange, as these clients will query their local OAB first. If an organization has all its clients running the Outlook Web App or Outlook in Online Exchange Mode, an OAB is not required.

Exchange 2007 and 2010 use one or multiple CASs and a web or Public Folder distribution method to distribute OABs, but the generation of an OAB is always bound to a single mailbox server. The obvious disadvantage here is that this server is a single point of failure and if it is unavailable for a long period of time, the generation of the OAB is affected and clients will not have an updated list of contacts.

Exchange 2013 changed the way OABs are generated and distributed. As for their generation, the OAB is now generated by the mailbox server that hosts a particular type of arbitration mailbox, the **Organization Mailbox**. If this mailbox is on a mailbox database that is part of a DAG, the server generating the OAB is the one hosting the active copy of the database. Not being bound to a particular server provides resilience in OAB generation because each mailbox server hosting an Organization Mailbox (there can be multiple) will generate *all* OABs defined in the environment.

Administrators can easily create extra Organization Mailboxes to provide fault tolerance or to serve users in a geographically-distributed environment. This is a two-step process where we first need to create the mailbox itself and then enable the OAB generation capability:

```
New-Mailbox -Arbitration -Name "OAB London" -Database LON-DB01
-UserPrincipalName oablon@letsexchange.com -DisplayName "OAB Mailbox for
London"
```

```
Set-Mailbox -Arbitration oablon -OABGen $True
```

An Organization Mailbox is a type of arbitration mailbox with the *OrganizationCapabilityOABGen* persisted capability, which is a new feature in Exchange 2013 (persisted capabilities define the purpose or function of an arbitration mailbox). To identify the Organization Mailbox (remember that there can be multiple), we use the following cmdlet for a non-DAG environment:

```
Get-Mailbox -Arbitration | Where {$_.PersistedCapabilities -match "oab"}
| Select Name, ServerName
```

We need to update this cmdlet in a DAG environment. First we get all the organization mailboxes and then we check on which servers the databases hosting them are currently mounted for each one of those:

```
$DBs = (Get-Mailbox -Arbitration | Where {$_.PersistedCapabilities -match
"oab"}).Database
```

```
$DBs | Get-MailboxDatabase -Status | Select Name, MountedOnServer
```

In previous versions of Exchange, the OAB generation was a scheduled process that would always run at a designated time even if the server was under a high load, for which the *Microsoft Exchange System Attendant* service was responsible. In Exchange 2013, this is now the responsibility of OABGeneratorAssistant, a mailbox assistant that runs under the *Microsoft Exchange Mailbox Assistants* service. Just like most mailbox assistants, this one is a throttled process that runs/pauses depending on the server workload.

Although there is a `Schedule` property for an OAB in Exchange 2013, this is no longer used and its generation is solely dependent on the `OABGeneratorWorkCycle` and `OABGeneratorWorkCycleCheckpoint` properties of the server hosting the Organization Mailbox.

```
Machine: EXMBX1.letsexchange.com                    ─  □  X

[PS] C:\>
[PS] C:\>Get-OfflineAddressBook | FL *schedule*


Schedule : {Sun.05:00-Sun.05:15, Mon.05:00-Mon.05:15,
            Tue.05:00-Tue.05:15, Wed.05:00-Wed.05:15,
            Thu.05:00-Thu.05:15, Fri.05:00-Fri.05:15,
            Sat.05:00-Sat.05:15}


[PS] C:\>
[PS] C:\>Get-MailboxServer EXMBX1 | FL *oab*


OABGeneratorWorkCycle           : 1.00:00:00
OABGeneratorWorkCycleCheckpoint : 1.00:00:00


[PS] C:\>
[PS] C:\>_
```

Although OAB files were located in the `%ExchangeInstallPath%\ExchangeOAB` folder before and then shared so that CASs could retrieve them for distribution to Outlook clients, these files are now first stored in the Organization Mailbox and then copied to the `%ExchangeInstallPath%\ClientAccess\OAB\` folder on the mailbox server hosting this mailbox.

As for the distribution method, Exchange 2013 supports only web distribution. Before, the *Microsoft Exchange File Distribution Service* on CASs would pull OAB files from the mailbox server where this was being generated and store them locally. Outlook clients would then receive the OAB URL from AutoDiscover, reach a CAS, and then authenticate and get the OAB from the files on the CAS. Outlook 2003 clients would get the OAB from Public Folders.

The problem with this web distribution method is that the OAB download fails if the CAS does not have the files stored locally, and clients will not receive updates if the File Distribution Service is not working.

To prevent this, OAB files in Exchange 2013 are not stored locally on CASs. All CASs do is proxy OAB download requests to the correct Mailbox server, thus removing the *File Distribution Service* from the CASs. In this scenario, Outlook clients receive the OAB URL from AutoDiscover and then reach a CAS, which performs the following:

1. Authenticates the user.
2. Queries Active Directory to determine the closest Organization Mailbox to the user and the mailbox database hosting it.
3. Queries Active Manager to determine on which server the mailbox database is mounted and proxies the request to it.
4. Gathers the OAB files and transmits them to the client.

As previously mentioned, a CAS will proxy OAB download requests to the *closest* mailbox server that hosts an organization mailbox. Therefore, it is recommended to have one organization mailbox active in each Active Directory site.

One important concept to keep in mind is that CASs will proxy these requests in a round-robin fashion if more than one organization mailbox is found in the same AD site. This might cause issues because each organization mailbox will have its own set of OAB files with different names and different generation times. As such, Outlook clients will download the full OAB each time they are proxied to a different organization mailbox because they see new filenames and generation times.

Best practices

In order to ensure that the Offline Address Book is always available to users and to improve the way it is distributed, there are three best practices that should be followed:

- Organization mailboxes should be hosted by a database that is part of a DAG.
- In an environment with multiple sites, there should be one organization mailbox per site. This way, users will download the OAB from a server closest to them.
- There should only be one organization mailbox active in each Active Directory site.

Summary

As we discovered throughout this chapter, the role of Mailbox in Exchange 2013 has undergone some great changes and it now hosts all the protocols and components that store, process, and render user data. Exchange 2013 improved the technology behind DAGs, making it more robust, fast, and resilient. By combining it with Windows Server 2012 Dynamic Cluster, administrators can further extend the capabilities of DAGs to allow more nodes to fail without bringing the entire cluster offline.

Other new features such as Automatic Reseed were also introduced; they allow administrators to increase the level of availability provided by any Exchange deployment, from a single to a multi-server environment.

We also had a look at the new Managed Store, the much improved modern Public Folders, and the Offline Address Book. All of these new or enhanced features take Exchange's high availability to a new level. However, proper attention is required in order to ensure everything is configured to make the most out of them.

The next chapter discusses site resilience for both the Client Access and Mailbox server roles, covering the new global namespace and database availability groups across multiple datacenters.

4
Achieving Site Resilience

Exchange 2013 continues to improve in areas such as high availability, storage, and site resilience. Even though **Database Availability Groups (DAGs)** and Windows Server Failover Clustering remain the technologies used to achieve site resilience for the Mailbox server role, site resilience, in general, has been considerably enhanced. With Exchange 2013, it becomes much simpler to configure and achieve site resilience due to all the underlying architectural changes introduced.

There is no doubt that with Exchange 2010 it was easier than ever to achieve site resilience. With good planning and by introducing DAGs and extending these across two or more datacenters, administrators could activate a second datacenter quicker than ever in order to continue to provide messaging services to users. This was done through a **datacenter switchover**, which although better than ever, was still a manual, complex, and usually time consuming process. Its complexity came from the fact that the recovery of the DAG was tied together with the recovery of the namespace used for client access. This caused a few challenges in some scenarios that are as follows:

- If a significant number of CASs, the array's VIP, or the majority of a DAG's members were lost, for example, then a datacenter switchover was necessary.

- A DAG could be split across two datacenters with its witness server located in a third datacenter that enabled automatic Mailbox role failover for either datacenter. However, this did not provide failover for the messaging service itself as the namespace still had to be switched over.

Let us have a look at how Exchange 2013 addressed these challenges.

Achieving site resilience for client access server

As we saw in *Chapter 1*, *Getting Started*, to deploy site resilience across two datacenters with Exchange 2010, many namespaces were needed. They were as follows:

- 2x Internet Protocol namespaces (primary and standby datacenters)
- 2x OWA failback namespaces (primary and standby datacenters)
- 1x OWA failback namespace (standby datacenters)
- 1x Autodiscover namespace
- 2x RPC Client Access namespaces (primary and standby datacenters)
- 1x Legacy namespace (in case of a migration scenario)
- Possibly a transport namespace for performing encryption with a partner organization

For example, in an active/passive datacenter scenario, one would typically have a namespace called `mail.letsexchange.com` for the active (primary) datacenter, and `mail.standby.letsexchange.com` for the passive (standby) datacenter, which would be used to provide services to users in case of a disaster with the active datacenter.

Besides the complexity involved in deploying and configuring so many namespaces, a major downside of Exchange 2010 was the single point of failure that was the namespace. If the CASs or the VIP for the CAS array were lost, a datacenter switchover would be needed. The datacenter, where services were switched over to, needed to have a different namespace, and updating the IP address for the CAS array FQDN was not easy due to the DNS latency, name resolution caches, and so on.

For starters, we already know that the RPC Client Access namespace has been removed in Exchange 2013; so, that is two less namespaces. We also know that a CAS now proxies requests to the Mailbox server hosting the mailbox's active database copy. Another difference in 2013 is that this proxy logic is not bound by the AD site where the CAS is located, meaning a CAS can proxy requests to the Mailbox servers located in different AD sites. This also means that no additional namespaces are required for site resilience (as long as latency and throughput are not the limiting factors), which eliminates two more namespaces: both OWA and the namespace for the Internet Protocol in the standby datacenter.

All of this has been made possible by the consolidation of server roles and both improvements and simplification of load balancing, which also enabled the separation of the recovery of a DAG from the recovery of a client access namespace. Administrators can now use a single and global namespace across datacenters, which enables Exchange to automatically failover between datacenters. With Exchange 2010, this requires manual intervention.

Global namespace

A global namespace means that the same **Fully Qualified Domain Name (FQDN)** that clients use to access Exchange can be used in multiple datacenters and AD sites such as `mail.letsexchange.com`. Using multiple IP addresses for the same namespace together with load balancing, Exchange 2013 leverages an inbuilt namespace fault tolerance. As most client-access protocols are now HTTP-based (Outlook Web App, Outlook, Outlook Anywhere, ActiveSync, and so on), clients have the capability of using multiple IP addresses and providing automatic failover at the client side. Administrators achieve this by configuring the DNS to reply to the client's name resolution requests with multiple IP addresses. For example, when a client queries `mail.domain.com`, DNS replies with two or more IP addresses. The client will then try to connect to one IP and, if unsuccessful, will wait for 20 seconds before trying the next IP. This means that if a CAS array VIP is lost, and there is a second VIP for another CAS array on a different site, all IP addresses returned by the DNS are used in a reliable way by the client and recovery happens automatically, typically within 21 seconds.

Any modern HTTP client works automatically with this redundancy. The HTTP stack accepts multiple IP addresses for a given FQDN, and in case the first IP that is tried fails (it simply cannot connect), it automatically tries the next IP on the list after 20 seconds. In case of a failure, where a connection is established but then lost, maybe due to an intermittent service failure or packet loss, the user may have to refresh the browser or client.

With this change, not every scenario in Exchange 2013 requires a datacenter switchover. As mentioned earlier, by correctly configuring Exchange and DNS, failover happens at the client side as it will automatically connect to another datacenter with an operational CAS array. These CASs, in turn, will proxy the connection back to the primary datacenter where the user's mailbox server remains unaffected by the failure or outage (as long as communication between datacenters is still possible).

Let us consider the following scenario: in Exchange 2010, a loss of a CAS array, or its VIP, in the primary datacenter required a datacenter switchover (assuming different AD sites). With Exchange 2013, nothing needs to be done with the exception of eventually fixing the load balancer. If a client is not already using the VIP on the second datacenter, it automatically connects to it without administrators having to perform a datacenter switchover, or make any changes to the namespace or even to the DNS.

Just compare the complexity of a datacenter switchover in Exchange 2010 where administrators had to manually run a number of PowerShell cmdlets and deal with DNS latency, with the automatic behavior of 2013 and an automatic failover between VIPs of around 21 seconds!

Let us look at an example. The company **LetsExchange** has two datacenters with good connectivity between them, one in New York and another one in New Jersey. In order to simplify the namespace architecture so that clients use only one namespace independently of their mailbox location, the following architecture is used:

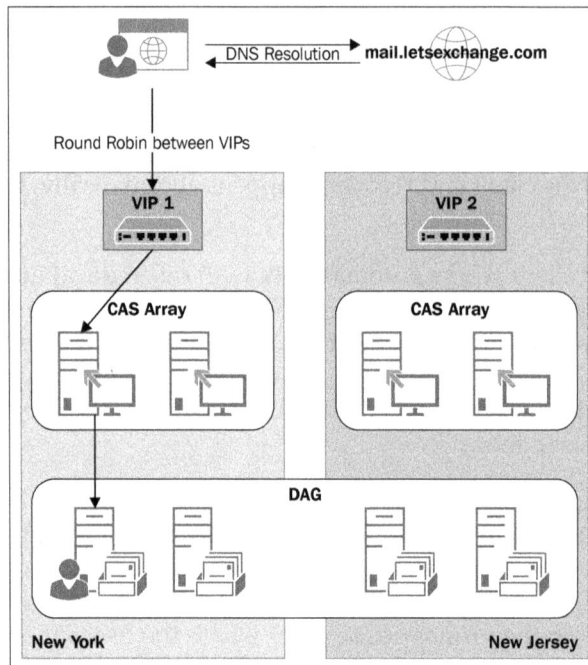

As bandwidth and latency between the two datacenters are not a concern, this deployment is configured in an active/active (or primary/primary) model with active mailbox copies on both datacenters. In this scenario, both CAS infrastructures are used to proxy and route the traffic to Mailbox servers in both datacenters. Here, an external DNS is configured to round robin each datacenter's load balancer VIP, thus achieving a site resilience namespace. The only downside of this scenario is the proxy of roughly half the traffic across datacenters, as users with a mailbox in **New York** might connect to a CAS in **New Jersey**, or vice-versa.

The connectivity flow in this scenario is as follows:

1. Linda's client (for example, **Outlook Web Access (OWA)**), does a DNS query for `mail.letsexchange.com` and in return receives `195.195.10.x` and `81.145.50.y`.

2. OWA tries to connect to the first IP address and reaches the load balancer's VIP1 in New York via HTTP, which, in turn, redirects the request to an available CAS.

3. The CAS queries the Active Manager to find out which Mailbox server is hosting the active copy of the user's database.

4. The CAS proxies the request to the appropriate Mailbox server.

If Linda's database is activated in the second datacenter, **VIP1** can still be used to establish a connection to the new server hosting the database (remember that CASs are no longer restricted to a single AD site).

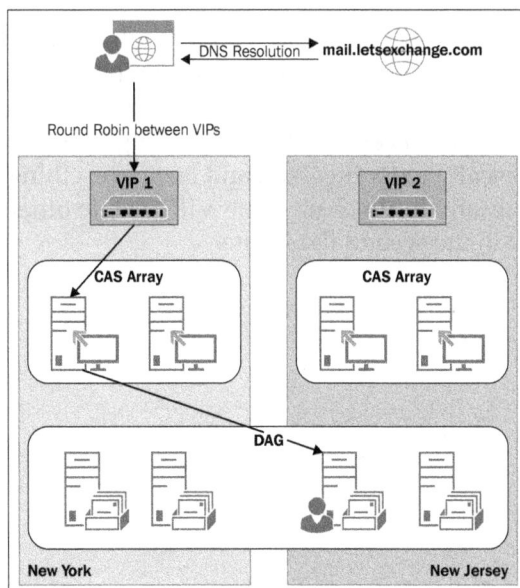

If, for some reason, VIP1 fails, clients trying to connect to it will wait 20 seconds, before automatically trying VIP2 as they already have it on their DNS cache:

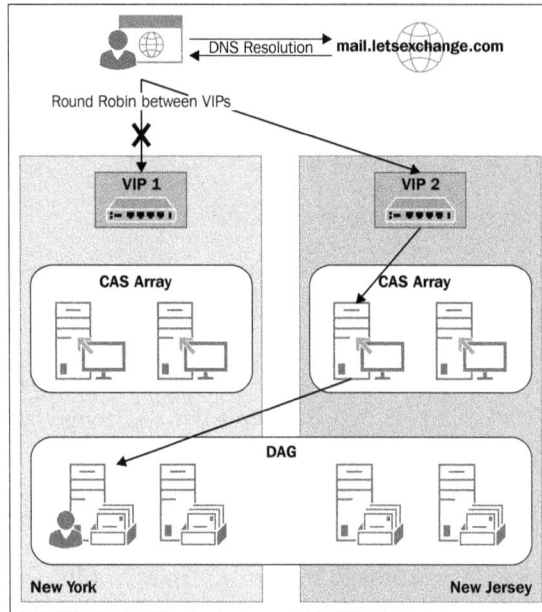

At this stage, depending on the nature of the problem with VIP1, administrators might choose to remove VIP1 from DNS to prevent future delays of new clients trying to connect to VIP1.

Administrators can tolerate this failover to happen without having to perform a switchback (often incorrectly referred to as failback). If the CAS service is lost in the primary datacenter (VIP1), resulting in a 20-second interruption for users, administrators might not be concerned about switching back. During this period, the main concern is typically to fix the issue and once everything is back to normal, new connections will automatically start using VIP1, while others will continue working through VIP2 in the second datacenter.

The connectivity flow in this scenario is as follows:

1. Linda's client (for example, OWA), does a DNS query for `mail.letsexchange.com` and in return receives `195.195.10.x` and `81.145.50.y`.

2. The browser tries to connect to the first IP address. However, because VIP1 is unreachable, it waits approximately 20 seconds and then tries the second IP address. The request reaches the load balancer's VIP2 in New Jersey via HTTP, which, in turn, redirects the request to an available CAS.

3. The CAS queries Active Manager to find out which Mailbox server is hosting the active copy of the user's database.

4. The CAS proxies the request to the appropriate Mailbox server in New York.

As you can see, even though the CAS infrastructure in New York failed, a datacenter switchover was not required. The CAS in New Jersey simply proxied the connection to the Mailbox server in New York.

Before proxying the connection, however, the CAS first decides if it will redirect or proxy the request to another CAS or array, as we saw right at the start of *Chapter 2, High Availability with the Client Access Server*. A CAS only redirects a connection under the following circumstances:

- The request is a telephony request (also discussed in *Chapter 2, High Availability with the Client Access Server*).

- For OWA requests, if the CAS determines that the user's mailbox is hosted on a different AD site and there is a CAS in that site available that has the `ExternalURL` attribute populated, then it will silently redirect the request. This is true unless `ExternalURL` in the target CAS is identical to the one used in the original site. In this case, which is similar to the scenario we looked at earlier (preceding diagram), the CAS will proxy the request to the target Mailbox server.

Some organizations, however, opt for an active/standby (or primary/secondary) scenario where all users' mailboxes are active in one datacenter and the second datacenter is only used in case of disaster recovery. In this scenario, connections going through the secondary datacenter during normal operation might not be desired. As such, two main options are available. They are as follows:

- Using a different namespace for the standby datacenter with clients configured to use `mail.letsexchange.com` by default. In this scenario, if mailbox databases are failed over to the standby datacenter, but the CASs in the primary datacenter are still operational (as is the network between the two sites), no changes are required as we have already seen. However, if the CAS infrastructure in the primary datacenter fails, then clients will have to be reconfigured to use `mail.standby.letsexchange.com` instead. This is identical to Exchange 2010.

- Deploying a single namespace across both datacenters, as already discussed, but controlling which VIP users connect to using DNS. By excluding, the VIP of the CAS array in the standby datacenter from the DNS, users will only be aware of the primary VIP. In case this VIP fails, then a DNS change will need to be made to make the standby VIP available to users, which will obviously cause downtime for users.

Whenever possible, a single and global namespace should always be used across datacenters in order to facilitate failover scenarios and minimize the user impact during the disaster recovery scenarios. However, due to network restrictions or even business requirements, this might not always be possible. In this case, a namespace controlling which VIP users connect using DNS is preferred, rather than using a different namespace as it will allow for an easier and quicker service recovery.

For organizations that want to use a single namespace but their Exchange environment expands a large area, such as a country or even multiple countries, geographic-aware DNS (or DNS geographical load balancing) might be a viable option. Here, Round Robin DNS is used to allow external users to cache multiple DNS entries (as before), but with the difference that DNS itself identifies which VIP is best suited for the user, based on where the user is connecting from (using IP identification).

> Geographic-aware DNS is still a feature only a few DNS hosting providers offer at the moment and it obviously adds extra cost. However, it is becoming common day by day.

Geographic-aware DNS ensures that the requests are always dealt with by the CASs closer to the users:

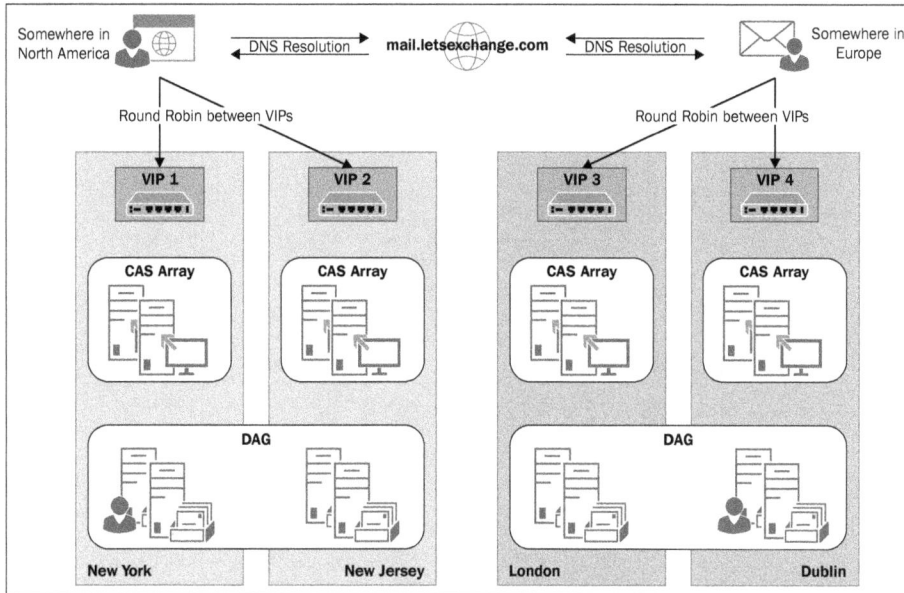

Achieving site resilience for the Mailbox server

Now that we have high availability and failover at the namespace level between datacenters, we need to achieve the same for the Mailbox server role. This is accomplished in a similar way to Exchange 2010, by extending a DAG across two or more datacenters.

An organization's SLA covering failure and disaster recovery scenarios is what mostly influences a DAG's design. Every aspect needs to be considered: the number of DAGs to be deployed, the number of members in the DAG(s), the number of database copies, if site resilience is to be used and whether it has to be used for all users or just a subset, if the multiple site solution will be active/active or active/passive, and so on. As to the latter, there are generally three main scenarios when considering a two-datacenter model.

Scenario 1 – active/passive

In an active/passive configuration, all users' databases are mounted in an active (primary) datacenter, with a passive (standby) datacenter used only in the event of a disaster affecting the active datacenter; this is shown in the following diagram:

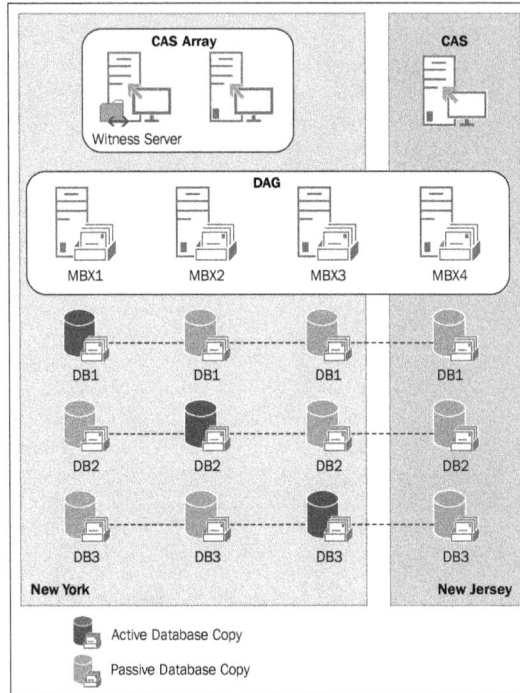

There are several reasons why organizations might choose this model. Usually, it is because the passive datacenter is not as well equipped as the active one and, as such, is not capable of efficiently hosting all the services provided in the active datacenter. Sometimes, it is simply due to the fact that most or all users are closer to the active datacenter.

In this example, a copy of each database in the New York datacenter is replicated to the **MBX4** server in the New Jersey datacenter so they can be used in a disaster recovery scenario to provide messaging services to users. By also having database replicas in New York, we provide intrasite resilience. For example, if server **MBX1** goes down, database **DB1**, which is currently mounted on server **MBX1**, will automatically failover to servers **MBX2** or **MBX3** without users even realizing or being affected.

In some failure scenarios where a server shutdown is initiated (for example, when an **Uninterruptible Power Supply** (**UPS**) issues a shutdown command to the server), Exchange tries to activate another copy of the database(s) that the server is hosting, before the shutdown is complete. In case of a hard failure (for example, hardware failure), it will be the other servers detecting the problem and automatically mounting the affected database(s) on another server.

In this scenario, we could lose up to two Mailbox servers in New York before having to perform a datacenter switchover (as discussed in *Chapter 3, High Availability with the Mailbox Server*). As New York is considered the primary datacenter, the witness server is placed in New York. If, for some reason, the primary site is lost, the majority of the quorum voters is lost, so the entire DAG goes offline. At this stage, administrators have to perform a datacenter switchover, just like in Exchange 2010. However, because the recovery of a DAG is decoupled from the recovery of the namespace, it becomes much easier to perform the switchover, assuming a global namespace is being used. All that the administrators need to do is run the following three cmdlets to get the DAG up and running again in New Jersey:

- Set the failed servers in the New York site as shown:

  ```
  Stop-DatabaseAvailabilityGroup <DAG_Name> -ActiveDirectorySite
  NewYork
  ```

- On the remaining DAG members, stop the Cluster service by running the following code line:

  ```
  Stop-Clussvc
  ```

- Activate the DAG members in New Jersey using the following code line:

  ```
  Restore-DatabaseAvailabilityGroup <DAG_Name> -ActiveDirectorySite
  NewJersey
  ```

It is true that placing the witness server in the passive datacenter (when a DAG has the same number of nodes in both datacenters) would allow Exchange to automatically failover the DAG to the passive datacenter if the active site went down. However, there is a major disadvantage of doing this: if the passive site were to go down, even though it does not host any active databases, the entire DAG would go offline as the members in the active datacenter would not have quorum. This is why, in this scenario, it is recommended to always place the witness server in the active site.

In order to prevent databases in New Jersey from being automatically mounted by Exchange, the `Set-MailboxServer` cmdlet can be used together with the `DatabaseCopyAutoActivationPolicy` parameter to specify the type of automatic activation on selected Mailbox servers. This parameter can be configured to any of the following values:

- **Blocked**: Prevents databases from being automatically activated on selected server(s).

- **IntrasiteOnly**: Only allows incoming mailbox database copies to be activated if the source server is on the same AD site, thus preventing cross-site activation or failover.

- **Unrestricted**: Allows mailbox database copies on selected server(s) from being activated independent of the location of the source database. This is the default value.

For the preceding example, we would run the following cmdlet in order to prevent database copies from being automatically activated on **MBX4**:

```
Set-MailboxServer MBX4 -DatabaseCopyAutoActivationPolicy Blocked
```

As New York and New Jersey are on different AD sites, setting the `DatabaseCopyAutoActivationPolicy` parameter to `IntrasiteOnly` would achieve the same result. In either case, when performing a database switchover, administrators need to first remove the restriction on the target server, as shown in the following code, otherwise they will not be able to mount any databases.

```
Set-MailboxServer MBX4 -DatabaseCopyAutoActivationPolicy Unrestricted
```

Scenario 2 – active/active

In this configuration, users' mailboxes are hosted across both datacenters. This is a very common scenario for deployments with a user population close to both locations. If Exchange fails for users in either of the datacenters, its services are activated on the other datacenter. Instead of simply having some active databases on the **MBX4** server (refer to the preceding diagram), multiple DAG members are deployed in the New Jersey datacenter in order to provide protection against additional failures and additional capacity so it can support the entire user population in case the New York datacenter fails.

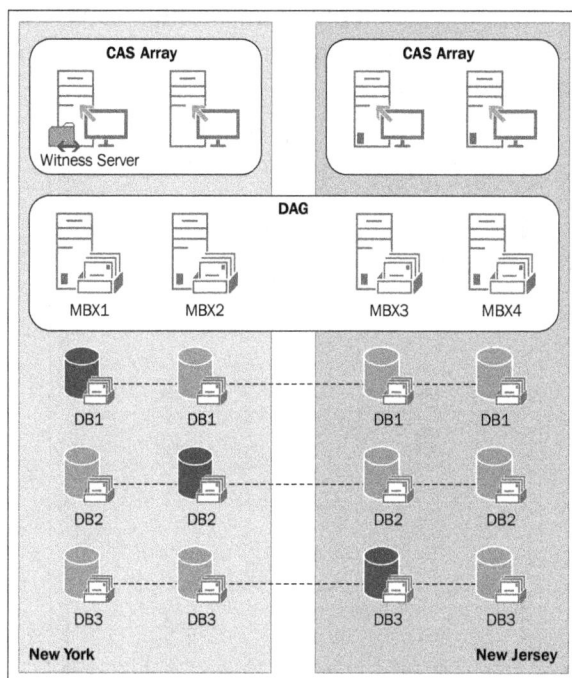

By having more than one member in each datacenter, we are able to provide both intrasite and intersite resilience. Proper planning is crucial, especially capacity planning, so that each server is capable of hosting all workloads, including protocol request handling, processing, and data rendering from other servers without impacting the performance.

In this example, the DAG is extended across both datacenters to provide site resilience for users on both sites. However, this particular scenario has a single point of failure: the network connection (most likely a WAN) between the datacenters. Remember that the majority of the voters must be active and able to talk to each other in order to maintain quorum. In *the preceding diagram*, the majority of voters are located in the New York datacenter, meaning that a WAN outage would cause a service failure for users whose mailboxes are mounted in New Jersey. This happens because when the WAN connection fails, only the DAG members in the New York datacenter are able to maintain the quorum. As such, servers in New Jersey will automatically bring their active database copies offline.

In order to overcome this single point of failure, multiple DAGs should be implemented, with each DAG having a majority of voters in different datacenters, as shown in the following diagram:

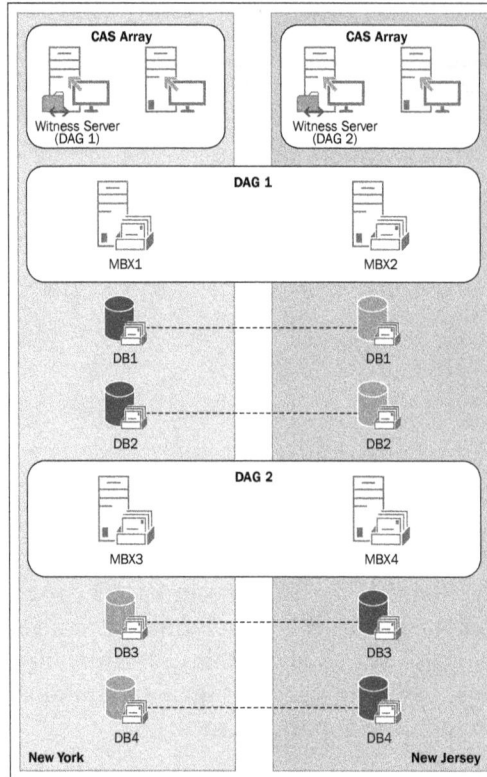

In this example, we would configure **DAG1** with its witness server in New York and **DAG2** with its witness server in New Jersey. By doing so, if a WAN outage happens, replication will fail, but all users will still have messaging services as both DAGs continue to retain quorum and are able to provide services to their local user population.

Scenario 3 – third datacenter

The third scenario is the only one to provide automatic DAG failover between datacenters. It involves splitting a DAG across two datacenters, as in the previous scenarios, with the difference that the witness server is placed in a third location. This allows it to be arbitrated by members of the DAG in both datacenters independent of the network state between the two sites. As such, it is a key to place the witness server in a location that is isolated from possible network failures that might affect either location containing the DAG members.

This was fully supported in Exchange 2010, but the downside was that the solution itself would not get automatically failed over as the namespace would still need to be manually switched over. For this reason, it was not recommended. Going back to the advantage of the namespace in Exchange 2013 not needing to move with the DAG, this entire process now becomes automatic as shown in the following diagram:

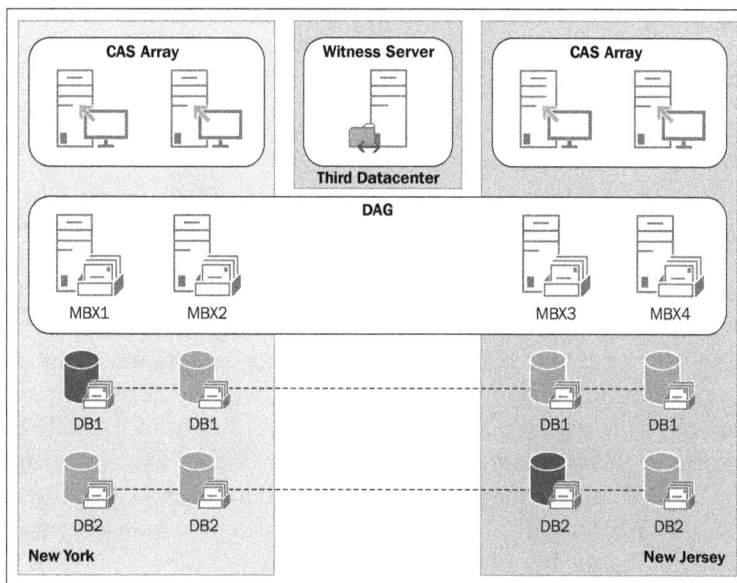

However, even though this scenario is now recommended, special consideration needs to be taken into account for when the network link between the two datacenters hosting Exchange mailboxes fail. For example, even though the DAG will continue to be fully operational on both datacenters, CASs in New York will not be able to proxy requests to servers in New Jersey. As such, proper planning is necessary in order to minimize user impact in such an event. One way of doing this is to ensure that DNS servers that are local to users only resolve the namespace to the VIP on the same site. This would cancel the advantages of single and global namespace, but as a workaround during an outage, it would reduce cross-site connections, ensuring users are not affected.

Windows Azure

Microsoft has been testing the possibility of placing a DAG's witness server in a Windows Azure **IaaS** (**Infrastructure as a Service**) environment. However, this infrastructure does not yet support the necessary network components to cater to this scenario. At the time of writing this book, Azure supports two types of networks: single site-to-site VPN (a network connecting two locations) and one or more point-to-site VPNs (a network connecting a single VPN client to a location). The issue is that in order for a server to be placed in Azure and configured as a witness server, two site-to-site VPNs would be required, connecting each datacenter hosting Exchange servers to Azure, which is not possible today. As such, the use of Azure to place a DAG's witness server is not supported at this stage.

Using Datacenter Activation Coordination (DAC)

DAC is a DAG setting that is disabled by default. It is used to control the startup behavior of databases.

Let us suppose the following scenario: a DAG split across two datacenters, like the one shown in the first diagram of the section *Scenario 2 – active/active*, and the primary datacenter suffers a complete power outage. All servers and the WAN link are down, so a decision is made to activate the standby datacenter. Usually in such scenarios, WAN connectivity is not instantly restored when the primary datacenter gets its power back. When this happens, members of the DAG in the primary datacenter are powered up but are not able to communicate with other members in the standby datacenter that is currently active. As the primary datacenter contains most of the DAG quorum voters (or so it should), when the power is restored, the DAG members located in the primary datacenter have the majority; so, they have quorum. The issue with this is that with quorum, they can mount their databases (assuming everything required to do so is operational, such as storage), which causes discrepancy with the actual active databases mounted in the standby datacenter. So now we have the exact same databases mounted simultaneously in separate servers. This is commonly known as **split brain syndrome**.

DAC was specifically created to prevent a split brain scenario. It does so through the **Datacenter Activation Coordination Protocol (DACP)** protocol. Once such a failure occurs, when the DAG is recovered, it will not automatically mount databases even if it has quorum. DACP is instead used to evaluate the DAG's current state and if databases should be mounted or not in each server by the Active Manager.

Active Manager uses memory to store a bit (a 0 or a 1); so, the DAG knows if it can mount databases that are assigned as active on the local server. When DAC is enabled, every time the Active Manager is started, it sets the bit to 0, meaning it is not allowed to mount any databases. The server is then forced to establish communication with the other DAG members in order to get another server to tell it if it is allowed to mount its local databases or not. The answer from the other members is simply their bit setting in the DAG. If a server replies that it has its bit set to 1, the server is permitted to mount databases and also set its own bit to 1.

On the other hand, when restoring the DAG in the preceding scenario, all the members of the DAG in the primary datacenter will have their DACP bit set to 0. As such, none of the servers powering up in the recovered primary datacenter are allowed to mount any databases because none of them are able to communicate with a server that has a DACP bit set to 1.

Besides dealing for split brain scenarios, enabling DAC mode allows administrators to use the site resilience built-in cmdlets to carry out datacenter switchovers:

```
Stop-DatabaseAvailabilityGroup
Restore-DatabaseAvailabilityGroup
Start-DatabaseAvailabilityGroup
```

When DAC mode is disabled, both Exchange and cluster management tools need to be used when performing datacenter switchovers.

Enabling the DAC mode

DAC can only be enabled or disabled using the `Set-DatabaseAvailabilityGroup` cmdlet together with the `DatacenterActivationMode` parameter. To enable DAC mode, this parameter is set to `DagOnly` and to disable it, it is set to `Off`:

```
Set-DatabaseAvailabilityGroup <DAG_Name> -DatacenterActivationMode DagOnly
```

Deciding where to place witness servers

When designing and configuring a DAG, it is important to consider the location of the witness server. As we have seen, this is very much dependent on the business requirements and what is available to the organization. As already discussed, Exchange 2013 allows scenarios that were not previously recommended, such as placing a witness server on a third location.

The following table summarizes the general recommendations around the placement of the witness servers according to different deployment scenarios:

Scenario		Place Witness Server In...
# DAGs	# Datacenters	
1	1	The datacenter where the DAG members are located.
1	2	The primary datacenter (refer to diagrams of section *Scenario 1 – active/passive* and *Scenario 2 – active/active*).
		A third location that is isolated from possible network failures that might affect either datacenter containing DAG members.
2+	1	The datacenter where the DAG members are located.
		The same witness server can be used for multiple DAGs.
		A DAG member can be used as a witness server for another DAG.
2+	2	The datacenter where the DAG members are located.
		The same witness server can be used for multiple DAGs.
		A DAG member can be used as a witness server for another DAG.
		A third location that is isolated from possible network failures that might affect either of the datacenters containing DAG members.
1 or 2+	3+	The datacenter where administrators want the majority of voters to be.
		A third location that is isolated from possible network failures that might affect either of the datacenters containing DAG members.

Summary

Throughout this chapter, we explored all the great enhancements made to Exchange 2013 in regards to site resilience. The removal of the limitation of CASs being bound to a single AD site, the introduction of a single and global namespace, and automatic failover at the client side all contribute to a much smoother datacenter recovery process with user impact being further reduced. As the recovery of a DAG is no longer tied together with the recovery of the client access namespace, each one of these components can be easily switched over between different datacenters without affecting the other component. This also allows administrators to place a witness server in a third datacenter in order to provide automatic failover for a DAG on either of the datacenters it is split across, something not recommended in Exchange 2010.

All in all, site resilience has come a long way and it is definitely one of the greatest improvements in Exchange 2013. In the next chapter, we will explore transport high availability, including the improvements made to shadow redundancy and safety nets so that no e-mails are lost while in transit.

5
Transport High Availability

Transport high availability seems to be one of those areas that Exchange Administrators do not really worry about—they just assume that an e-mail, once in Exchange, will always be delivered as long as the target mailbox is available. However, what if a server trying to send a newsletter to 40 recipients fails all of a sudden? What happens to those 40 e-mails? High availability for the Exchange transport pipeline is crucial to guarantee that no e-mails are lost while in transit. This is also very important in large deployments with dozens of servers, where e-mails sometimes cross countries before being delivered to their destination mailbox.

Before we delve into how Exchange 2013 further improves transport high availability, we first need to understand how the transport pipeline works in Exchange 2013. Please note that this is simply a high-level overview and not an in-depth explanation, as the main objective of this chapter is to understand how Exchange 2013 protects e-mails while in transit, and not how they are routed and delivered.

Servicing of the transport pipeline

Mail flow takes place in Exchange through the transport pipeline, which includes components, connections, services, and queues working collectively to route e-mails. With all the architectural changes introduced in Exchange 2013, three different services are part of the transport pipeline, and they are as follows:

- **Front End Transport service**: Running on CASs, this service is a stateless proxy for the external SMTP traffic, which is both inbound and outbound. It communicates only with the Transport service on Mailbox servers, and does not inspect or queue any e-mails.

- **Transport service**: Running on Mailbox servers, this service is similar to the previous Hub Transport server role. It handles the mail flow within the organization, and performs content-inspection and e-mail categorization. It is capable of queuing e-mails, but it does not communicate with mailbox databases; it simply routes e-mails between the Front End Transport service and the Mailbox Transport service.

- **Mailbox Transport service**: Running on Mailbox servers as well, this service is made up of two services:

    ◦ **Mailbox Transport Submission service**: This uses **Remote Procedure Calls (RPC)** to connect to mailbox databases in order to retrieve e-mails and submit them to the Transport service using SMTP. It does not queue e-mails.

    ◦ **Mailbox Transport Delivery service**: This receives e-mails from the Transport service over SMTP and uses RPC to connect to the target's mailbox database in order to deliver the e-mail. If the server is part of a DAG, the e-mail is only accepted by the Mailbox Transport service on the server holding the mailbox database's active copy.

E-mails received from the Internet are delivered to Exchange using a third-party smart host, an Edge server, or through the Front End Transport service of an Exchange 2013 CAS by a Receive connector. Before Hub Transport servers were configured out of the box to reject e-mails from the Internet. However, all Exchange 2013 CASs now have a Receive connector called `Default Frontend <server_name>`, which is configured by default to allow **Anonymous users** to connect to it:

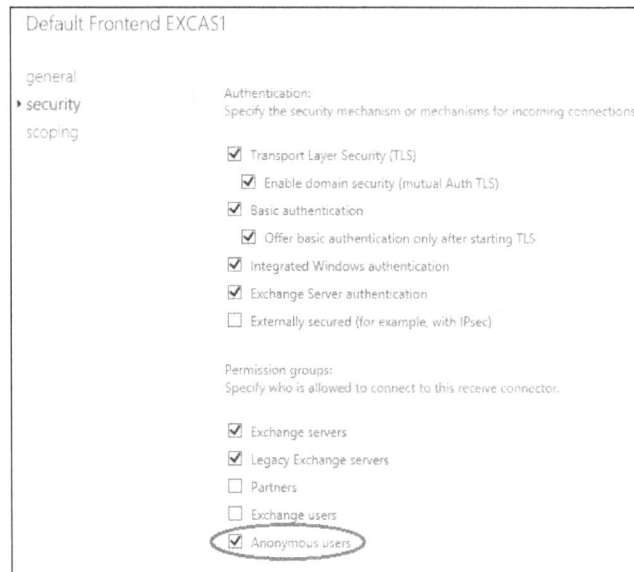

Regarding internal e-mails, these arrive at the Transport service through one of the following four methods:

- The Receive connector.
- Pickup and replay directories.
- The Mailbox Transport service.
- Transport agent submission. (Transport agents provide administrators with the ability to install custom software on an Exchange server in order to process e-mails passing through the transport pipeline. This might be software written by Microsoft, by a third-party vendor, or by an organization's developer.)

The Transport service itself consists of the following processes and components:

- **SMTP receive**: This performs content inspection and applies transport rules. It also performs anti-malware/anti-spam inspection (if enabled). The e-mail is then placed in the Submission queue if it does not get rejected by the SMTP receive.
- **Submission**: The e-mail is placed in the Submission queue through one of three methods, which are a Receive connector, replay and pickup directories (now residing on Mailbox servers), or a transport agent.
- **Categorizer**: This takes e-mails from the Submission queue, one at a time, and performs the following actions:
    - Recipient resolution, which determines if it is an internal or external user to the Exchange organization.
    - Routing resolution, which determines the destination of the e-mail, the route to that destination, and the next hop.
    - Content conversion, which enables the e-mail to be sent in a readable format by the recipient. E-mails might be converted to HTML, a plain text or rich text format, MAPI to MIME, and so on.

> Mail flow rules are also applied at this stage. After an e-mail has been categorized, it is placed in a delivery queue.

- **SMTP send**: Based on the recipient's location, the e-mail is routed to the following destinations:

  ° The same Mailbox server (Mailbox Transport service)

  ° A different Mailbox server (Mailbox Transport service) that is a member of the same DAG

  ° A different Mailbox server (Transport service) that is a member of a different DAG, AD site, or AD forest

  ° A CAS (Front End Transport service) for delivery out to the Internet

The following diagram taken from Microsoft TechNet (`http://technet.microsoft.com/en-us/library/aa996349(v=exchg.150).aspx`) puts everything discussed so far together, and shows the relationships between the different transport pipeline components in Exchange 2013:

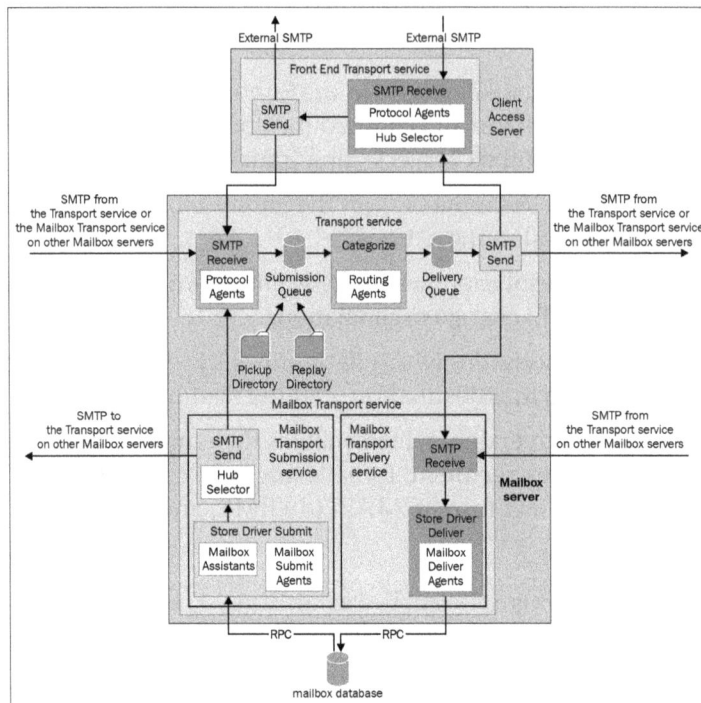

The main objective of the Transport service is to route e-mails to their final destination, with routing decisions being made during the categorization stage. Because this service is hosted by Mailbox servers in Exchange 2013, the routing process is now fully DAG-aware and uses DAGs as routing boundaries. This means that if a Mailbox server is a DAG member, the primary mechanism used to route e-mails is closely aligned with the DAG. This is because if the DAG is spread across more than one AD site, it would be inefficient to use the AD site as the routing boundary. However, the AD site membership is still used as routing boundaries for servers that are not part of a DAG, or while routing e-mails to Exchange 2007/2010.

Front End Transport service routing

For **outgoing** e-mails, administrators need to create a Send connector, as Exchange 2013 by default does not allow sending e-mails outside of a domain. The Transport service will then use this Send connector to route e-mails out to the Internet. However, such Send connectors should be configured so that the Transport service proxies these messages through the Front End Transport service on a CAS.

To do this, we can use the Shell and the cmdlet `Set-SendConnector <Connector_Name> -FrontendProxyEnabled $True`, or enable the **Proxy through client access server** option in the EAC, shown as follows:

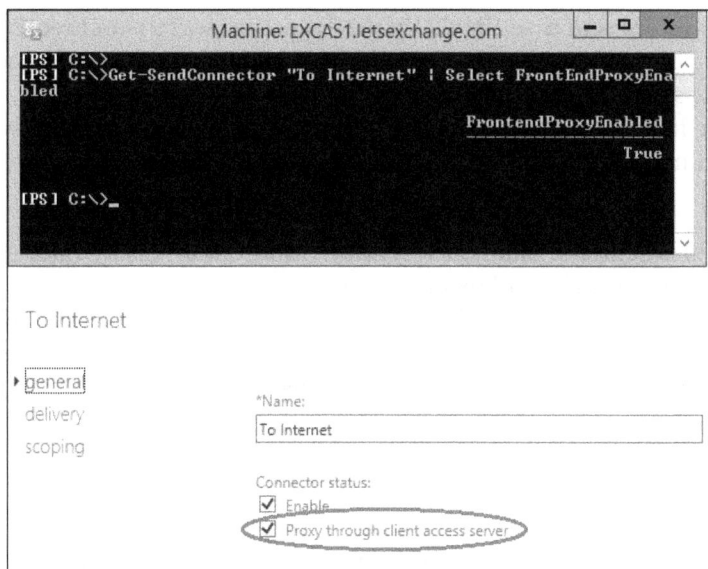

Regarding **incoming** e-mails, the Front End Transport service tries to find one Mailbox server with its Transport service in a healthy state in order to receive the e-mail. If it is unable to do so, the external sender will perceive the service as being unavailable, as this service does not queue e-mails. The Front End Transport service then queries the AD to resolve the recipients to mailbox databases (unless the e-mail is, for example, for a distribution group). For each database, it checks the delivery group, which can be a DAG, a mailbox, or an AD site, and its routing information.

Based on the type and number of recipients, one of the following actions is performed by the Front End Transport service:

- If the e-mail has a single recipient, it selects a Mailbox server in the target delivery group, giving preference to a server based on the proximity of the AD site.

- If the e-mail has multiple recipients, it uses the first 20 recipients to select a Mailbox server in the closest delivery group, again based on the proximity of the AD site. As e-mail bifurcation does not happen in the Front End Transport service, only one Mailbox server is selected, independent of the number of recipients.

Mailbox Transport service routing

Incoming e-mails are sent over SMTP by the Transport service and received by the Mailbox Transport Delivery service, which then establishes an RPC connection to the local database in order to deliver the e-mail. As for outgoing e-mails, this service connects to the local database, again using RPC, to collect e-mails, and then submits them to the Transport service over SMTP. This is a stateless service that does not queue e-mails.

When an e-mail is sent, the Mailbox Transport Submission service queries the AD to resolve the recipients to mailbox databases (unless the e-mail is for a distribution group, for example). For each database, it identifies the delivery group, which can be a DAG, a mailbox, or an AD site, and its routing information. Based on the type and number of recipients, one of the following actions is performed:

- If the e-mail has a single recipient, it selects a Mailbox server in the target delivery group, giving preference to a server based on the proximity of the AD site.

- If the e-mail has multiple recipients, it uses the first 20 recipients to select a Mailbox server in the closest delivery group, again based on the proximity of the AD site.

The Mailbox Transport Delivery service is only able to deliver e-mails to a recipient whose mailbox database is mounted locally. If that is not the case, it sends a non-delivery response back to the Transport service. This situation might happen, for example, if the mailbox database's active copy was very recently moved to a different server, and the Transport service wrongly forwarded the e-mail to the Mailbox server that was hosting the active copy but now only hosts a passive copy. This non-delivery response can be one of the following:

- Retry delivery
- Non-delivery report
- E-mail reroute

Improving on transport high availability

Now that we understand how the transport pipeline works in Exchange 2013 and how e-mails are routed, let us look at how high availability is achieved to ensure no e-mails are lost while in transit. This is done by keeping redundant copies of e-mails both before and after they are successfully delivered. **Transport dumpster** was introduced in Exchange 2007, and **shadow redundancy** in Exchange 2010. Exchange 2013 took these two features a step further.

As a brief summary, the following are the main improvements in transport high availability:

- Shadow redundancy generates a redundant copy of an e-mail on a different server before it is accepted. If shadow redundancy is not supported by the sending server, this is not a problem, as we will see shortly.

- Shadow redundancy uses both DAGs and AD sites as boundaries for transport high availability, which eliminates unnecessary redundant e-mail traffic across DAGs or AD sites.

- The transport dumpster feature, now called Safety Net, has been further improved. Safety Net temporarily stores e-mails that are processed successfully by the Transport service.

- Safety Net is now made redundant on a different server, avoiding a single point of failure, as mailbox databases and the Transport service are located on the same server.

The following diagram shows at a higher level an overview of transport high availability in action in Exchange 2013:

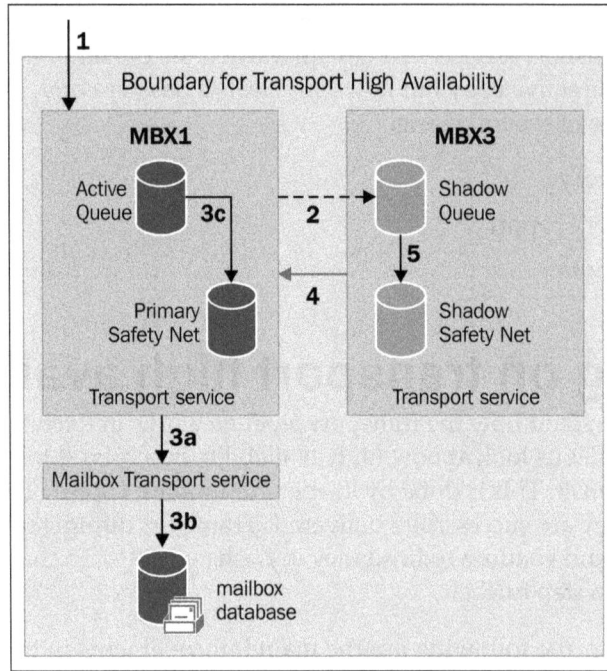

The description of the preceding diagram is as follows:

1. The Mailbox server, **MBX1**, receives an e-mail from a server outside the boundary for transport high availability.

2. Before acknowledging that the e-mail was received, **MBX1** starts an SMTP session to another Exchange 2013 Mailbox server named **MBX3** within the boundary for transport high availability, and **MBX3** creates a shadow copy of the e-mail. In this scenario, **MBX1** holds the primary e-mail (primary server) and **MBX3** holds the shadow e-mail (shadow server).

3. On **MBX1**, the Transport service processes the primary e-mail as follows:

    1. As the recipient's mailbox is hosted by **MBX1**, the Transport service passes the e-mail to the local Mailbox Transport service.

    2. The e-mail is delivered to the local database by the Mailbox Transport service.

    3. **MBX1** queues a discard status for **MBX3**, indicating that the primary e-mail was processed successfully, and moves a copy of the primary e-mail to the local **Primary Safety Net** (the e-mail remains in the same queue database, but moves to a different queue).

4. **MBX3** polls **MBX1** periodically for the status of the primary e-mail.

5. **MBX3** eventually determines that **MBX1** processed the primary e-mail successfully and moves the shadow e-mail to the local **Shadow Safety Net** (again, the e-mail remains in the same queue database, but moves to a different queue).

The e-mail is kept in both the **Primary Safety Net** and **Shadow Safety Net** until it expires, based on a configurable timeout value (2 days by default). In case a database failover happens before this timeout period is reached, the **Primary Safety Net** on **MBX1** resubmits the e-mail. If **MBX1** is not available, **MBX3** resubmits the e-mail from its **Shadow Safety Net**.

Revisiting shadow redundancy

Shadow redundancy was introduced in Exchange 2010 as a mechanism to generate redundant copies of e-mails before being delivered to mailboxes. It delayed deleting an e-mail from the transport database on a Hub Transport server until the server confirmed that the next hop in the delivery path for the e-mail had completed its delivery. In case the next hop crashed before having the chance to report a successful delivery back to the transport server, the transport server would resubmit the e-mail to that next hop. The XSHADOW command was used to advertise shadow redundancy support.

We already saw that CASs do not queue e-mails locally, and that it does not matter if shadow redundancy is not supported by the sending server. The Front End Transport service will keep the SMTP session open on the sending server while the e-mail is being transmitted to the Transport service, and a shadow copy is created on a different Mailbox server. Only after this happens is the SMTP session with the sending server terminated, ensuring that an e-mail acknowledgment is only sent to the server if the e-mail is made redundant in Exchange.

The main enhancement to shadow redundancy in Exchange 2013 is the creation of a redundant copy of any of the e-mails before acknowledging to the sending server that is successfully receiving them. As a sending server does not need to support shadow redundancy, any e-mails entering the transport pipeline in Exchange 2013 are made redundant while in transit.

As we saw in the preceding diagram, more than one Exchange 2013 Mailbox server (standalone or multirole) is required for shadow redundancy. However, other restrictions applied are as follows::

- If it is not a DAG member, the other server has to be in the local AD.
- If it is a DAG member, the other server has to be a member of the same DAG. In this case, the other server can be in the local or in a remote AD site, with preference given to a server in a remote site for site resiliency.

Unfortunately, there are three scenarios under which shadow redundancy is not able to protect e-mails in transit, which are as follows:

- In an environment with a single Exchange server
- When a DAG has no more nodes to fail over to
- When both primary and shadow servers fail simultaneously

Creating shadow e-mails

The purpose of shadow redundancy is to have two copies of an e-mail within the boundary of transport high availability while it is in transit. In which server and at what stage the redundant copy gets created will depend on where the e-mail comes from and where it is going, according to the following factors:

- E-mails arriving from outside the boundary of transport high availability
- E-mails sent outside the boundary of transport high availability
- E-mails arriving from a Mailbox server within the boundary of transport high availability

As we have seen, a boundary for transport high availability is either a DAG for servers that are DAG members (including DAGs across multiple AD sites) or an AD site for servers that are not DAG members. This means that if an e-mail crosses a boundary, shadow redundancy is initiated or restarted, as it never tracks e-mails beyond a boundary.

Coexistent scenarios with Exchange 2010 Hub Transport servers are a different case, which we will explore shortly.

E-mails arriving from outside the boundary of transport high availability

When the Transport service receives an e-mail arriving from outside the boundary of transport high availability, it does not matter if the sending server supports shadow redundancy or not. Shadow redundancy will create a redundant copy of the e-mail on a different Mailbox server within the boundary while the initial SMTP session with the sending server remains active. Only when the primary zserver receives an acknowledgement that the shadow e-mail was created successfully does it acknowledge the receipt of the e-mail back to the sender and close the SMTP session.

E-mails sent outside the boundary of transport high availability

When an e-mail is sent outside the boundary of transport high availability, and the receiving SMTP server acknowledges that it received the e-mail successfully, the sending Exchange 2013 server moves the e-mail into Safety Net. After the primary e-mail is transmitted successfully across the boundary, it cannot be resubmitted from Safety Net.

In the following screenshot, we can see an internal user sending an e-mail to an external recipient and the Mailbox server, EXMBX1, creating a shadow copy of that e-mail on the server EXMBX2. The following screenshot was captured by running the following cmdlet:

```
Get-TransportService | Get-MessageTrackingLog | Sort TimeStamp
```

E-mails arriving from a Mailbox server within the boundary of transport high availability

When the Transport service on a server accepts an e-mail whose destination is the same DAG or AD site, the next hop for the e-mail is generally the final destination itself. Shadow redundancy is achieved by keeping another copy of the e-mail anywhere in the same DAG or AD site.

Shadow redundancy with legacy Hub Transport servers

In a coexistent scenario with Exchange 2010 servers (not 2007), shadow redundancy is maintained as well. For example, when an e-mail is sent within the same AD site from a 2010 Hub Transport server to a 2013 Mailbox server, the Hub Transport server uses the XSHADOW command to advertise that it supports shadow redundancy. However, the 2013 server does not advertise its support in order to prevent the 2010 server from creating a shadow copy of the e-mail on a 2013 Mailbox server.

When an e-mail is sent within the same AD site from a 2013 Mailbox server to a 2010 Hub Transport server, the 2013 server shadows the e-mail on behalf of the 2010 server. When the 2013 server receives acknowledgement from the 2010 server that the e-mail was successfully received, the 2013 server moves the e-mail into Safety Net. However, once the e-mail is moved into Safety Net, it is never resubmitted to the 2010 Hub Transport server.

Configuring shadow redundancy

Shadow redundancy is a global setting that is enabled by default (it is not possible to enable or disable shadow redundancy on a per-server basis). To disable it, we use the `Set-TransportConfig` cmdlet to set the `ShadowRedundancyEnabled` parameter to `$False`:

It is possible that while trying to create a redundant copy of an e-mail, the SMTP connection between the primary and the shadow servers, or the one between the sending and the primary servers, times out. If this happens, or if for some reason a Mailbox server is unable to generate a redundant copy, the e-mail is not rejected by default. However, if generating a redundant copy for every e-mail entering the organization is paramount, Exchange can be configured to reject an e-mail if a redundant copy of it is not generated. This is done by using the `Set-TransportConfig` cmdlet to set the `RejectMessageOnShadowFailure` parameter to `$True`:

In this scenario, the e-mail will be rejected with a **451 4.4.0 Message failed to be made redundant** SMTP response code, but the sending server can retransmit it again.

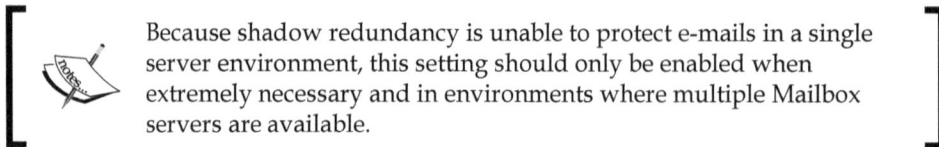

> Because shadow redundancy is unable to protect e-mails in a single server environment, this setting should only be enabled when extremely necessary and in environments where multiple Mailbox servers are available.

If a shadow copy of the e-mail gets created but the SMTP session between the sending and primary servers times out, the primary e-mail is accepted and processed by the primary server, but the sending server will try to redeliver the unacknowledged e-mails. Exchange's duplicate e-mail detection kicks in and prevents the recipient from receiving two identical e-mails, even though the primary server generates another shadow copy of the e-mail upon resubmission.

The following Set-TransportConfig parameters control how shadow e-mails are created:

- ShadowMessagePreferenceSetting: This controls where a shadow copy of an e-mail gets generated. It can be set to PreferRemote (the default value) to try to create a copy in a different AD site LocalOnly, to only create a copy in the local AD site, or RemoteOnly, to only create a copy in a different AD site. This parameter is used only for members of a DAG spread across multiple AD sites.

- MaxRetriesForRemoteSiteShadow: This specifies how many times (4 by default) a Mailbox server attempts to generate a shadow copy of an e-mail on a remote AD site (if ShadowMessagePreferenceSetting = RemoteOnly) or on a remote site before trying to create it in the same local AD site (if ShadowMessagePreferenceSetting = PreferRemote). If unable to, the e-mail will either be rejected or accepted depending on the setting of the RejectMessageOnShadowFailure parameter.

- MaxRetriesForLocalSiteShadow: This specifies how many times (2 by default) a Mailbox server attempts to generate a shadow copy of an e-mail on the same local AD site. This parameter is used when ShadowMessagePreferenceSetting = PreferRemote, or ShadowMessagePreferenceSetting = LocalOnly, when the Mailbox server is not a DAG member or if its DAG is on a single AD site. If unable to, the e-mail will either be rejected or accepted depending on the setting of the RejectMessageOnShadowFailure parameter.

Both Receive and Send connectors have a `ConnectionInactivityTimeOut` setting that can be used to specify the duration for which an SMTP connection can remain idle before it is closed. Receive connectors have an additional parameter, `ConnectionTimeout`, to specify for how long an SMTP connection can remain open before it is closed, even if data is still being transmitted.

Maintaining shadow e-mails

The work of shadow redundancy does not stop when a shadow e-mail is created, as the primary and shadow servers have to remain in contact so that they can track the status and progress of the e-mail. When it is transmitted successfully to the next hop by the primary server, and the next hop acknowledges the receiving of the e-mail, the **discard status** of the e-mail is updated to the **delivery complete** status by the primary server. This discard status is simply a message containing a list of e-mails being monitored by shadow redundancy.

When an e-mail is delivered successfully, there is no need to keep it in a shadow queue. Therefore, when the shadow server realizes that the e-mail was successfully transmitted to the next hop by the primary server, it moves the shadow e-mail into Safety Net.

In order for a shadow server to determine the discard status of shadow e-mails in its own shadow queues, it queries the primary server and issues a `XQDISCARD` command. The primary server then responds with the **discard notification** for e-mails that apply to that shadow server. Discard notifications are not stored in memory but on the disk, so they persist if the server or the Microsoft Exchange Transport service restarts.

This communication between the primary and shadow servers is also used as a heartbeat to determine the servers' availability. If the shadow server is unable to establish a session with the primary server after a certain amount of time (three hours, by default, configurable using the `ShadowResubmitTimeSpan` parameter), the shadow server will promote itself to the primary server, promote the shadow e-mails to primary e-mails, and transmit them to the next hop.

Several parameters of the `Set-TransportConfig` cmdlet are used to control how shadow e-mails are maintained. They are as follows:

- `ShadowHeartbeatFrequency`: This specifies the duration (two minutes, by default) for which a shadow server waits before checking for the discard status by establishing a session with the primary server.

- `ShadowResubmitTimeSpan`: This specifies the duration (3 hours, by default) for which a server waits before determining that a primary server has failed and so assumes control of shadow e-mails in the shadow queue for the unreachable primary server.

- `ShadowMessageAutoDiscardInterval`: This specifies the duration (2 days, by default) for which the discard events will be retained of e-mails that are successfully delivered. A primary server queues the discard events until the shadow server queries it. If it is not queried during the time specified in this parameter, the queued discard events are deleted by the primary server.

- `SafetyNetHoldTime`: This specifies the duration (2 days, by default) for which the successfully processed e-mails are kept in Safety Net. Shadow e-mails that are not acknowledged expire from Safety Net after the time period of `SafetyNetHoldTime` + `MessageExpirationTimeout`.

- `MessageExpirationTimeout`: A part of the `Get-TransportService` cmdlet specifies the duration (2 days, by default) for which e-mails can remain in a queue before expiring.

Shadow redundancy after an outage

When a server outage occurs, shadow redundancy will minimize e-mail loss. When the failed Mailbox server is brought back online, two scenarios are possible:

- The server has a new transport database, and therefore, it is recognized by other transport servers in the organization as being a new route. As such, servers with shadow e-mails queued for the recovered server assume ownership of these e-mails and resubmit them. The e-mails are then delivered to their destinations. E-mails are delayed for a maximum amount of time specified by `ShadowHeartbeatFrequency`.

- The server has the same transport database, but is offline long enough for the shadow server to take ownership of the e-mails and resubmit them. When the server is brought back online, it delivers the e-mails in its queues, resulting in duplicate delivery as the shadow server had already delivered these e-mails. However, duplicate e-mail detection prevents recipients from receiving duplicate e-mails. E-mails are delayed for a maximum amount of time specified by `ShadowResubmitTimeSpan`.

Safety Net

Safety Net, as already mentioned, is the enhanced version of transport dumpster. Introduced in Exchange 2007, this feature provided redundant copies of e-mails in case of a lossy failover in the **Cluster Continuous Replication (CCR)** or **Local Continuous Replication (LCR)** environments by having Hub Transport servers located in the same AD site automatically redeliver those e-mails in the transport dumpster queue. Transport dumpster in Exchange 2010 provided the same level of protection, but only for e-mails that had not yet been replicated to the passive database copies in a DAG. If a failure required an out-of-date database copy to be activated, e-mails would be automatically resubmitted from the transport dumpster to the new active copy.

In Exchange 2013, this functionality has been improved and is now called Safety Net.

Obviously, there are a few similarities and differences between the transport dumpster in Exchange 2010 and the new Safety Net, which are as follows:

Similarities	Differences/Improvements
Safety Net remains a queue associated with a Mailbox server's Transport service that keeps copies of e-mails processed successfully by the server.	DAGs are not required for Safety Net. If a Mailbox server is not a DAG member, Safety Net will store a copy of the delivered e-mails in another Mailbox server in the same AD site.
It is possible to specify how long the copies of successfully processed e-mails should be kept by Safety Net before they expire and are deleted (2 days by default).	Safety Net is not a single point of failure anymore. Primary Safety Net and Shadow Safety Net provide resiliency for this feature — if the Primary Safety Net becomes unavailable for over 12 hours, e-mails are redelivered from the Shadow Safety Net.
	Safety Net works in conjunction with shadow redundancy in a DAG environment. Shadow redundancy is not required to store another copy of the delivered e-mail in a shadow queue while it waits for the delivered e-mail to replicate to a database's passive copies. The copy of the delivered e-mail is already kept in Safety Net, and so, if required, it can be resubmitted from Safety Net.
	Transport high availability is no longer a best effort, and Exchange 2013 tries to ensure e-mail redundancy. For this reason, it is no longer possible to specify a maximum size limit for Safety Net, except for how long e-mails should be kept before automatic deletion.
	Safety Net also applies to public folders.

The working of Safety Net

While shadow redundancy preserves a redundant copy of the e-mail while it is in transit, Safety Net preserves a redundant copy of the e-mail after it is processed successfully. Basically, Safety Net begins where shadow redundancy ends. Safety Net uses the same concepts of boundary as transport high availability, primary e-mails, primary servers, shadow e-mails, and shadow servers.

The Primary Safety Net, shown in the diagram in the *Improving on transport high availability* section, is located on the server that was holding the primary e-mail before it was processed successfully by the Transport service. This does not necessarily mean the destination Mailbox server, for example, as the e-mail could have come through a Mailbox server in an AD site through which all e-mails are routed. After the primary e-mail is processed by the primary server, it is moved to the Primary Safety Net on the same server from the active queue.

The Shadow Safety Net, also shown in the diagram in the *Improving on transport high availability* section, is located on the server that was holding the shadow e-mail. When the shadow server determines that the e-mail was processed successfully, it moves the shadow e-mail to the Shadow Safety Net on the same server from the shadow queue.

> As Safety Net and shadow redundancy are very much interlinked, shadow redundancy needs to be enabled for the Shadow Safety Net to work, which it is by default.

The following `Set-TransportConfig` parameters are used by Safety Net:

- `ShadowRedundancyEnabled`: Enables (`$True`) or disables (`$False`) shadow redundancy for all transport servers. Remember that shadow redundancy needs to be enabled for a redundant Safety Net.

- `SafetyNetHoldTime`: Specifies the duration (2 days, by default) for which the successfully processed e-mails are kept in the Primary Safety Net, and for how long the acknowledged shadow e-mails are stored in the Shadow Safety Net. You can also set this value using the EAC by navigating to **mail flow | receive connectors**. Click on the more options icon and then navigate to **Organization transport settings | safety net | Safety Net hold time (days)**. Shadow e-mails that are not acknowledged expire from the Shadow Safety Net after the time period of `SafetyNetHoldTime` + `MessageExpirationTimeout`. While using lagged database copies, in order to prevent data loss during Safety Net resubmits, `SafetyNetHoldTime` has to be the same or greater than `ReplayLagTime` on `Set-MailboxDatabaseCopy`.

The `MessageExpirationTimeout` parameter on `Set-TransportService` specifies for how long an e-mail remains in a queue before expiring (2 days, by default).

Please note that while running the `Get-TransportConfig` cmdlet, we can still see the `MaxDumpsterSizePerDatabase` and `MaxDumpsterTime` parameters:

However, both these parameters are only used by Exchange 2010 and not 2013. The `MaxDumpsterSizePerDatabase` parameter has no replacement in Exchange 2013, while the `MaxDumpsterTime` parameter is replaced by the `SafetyNetHoldTime` parameter as already discussed.

Resubmitting e-mails from Safety Net

Active Manager is the component responsible for initiating an e-mail resubmission from Safety Net, and no manual action is required. E-mails are resubmitted from Safety Net in two basic scenarios:

- After a failover (either automatic or manual) of a database in a DAG
- After a lagged database copy is activated

What is different between these two scenarios is the period of time from which e-mails will be resubmitted. During a DAG failover, the new active database copy is typically only seconds or minutes behind the old active copy, which means Safety Net only had to resubmit e-mails sent and received during this short period of time. However, activating a lagged copy requires Safety Net to resubmit e-mails that were sent and received during an extended period of time, usually several days.

As we saw in the previous section, in order for Safety Net to be successful in resubmitting e-mails for a lagged copy, it is important that e-mails are stored in Safety Net for at least the same time as that of the lag time of the lagged copy. Therefore, the `SafetyNetHoldTime` parameter has to be greater or equal to the `ReplayLagTime` parameter for the lagged copy.

Resubmitting e-mails from Shadow Safety Net

Resubmission of e-mails from the Shadow Safety Net is also completely automated, and manual intervention is not required.

When the Active Manager requests e-mails to be resubmitted from Safety Net for a specific period in time, this request is sent to the Mailbox servers where the Primary Safety Net is storing the e-mail copies for the required time period. In vast deployments, it is common that the required e-mails are kept in Safety Net on several Mailbox servers, especially for a large requested time period.

Resubmitting e-mails from Safety Net is likely to produce a large number of duplicate e-mails. This is overcome by duplicate e-mail detection, which prevents internal users from receiving duplicate e-mails on their mailboxes. However, this only works for e-mails within the Exchange organization. When these are sent to external recipients, duplicate e-mail detection does not work. To cater to this scenario, resubmission of e-mails from Safety Net is optimized to reduce duplicate e-mail delivery.

If, for some reason, Active Manager is unable to communicate with the Primary Safety Net, it will continue to try contacting it for 12 hours. After this 12-hour period, a broadcast to all Mailbox servers within the boundary of transport high availability is sent looking for other Safety Nets that contain e-mails for the target database for the required time period. A Shadow Safety Net will then respond and resubmit the e-mails matching the criteria.

It is worth exploring a particular scenario to show the intelligence of Safety Net. Let us assume the following scenario:

1. The queue database holding the Primary Safety Net got corrupted and a new one was created at 15:00. As such, all of the primary e-mails kept in the Primary Safety Net from 10:00 to 15:00 are lost, but the server is able to keep copies of successfully delivered e-mails in Safety Net starting from 15:00.

2. Active Manager requests the e-mails to be resubmitted from Safety Net for a particular database from 10:00 to 17:00.

3. The Primary Safety Net resubmits all the e-mails it has for the requested time period, which, due to problems with its queue database, is only from 15:00 to 17:00.

4. The Primary Safety Net then sends a broadcast to all Mailbox servers within the boundary of transport high availability, searching for further Safety Nets that contain e-mails for the target database for the time period 10:00 to 15:00, for which the Primary Safety Net has no e-mails. A second resubmit request is generated on behalf of the Primary Safety Net by the Shadow Safety Net, so shadow e-mails for the target database for the time interval 10:00 to 15:00 are resubmitted.

Making an inbound and outbound e-mail flow resilient

Here, we will see how inbound and outbound e-mail flow is more resilient in Exchange 2013.

Outbound

Send connectors are used to control the flow of outbound e-mails to the receiving server, and are configured on Mailbox servers running the Transport service. These are commonly used to send outbound e-mails to an Edge server, a smart host or directly to the Internet.

With the changes in the transport pipeline, Send connectors now behave slightly different. For example, as we saw in the beginning of this chapter, they can be configured on a Mailbox server (Transport service) to route outbound e-mails through a CAS (Front End Transport service) in the local AD site by using the FrontEndProxyEnabled parameter. This is useful to simplify and consolidate e-mail flow, especially in environments with a large number of Exchange servers.

While using Send connectors to send e-mails out to the Internet, administrators have two choices to resolve the recipients' domains:

- Using Edge servers or smart hosts to send e-mails to the Internet
- Using DNS MX records in order to resolve Internet addresses on the Exchange servers

A common misconception is that outbound traffic can be load-balanced simply by creating two Send connectors with the same cost, with each one using DNS to route e-mails directly to the Internet or through different smart hosts or Edge servers. However, when two Send connectors have the same cost, and their source servers are the same or in the same site, Exchange will just choose the one with the alphanumerically lower name. It will not load-balance outgoing e-mails across both connections.

In order to effectively load balance outgoing traffic, a single Send connector with multiple smart hosts or Edge servers should be used. At the same time, by using this method, we are also achieving high availability. If one Edge server fails, Exchange will continue using the other one.

Inbound

Receive connectors control the flow of inbound e-mails into an Exchange organization by acting as an inbound connection point that administrators set up to accept connections from servers or clients limited to certain, or any, IP addresses and port numbers. In Exchange 2013, these can be configured on Client Access servers (Front End service), Mailbox servers (Transport service), or on Edge servers (for inbound Internet e-mails). However, one Receive connector can only be associated with one server.

By default, the required Receive connectors for an internal e-mail flow are created automatically when a Mailbox or CAS is installed. As we saw in the diagram at the beginning of this chapter, in most cases, creating a Receive connector to explicitly receive e-mails from the Internet is not required, because a Receive connector (named `Default Frontend <server_name>`) to accept mail from the Internet is automatically created upon installation of Exchange.

Usually, the default Receive connectors are sufficient to meet the needs of the messaging infrastructure. However, there are cases where additional Receive connectors might be desired or even required. The two most common cases are to turn off authentication for specific clients (printers, line of business [LOB] applications, and so on) and to allow relaying of e-mails from specific clients.

While Exchange automatically load-balances intra-organization e-mail traffic between servers, this does not happen for e-mails received from non-Exchange sources such as LOB applications, printers, external mail servers, and POP and IMAP-based clients. In these situations, organizations typically choose to load-balance this type of traffic using a unified SMTP namespace (such as `smtp.domain.com`). This is done to distribute e-mails across the transport servers within the organization and to prevent a server failure from causing these applications and devices from being able to send e-mails. DNS Round Robin, Windows NLB, or a hardware/software load-balancing solution are the usual choices to achieve this. As the pros and cons of each of these technologies have already been discussed, let us focus on the general idea and what to consider while load-balancing this type of traffic.

Non-Exchange internal e-mails

While planning to load-balance SMTP traffic, a separate Receive connector for this purpose should always be created and configured to use an additional IP address on the receiving server. Additionally, the **Exchange Server authentication** checkbox should be disabled to make sure Exchange traffic is not routed through this Receive connector.

A common scenario is when devices or applications do not support authenticated SMTP; in which case, administrators enable the **Anonymous users** permissions on the Receive connector.

A problem with some load-balancing configurations is that the receiving Exchange server is only aware of the IP address of the load-balancer, and not that of the actual application or printer. For example, a printer is configured to send e-mails to `smtp.letsexchange.com`, which resolves to a load-balancer VIP. However, because the load-balancer terminates the connection from the printer and establishes a new one between itself and an Exchange server, the Exchange server "sees" the connection as coming from the load-balancer, and not the original IP address. This is problematic as the scoping settings on the receive connector, specifically the **Receive mail from servers that have these remote IP addresses** option, will be rendered useless, and everyone that knows the SMTP VIP will be able to send e-mails through this Receive connector, possibly in a non-authenticated way. This also means that protocol logging and message tracking logs will not have complete information regarding the sender.

As such, it is crucial that the source IP address is passed on to the Exchange server so that it can validate if that particular IP address is authorized to use the Receive connector or not. This gives administrators the control and security they are used to having using the Exchange tools over exactly what connects to Exchange.

Inbound Internet e-mails

As already mentioned, incoming e-mails from the Internet can be delivered to Exchange using a third-party smart host, an Edge server, or through a 2013 CAS. While handling this traffic, administrators do not need to deploy a load-balancing solution in order to distribute the load across the receiving servers; this can be accomplished by using DNS Round Robin and **mail exchange** (**MX records**) as described next.

While running a mail server, no matter its version or make, if it uses SMTP as the e-mail transfer mechanism, the DNS MX records need to be configured for the domain that will be receiving the e-mail. An MX record is a particular type of DNS record that defines the name and the preference of one or more e-mail servers responsible for accepting e-mails for a particular domain. Without MX records, an organization is only capable of sending and receiving internal e-mails, as other e-mail servers external to the organization will not know how to reach a server in order to deliver e-mails into the organization.

MX records follow the format below, where `10` signifies the preference or order (between 0 to 65535, with 0 having the highest preference) in which mailers select MX records while attempting mail delivery to the host:

```
domain.com. IN MX 10 host.domain.com
```

Multiple MX records can be used for a single domain, sorted in the preference order. For example, if a domain has three MX records configured, a sending server will try to use all three records before queuing or rejecting the e-mail.

There are several different ways of configuring MX records to control inbound Internet mail flow. This configuration will depend on several factors, such as the number of datacenters where Exchange is deployed and the number of devices capable of routing Internet mail into the organization. As this book is about high availability, let us assume a deployment with two datacenters with both locations capable of routing e-mails. There are three main possibilities for this scenario:

- One primary datacenter and a standby datacenter
- Both datacenters are used for mail flow
- A single MX record

In a primary/standby datacenter scenario, organizations usually choose to have all inbound and outbound traffic flowing through the primary datacenter, with the standby one only being used in a disaster-recovery situation. To achieve this, we configure the MX records for the first datacenter with a lower cost. Assuming New York to be the primary datacenter and New Jersey the standby one, the DNS configuration would be as follows:

```
letsexchange.com.             IN MX 10 newyork.letsexchange.com
newyork.letsexchange.com      A <IP_Address_1>
newyork.letsexchange.com      A <IP_Address_2>
(...)


letsexchange.com.             IN MX 20 newjersey.letsexchange.com
newjersey.letsexchange.com    A <IP_Address_3>
newjersey.letsexchange.com    A <IP_Address_4>
(...)
```

With this configuration, both MX records are provided to the sending SMTP server, but the lowest-cost MX record (New York) is used first. When the address for `newyork.letsexchange.com` is resolved, DNS uses Round Robin to alternate between the address values that it returns, ensuring that the `newyork.letsexchange.com` hosts are used equally for receiving inbound e-mail. This approach guarantees that e-mail traffic is balanced efficiently across all mail hosts in the primary datacenter, whether these are Edge servers, CASs, or third-party appliances. In case of a disaster, all that needs to be updated is the `newjersey.letsexchange.com` MX record to a lower cost than than 10 (that of the New York record). This way, the `newjersey.letsexchange.com` MX record becomes the primary record, directing all traffic to the New Jersey datacenter. Alternatively, you can increase the cost of the `newyork.letsexchange.com` MX record.

Note that this scenario will increase the traffic on the WAN between the datacenters as some messages that enter the New York datacenter will be destined for recipients in New Jersey and vice versa.

For the second scenario, which is typically an active/active datacenter deployment with users working from both datacenters, both MX records are set to have equal cost:

```
letsexchange.com.               IN MX 10 newyork.letsexchange.com
newyork.letsexchange.com        A <IP_Address_1>
newyork.letsexchange.com        A <IP_Address_2>
(...)


letsexchange.com.               IN MX 10 newjersey.letsexchange.com
newjersey.letsexchange.com      A <IP_Address_3>
newjersey.letsexchange.com      A <IP_Address_4>
(...)
```

By having both MX records with the same cost, both datacenters will be used to receive inbound Internet e-mail. Please note that depending on the sending SMTP server, this solution might not guarantee equal distribution of e-mails between the two datacenters as some message transfer agents always pick the same MX record independently from how many MX records are configured for a domain. It does guarantee, however, equal distribution of e-mails for a particular MX record as the first scenario does.

In case of a disaster with one of the datacenters, its MX record should be updated with a higher cost or even deleted so sending SMTP servers do not try to use it.

As for the third scenario, a single MX record can be used:

```
letsexchange.com.              IN MX 10 mail.letsexchange.com
mail.letsexchange.com          A <IP_Address_1>
mail.letsexchange.com          A <IP_Address_2>
mail.letsexchange.com          A <IP_Address_3>
mail.letsexchange.com          A <IP_Address_4>
(...)
```

With this configuration, the MX record references all mail hosts in both datacenters, ensuring an equal distribution of e-mails between all the hosts in both datacenters. This is usually the best approach when mail flow is desired to come into both datacenters. However, the first scenario is the best option when the objective is to ensure that e-mail flow is controlled in terms of datacenter usage.

In case of a disaster in this scenario, the records associated with hosts on the failed datacenter would need to be deleted from DNS and recreated once the datacenter is reactivated.

Although a load-balancer is not strictly required, it can obviously be used to distribute incoming Internet e-mails, which will bring additional functionality and increase high availability due to its health-check capabilities. In this case, a single MX record pointing to the load-balancing solution is published. The load-balancer then distributes incoming e-mails to all receiving servers listed in its configuration.

Despite all the advantages of using a proper load-balancing solution, there are some points to be aware of while using a physical/virtual load-balancer for SMTP traffic:

- **Priority**: There might be cases where a certain preferred server needs to be considered first for a new connection (if available). If this is not the case, then ensure that all receiving servers have the same priority or weight.

- **Load-balancing method**: In order to not create SMTP traffic imbalances, a suitable load-balancing method (algorithm) should be used. Usually, Round Robin is fine, but different ones might be used, especially if servers have different priorities. Always ensure whether the current configuration is the best suited.

- **Source IP address**: Ensure that the Exchange servers see the source IP server for the reasons already discussed.

- **Health monitors**: Make sure that the load-balancer's health monitors meet your requirements. For example, one that only establishes an SMTP connection to a server, waits for the SMTP banner to be returned or for a HELO response, and then disconnects, might not be sufficient as it detects service failures but not back-pressure.

- **Single point of failure**: Plan for a pair of load-balancers so that they do not become a single point of failure for all inbound e-mail traffic.

Summary

In this chapter, we have explored all the improvements made by Exchange 2013 to transport high availability, namely shadow redundancy and Safety Net. Together, these two features guarantee that no e-mail is lost while in transit by keeping redundant copies of e-mails both before and after they are successfully delivered.

We also explored different methods used to load-balance both inbound and outbound mail flow at the same time, increasing high availability by preventing single points of failure.

Although shadow redundancy and Safety Net do a great job out of the box, business requirements will ultimately determine the configuration of these transport high availability features as well as the configuration of inbound and outbound mail flow.

In the next chapter, we will explore high availability for the Unified Messaging role.

6
High Availability of Unified Messaging

Unified Messaging (**UM**) refers to the integration of different electronic messaging and communications media, such as e-mails, fax, or voicemail technologies, into a single interface, accessible from a variety of different devices. Before Exchange UM was introduced in Exchange 2007, IT administrators frequently managed an organization's voicemail/telephony network and e-mail systems/data networks as separate systems. E-mails and voicemails were located in distinct inboxes hosted by different servers and accessed through e-mail clients and telephones.

With the introduction of Exchange UM, administrators were finally able to combine e-mails, voicemails, and incoming fax into one universal inbox located on Exchange. This allows users to listen to their voicemail in their inbox, which can even be automatically transcribed into the e-mail, or by using any telephone and the Outlook Voice Access functionality.

Introducing the new features of UM

UM in Exchange 2013 is very similar to the previous editions of Exchange in terms of its functionality. However, there have been architectural changes, and new features have also been added. Although Exchange 2013 UM includes the same features as Exchange 2010, it is now a component of the voice features of Exchange 2013 and is no longer a separate server role. UM-related services and UM components (such as auto attendants, dial plans, UM mailbox policies, and UM IP gateways) can still be managed through the shell, or by using the new **Exchange Admin Center** (**EAC**) and the unified messaging page.

The following is just a list of the new features and improvements introduced in UM in Exchange 2013:

- Voice architectural changes
- IPv6 support
- Improvements to voicemail preview
- Updates to the UM cmdlets
- Improvements to caller-ID support
- Improvements to the speech platform and recognition

In this chapter, we will only explore the new architecture of UM, as it is crucial to understand how it works to enable you to plan for high availability.

Architectural changes

Exchange 2013's architecture is very different from Exchange 2010 as we have seen in the last few chapters. In the previous versions of Exchange, all the components for UM were located on a server with the UM server role installed. With the new architecture of Exchange 2013, the UM server role has been eliminated, and the UM functionality now exists across the CAS and Mailbox server roles.

Two new services are used in Exchange 2013 for UM:

- **Microsoft Exchange Unified Messaging Call Router** service (`MSExchangeUMCR` or `Microsoft.Exchange.UM.CallRouter.exe`) running on CASs and listening on TCP port 5060
- **Microsoft Exchange Unified Messaging** service (`MSExchangeUM` or `umservice.exe`) running on Mailbox servers

The **UM Worker Process** (`UMWorkerProcess.exe`) is still present and runs on Mailbox servers. This process, which listens on TCP port 5065 or 5067, is created during the startup of the Unified Messaging service and interacts with incoming and outgoing requests received by the Unified Messaging service.

The process for connecting to UM in Exchange 2013 starts with a connection to TCP port 5060 on a CAS. When the CAS receives an incoming call, the **Session Initialization Protocol (SIP)** traffic gets redirected by the call router service to TCP port 5065 or 5067 on a Mailbox server. A media channel (**Realtime Transport Protocol (RTP)** or **Secure Realtime Transport Protocol (SRTP)**) then gets established to the Mailbox server that is currently hosting the user's mailbox from the **Voice over IP (VoIP)** gateway, **Session Border Controller (SBC)**, or **IP Private Branch eXchange (PBX)**, as shown in the following diagram:

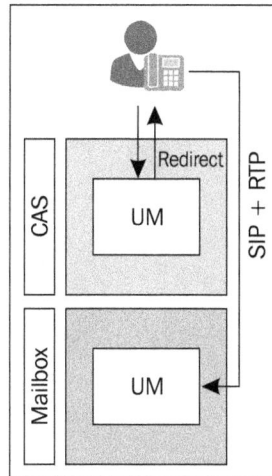

The reason for using both 5065 and 5067 TCP ports is that Exchange starts listening on 5065, and after seven days, it starts another process listening on port 5067. When the process listening on port 5065 finishes handling all its calls, it gets stopped. This is to reset the worker process because of the heavy loads due to voicemails, transcriptions, and so on. This way, Exchange does not need to restart the service if it crashes; it simply starts a new process on the other port and directs all new calls to it.

After the media channel has been established, the Unified Messaging service plays the user's voicemail greeting, processes any call-answering rules the user might have, and asks the caller to leave a message. The Mailbox server records the message, creates a transcription, and delivers it to the user's mailbox.

> SIP is a signaling protocol for VoIP used to initiate, modify, and end a user's session involving multimedia elements such as voice, video, or instant messaging. SIP clients connect to SIP servers using TCP or UDP port 5060. SIP is only used for starting and terminating calls. RTP defines a standard packet format for the delivery of only audios and videos over a network. A static or standard TCP/UDP port is not required by RTP. RTP is typically configured to use ports 1024 to 65535, but there is no standard port range defined.

Using a software PBX, in this case Asterisk, we can see a part of the UM flow discussed previously, as shown in the following screenshot:

```
== Using SIP RTP CoS mark 5
   -- Called SIP/ToExchange/4444
   -- Got SIP response 302 "Moved Temporarily" back from 192.168.1.100:5060
   -- Now forwarding SIP/4001-00000004 to 'SIP/4444:::::TCP@exmbx1.letsexchange.c
om:5062' (thanks to SIP/ToExchange-00000005)
== Using SIP RTP TOS bits 184
== Using SIP RTP CoS mark 5
[2013-10-20 16:32:04] NOTICE[2830]: app_dial.c:883 do_forward: Not accepting cal
l completion offers from call-forward recipient SIP/exmbx1.letsxchange.com:5062-
00000006
   -- Got SIP response 302 "Moved Temporarily" back from 192.168.1.106:5062
   -- Now forwarding SIP/4001-00000004 to 'SIP/4444:::::TCP@exmbx1.letsxchange.c
om:5065' (thanks to SIP/exmbx1.letsxchange.com:5062-00000006)
== Using SIP RTP TOS bits 184
== Using SIP RTP CoS mark 5
[2013-10-20 16:32:04] NOTICE[2830]: app_dial.c:883 do_forward: Not accepting cal
l completion offers from call-forward recipient SIP/exmbx1.letsxchange.com:5065-
00000007
   -- SIP/exmbx1.letsxchange.com:5065-00000007 is ringing
   -- SIP/exmbx1.letsxchange.com:5065-00000007 answered SIP/4001-00000004
```

In the preceding console session, we can see what happens when a user with an extension of 4001 calls the subscriber access number 4444:

```
Called SIP/<Trunk_Name>/4444
```

```
Got SIP response 302 "Moved Temporarily" back from CAS_Server_IP>:
5060
```

```
Now forwarding SIP/<CallID> to 'SIP/4444:::::
TCP@<Mailbox_Server_FQDN>:5062' (thanks to SIP/<Trunk_Name-CallID)
```

The connection has now been routed from the CAS to the Unified Messaging service on the Mailbox server holding the user's mailbox. It is this service that knows the current port that the UMWorkerProcess is running on (5065 or 5067). The connection flow continues, and the output is as follows:

```
Got SIP response 302 "Moved Temporarily" back from <Mailbox_Server_
IP>:5062
```

```
Now forwarding SIP/<CallID> to 'SIP/4444:::::
TCP@<Mailbox_Server_FQDN>:5065' (thanks to SIP/<Mailbox_Server_
FQDN>:5062-<CallID>)
```

```
SIP/<Mailbox_Server_FQDN>:5065-<CallID> is ringing
```

```
SIP/<Mailbox_Server_FQDN>:5065-<CallID> answered SIP/4001-CallID
```

CASs only act as SIP redirectors. They only handle SIP requests from SIP peers (such as VoIP gateways, SBCs, or IP PBXs); they do not receive any media traffic. RTP/SRTP media traffic is only between Mailbox servers and SIP peers, not CASs.

Mailbox servers do not answer SIP requests from incoming calls; they only receive SIP traffic from CASs and then establish RTP/SRTP connections to the SIP peer.

> While deploying Exchange 2013 UM, SIP peers need to be configured to point to the CASs that are installed so that incoming calls can be correctly routed for UM.

While integrating the Exchange UM with **Office Communications Server (OCS)** 2007 R2 or Lync, RTP/SRTP and SIP for incoming calls are handled by the OCS/ Lync and Mailbox servers. To Lync, Mailbox and CASs are trusted peers as both server roles need to be in the SIP dial plan. Lync uses the inbound routing component to route incoming calls, which communicates with the CAS using SIP and then routes the call to a Mailbox server, as shown in the following diagram:

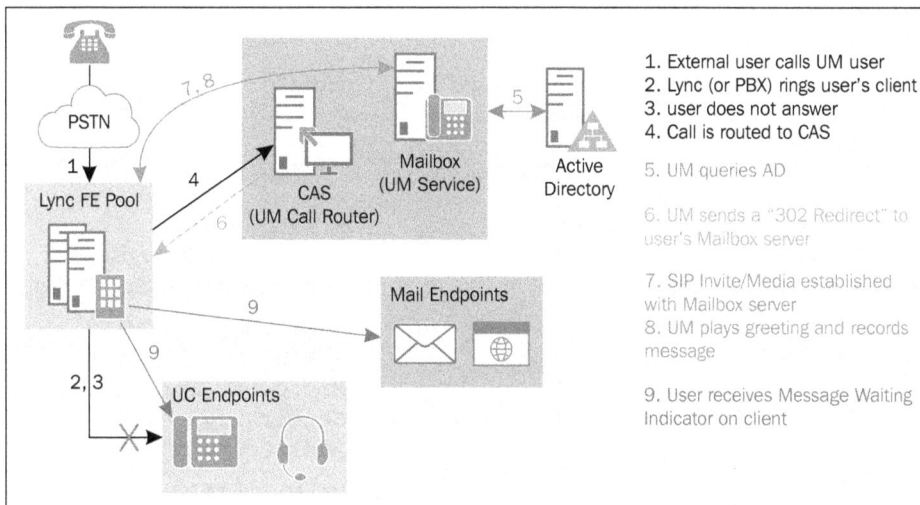

Unified Messaging ports

The call router service uses SIP over TCP or a mutual **Transport Layer Security (TLS)** in order to communicate with Mailbox servers that run the Unified Messaging service. To avoid port conflicts, the call router service and the Unified Messaging service listen on different TCP ports. They are able to accept both secured and unsecured connections, subject to mutual TLS being used with RTP and SIP traffic or not.

By default, CASs listen for SIP requests on the TCP ports 5060 (unsecured) and 5061 (secured using mutual TLS). Both these ports are easily configurable through the `Set-UMCallRouterSettings` cmdlet. As the call router does not handle media traffic, only TCP ports are used instead of UDP.

By default, the Unified Messaging service on Mailbox servers listens for SIP requests on TCP ports 5062 (unsecured) and 5063 (secured using mutual TLS). These ports cannot be changed.

The following table lists the ports and protocols used in Exchange 2013:

Protocol	UDP port	TCP port	Can ports be changed?
SIP (Calls router services in the CAS)	N/A	5060 (unsecured) and 5061 (secured)	Yes
SIP (Unified Messaging service on the Mailbox server)	N/A	5062 (unsecured) and 5063 (secured)	No
SIP (UM worker process on the Mailbox server)	N/A	TCP 5065 and 5067 (unsecured), and mutual TLS 5066 and 5068 (secured)	No
RTP (UM worker process on the Mailbox server)	1024 to 65535	N/A	Yes, through the registry (however, it is not supported!): `HKEY_LOCAL_MACHINE\ SOFTWARE\Microsoft\ Microsoft Speech Server\2.0\ AudioConnectionMinPort` `HKLM\SOFTWARE\ Microsoft\Microsoft Speech Server\2.0\ AudioConnectionMaxPort`

Unified Messaging availability

For many organizations, e-mails and voicemails are critical for daily operations. Although the requirements for the minimum uptime may change, every organization desires to achieve a high level of availability. A factor that needs to be considered while deploying a UM system is the ability to continue to provide service to users when a key component, such as an IP gateway or Exchange server, becomes unavailable. In order to guarantee continuous access to e-mails and voicemail, you have to correctly plan and implement a solution that ensures the availability of all components providing these services.

UM requires the integration of an Exchange deployment with the existing telephony system. A successful deployment requires not only consideration around Exchange, but also a detailed analysis of the telephony infrastructure in place. Whether you are deploying UM using IP PBXs, VoIP gateways, or Lync, all the deployment options for UM have several steps in common. The following components are all required in order to create a highly available and scalable system that is able to support a large number of users:

- Deploy and configure telephony components or Lync with UM
- Verify the correct installation of Mailbox servers running the Unified Messaging service and CASs running the call router service
- Create and configure all the required UM components, such as IP gateways, dial plans, mailbox policies, and hunt groups
- Complete any post-deployment tasks required, such as obtaining certificates for a mutual TLS, configuring faxing, or creating auto attendants

Next, we will focus on the aspects that are crucial for high availability.

Exchange servers

The UM worker process automatically deals with outages in Mailbox servers. For example, if a user's mailbox becomes unavailable, UM will continue to accept calls destined for the user. However, the user's custom greetings will not be played; instead, a standard greeting will be used for calls to that particular user.

Still, it is recommended to make use of DAGs to ensure that the failure of a Mailbox server does not affect voicemail functionality in any way. If a database for a user receiving a call fails over to a different server, CASs will be notified and will redirect calls to the right Mailbox server. As the UM service is now part of the Mailbox server role, no further action is required to make this service highly available.

IP gateways

Before explaining what an IP gateway is, we need to first look at the definition of two different network types: packet-switched and circuit-switched networks. Packet-switched networks are networks where packets are individually routed between devices such as switches, routers, IP PBXs, VoIP gateways, and SBCs; circuit-switched networks, on the other hand, establish a dedicated connection between the two nodes for exclusive use by them for the duration of the communication.

A UM IP gateway is a representation of an IP PBX, a physical VoIP gateway, or an SBC hardware device. Before any of these devices can be used to send outgoing calls or answer incoming calls, a UM IP gateway has to be created. Traditionally, gateway is a term used to describe a physical device connecting two incompatible networks. Within Exchange UM and other unified messaging platforms, VoIP gateways are deployed to translate a circuit-switched-based telephony network, such as a **Public Switched Telephone Network (PSTN)**, and a packet-switched data network, such as IP. IP PBXs are also able to translate between PSTN networks and packet-switched networks, so a VoIP gateway is not necessary.

Incoming calls

PBXs need to be configured in order to send the incoming calls that they receive to different IP gateways. Once set up, most PBXs can detect failures and redirect calls to an IP gateway that is able to answer incoming calls.

Usually, IP gateways can be configured to route calls to Exchange servers in a round-robin manner. Each IP gateway is configured with the CASs responsible for answering calls. These are the servers in the same dial plan to the IP gateway object representing the IP gateway. The IP gateway will forward calls to CASs within the same dial plan. In case the call gets sent to a server that is not available, it will try to contact the server again. If it is still unsuccessful, it then uses the next server in the list configured on the IP gateway. However, be aware that not all IP gateways can be configured to load balance and detect when servers have been taken offline or have failed.

Outgoing calls

From an Exchange perspective, multiple UM IP gateways should be used. For example, in order to provide for the availability of an IP gateway, assuming a two-IP-gateway scenario, you can configure and enable one IP gateway, and configure the second IP gateway, but leave it disabled so that you have an IP gateway that can be used to take the place of the first gateway in case this fails or is taken offline.

While creating an IP gateway in Exchange, you can configure it with either an IP address or an FQDN. While using an FQDN, you must ensure that a DNS record for the gateway has been correctly configured to allow the hostname to be resolved to the correct IP address. Here, you can use a basic round-robin and configure two DNS records with the same name to resolve to two different gateways. However, this method has the already discussed disadvantages of not detecting failures (load balancing, but no high availability).

Also, while using FQDNs instead of IP addresses, in case the UM IP gateway's DNS configuration changes, the UM IP gateway must be disabled and then re-enabled in order to ensure the UM IP gateway configuration information is updated correctly.

SIP load balancing

As already discussed, SIP connections are established from SIP peers to CASs on port 5060. As long as the SIP peers support FQDNs (and not just IP addresses), the DNS round-robin can be used to distribute the workload among multiple CASs. However, as we have seen in the previous chapters, round-robin does not provide failure detection. If one of the servers fails and if the IP gateway cannot detect that the server is unavailable as described earlier, it continues sending incoming calls to the server until administrators update the dial plan by removing the failed server.

UM itself does not use DNS round-robin or NLB to load-balance incoming calls. A way to balance the load between the servers in a dial plan is to configure the IP gateway with the FQDNs or IP addresses of the CASs in the dial plan. It will then use this list to help distribute the load across all CASs and plan and detect a server failure (if this functionality is supported).

A load-balancing device can also be used to distribute SIP traffic. However, nowadays, as most IP gateways are able to detect server failures and distribute load automatically, load-balancer devices are generally not required or recommended.

Summary

In this chapter, we explored in more detail the new architecture of Unified Messaging in Exchange 2013 and the typical flow of a telephone call. Achieving a high level of availability for an entire UM deployment requires proper planning and consideration. It is not just about Exchange, but all the components that are part of the deployment, from Exchange to SIP peers. By default, most IP PBXs and IP gateways possess good load-balancing capabilities as well as the ability to detect failures out of the box, meaning little or no manual configuration is required. On the Exchange side, the deployment of multiple CASs, DAGs, and the correct configuration of UM IP gateways and dial plans ensure that the service remains available if any of these devices fail.

7
Backup and Recovery

Designing and maintaining a highly available and resilient Exchange infrastructure is not just about DAGs, load balancers, and multiple servers. After all, what good is a DAG if the data gets corrupted and there is no way of recovering it?

Backups have been around for many decades. Disk failures, power outages, administrative errors, software and hardware errors, and many other causes raise the potential of data loss on any computer system. As long as data loss is a possibility, then backups are likely to be needed in order to be able to recover from most disaster scenarios. The introduction of DAGs and other features have enabled new possibilities, making administrators question their backup strategy and sometimes even the need for backups. Many already consider that backups are no longer needed. One thing is certain: *Exchange is changing the reasons why administrators back up their Exchange environment and how they do it.*

Understanding the importance of backups

As we have seen throughout the previous chapters, Exchange 2013 has made great improvements in terms of high availability and resilience, making it easier than ever to deploy highly available and redundant databases. But even the best forms of fault tolerance and redundancy cannot protect against disaster or failure. It is essential for every organization to ensure that there is sufficient and adequate protection for all Exchange critical data.

As part of any data protection plan, it is crucial to understand which methods can be used to protect data and to determine the best method to meet the needs of the organization. Data protection planning relies on numerous decisions made during the planning phase of an Exchange deployment, and it is a complex process.

To perform Exchange 2013 backups and restores, you need Exchange-aware software that supports the **Volume Shadow Copy Service (VSS)** writer for Exchange 2013, such as **System Center Data Protection Manager (DPM)** 2012, Windows Server Backup, or third-party software. The following are some limitations when using VSS to back up/restore Exchange data that you should also be aware of:

- The Exchange 2013 VSS plugin can be used to back up volumes that contain non-replicated standalone mailbox databases or active mailbox database copies only. This means that you cannot use it to back up volumes that contain passive copies. To do this, you must use DPM or a third-party software.

- Passive copies are backed up using a distinct VSS writer, which is part of the Exchange Replication service, but it does not support restores. Even though you can back up a passive copy using DPM, for example, you are not able to perform a VSS restore directly into a passive copy. What you can do is perform a VSS restore to an alternative location, interrupt replication to the passive copy, and then copy the restored database and log files to the location of the passive copy.

> The VSS writer architecture in Exchange 2013 underwent a significant change from the previous versions of Exchange. Earlier versions had two separate VSS writers, one on the Exchange Replication service and another on the Exchange Information Store service. The VSS writer previously found in the Information Store service is now part of the Replication service in Exchange 2013. This new writer, called **Microsoft Exchange Writer**, is now used by VSS-based software, which is Exchange-aware, to back up and restore active or passive database copies.

Although this writer runs in the Replication service, it still depends on the Information Store service to advertise it. As such, both these services are necessary to back up or restore Exchange databases.

Listing vital components to back up

Most of the Exchange 2013 configuration settings for both Client Access and Mailbox servers are stored in Active Directory. Exchange 2013, as well as previous versions of Exchange, also includes the Setup parameter `/mode:RecoverServer` that is used to rebuild a failed server using the configuration information and settings stored in AD. Nonetheless, there is some information that does not get stored in AD, as we will shortly see, that might be important to an organization. As such, you should always back up the local filesystem and System State data of every Exchange server in the organization.

The new architecture of Exchange 2013 makes it slightly easier to back up, as administrators now only need to worry about backing up two different roles: Mailbox and Client Access Servers. However, backing up Exchange servers might not be enough. You still need to consider backing up the following:

- Active Directory
- Client data such as PSTs or POP3 mailboxes
- Anti-virus/anti-spam software or its configuration

Client Access Servers

The CAS role stores configuration data in AD, in local configuration files, and in the IIS metabase. Because data stored in IIS and AD is not synchronized or duplicated, `Setup /mode:RecoverServer` restores CASs to the default installation state and ignores any customization work done post-installation.

If the IIS metabase and AD are not synchronized because of a recovery operation, the CAS could experience errors. Because of this, it is not recommended to recover the IIS metabase to a CAS after running `Setup /mode:RecoverServer`. You should keep a detailed change log of all customizations performed on CASs so that in the case of one or more requiring recovery, any customization done can be reapplied by referring to the change log.

Part of these customizations might include changes to the default Outlook Web App logon page made by changing files in `%programfiles%\Microsoft\Exchange Server\V15\FrontEnd\HttpProxy\owa`.

When customizing the CAS role, most of these changes will be done to files located in `%programfiles%\Microsoft\Exchange Server\V15\FrontEnd`. As such, and at the very least, you should always include this directory in your backups. However, it is still recommended that you back up the entire Exchange directory.

Mailbox servers

Due to all the architectural changes in Exchange 2013, backing up the Mailbox server role is now even more important. Not only does it contain the users' mailbox data and public folders, it now also contains Transport and Unified Messaging data.

Databases and transaction logs

An Exchange 2013 mailbox database contains all the end user information as well as Public Folder data. Use an Exchange-aware backup application such as Windows Server Backup, DPM, or an other third-party tool to back up all Exchange databases on a regular basis.

After the transaction logfiles are committed, they are protected by backups and Exchange deletes them from the filesystem. If regular backups fail or are not performed, transaction log files do not get committed and deleted. When this happens, they can consume all of the available space on your hard disks. If this happens, Exchange dismounts its databases and stops accepting data until more space is made available.

This is true, assuming circular logging is not enabled. With circular logging, Exchange overwrites transaction logfiles once data in the logfile has been committed to the database. By enabling it, administrators can reduce storage space requirements. The problem is that it is not possible to recover any data since the last full backup without transaction logs. As a result, circular logging is not recommended for production environments.

> Regularly backing up databases will also ensure that administrators can recover important mailbox items deleted by users. This is one of the main reasons why backups are still performed nowadays.

Offline address book

As we have already seen, Exchange 2013 changed the way OABs are generated and distributed. OABs are now generated by the Mailbox server that hosts a particular type of arbitration mailbox, the **Organization Mailbox**, and then copied to the folder `%programfiles%\Microsoft\Exchange Server\V15\ClientAccess\OAB\` on the Mailbox server hosting this mailbox.

If the Organization Mailbox is not hosted by a database that is part of a DAG, you might want to consider backing up the OAB. If your organization is of small to medium size, it might be quicker and easier to simply rebuild the OAB in case of a disaster recovery scenario. However, bear in mind that this will force all your Outlook clients to perform a full download of the entire OAB.

Customizations and logfiles

Similar to CASs, customizations can be made to Mailbox servers that are not stored in AD. For example, if you change the `%programfiles%\Microsoft\Exchange Server\V15\Bin\MSExchangeMailboxReplication.exe.config` file so that you can move more mailboxes concurrently, you should back up this directory.

In the folder `%programfiles%\Microsoft\Exchange Server\V15\TransportRoles`, we have all the protocol log files, message tracking logs, queue database, pickup and replay directories, and more. As such, it is also important to back up this directory.

If you make use of the Unified Messaging features of Exchange, there is a chance you will have custom audio prompts. If this is the case, do not forget to include the `%programfiles%\Microsoft\Exchange Server\V15\UnifiedMessaging\prompts` folder in your backup job.

Similar to the CAS role, it is a best practice to back up the entire Exchange directory.

Unified contact store

The contact card in Lync Server 2010 aggregated all data associated with a contact, but it did not offer a single location to store all of this contact-related data. With Lync Server 2013, when integrated with Exchange 2013, this is no longer the case. The **Unified Contact Store (UCS)** provides users with a single contact list available in multiple applications such as Lync 2013, Outlook 2013, and OWA. When UCS is enabled for a user, that user's contacts are not stored in Lync and are retrieved using the **Session Initiation Protocol (SIP)**. Instead, contacts are stored in Exchange and retrieved using Exchange Web Services. This presents both a single storage location and a unified view of all this data.

> Contact information is stored in a couple of folders in the user's mailbox. Contacts themselves are stored in the *Lync Contacts* folder that is visible to users. Metadata about the contacts, on the other hand, is stored in a subfolder not visible to users.

The problem with restoring a UCS-migrated mailbox is that the IM contact list for the user might be affected. For example, if you restore the mailbox of a user that got migrated after the last backup, he/she will lose all his/her contacts. In other scenarios, modifications done to the contact list since the last backup will be lost. In order to prevent this, make sure the user gets migrated back to the IM server prior to restoring his/her mailbox.

Exploring Windows Integrated Backup

Exchange 2013 has a plugin for Windows Server Backup, which enables administrators to create VSS backups of Exchange, allowing them to back up and restore Exchange databases. This new plugin is an executable file named WSBExchange.exe, which runs as a service called Microsoft Exchange Server Extension for Windows Server Backup. This plugin automatically gets installed on Exchange 2013 Mailbox servers and enables Windows Server Backup to generate Exchange-aware VSS backups.

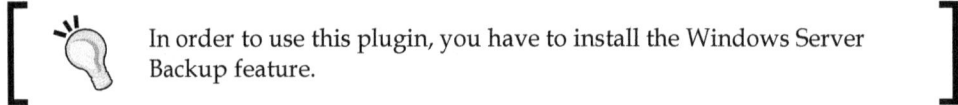

> In order to use this plugin, you have to install the Windows Server Backup feature.

In Windows Server 2012, Microsoft made some improvements to help protect data. One of these improvements is the new **Resilient File System (ReFS)**, which can be used to hold Exchange backup data. ReFS maximizes data availability by preventing errors that in previous editions would typically cause data loss. Data integrity safeguards critical data by protecting it from errors and making it available when needed. If corruption occurs, ReFS can detect and automatically repair the corruption. ReFS is designed to rapidly recover from system errors without user data loss. It periodically scans the volume in an attempt to identify corruption, and if any is found, a repair of that corrupt data is triggered.

Before you back up Exchange data using Windows Server Backup, you need to be aware of the following:

- The backup has to be run locally on the server that you want to back up, since you cannot perform remote VSS backups.
- You can store the backup on a remote network share or on a local drive.
- You can only perform full backups.
- When performing a restore, you can only restore Exchange data. This can be restored to its original or to an alternative location. When restoring to the original location, the recovery process will be handled automatically by Windows Server Backup and the plugin. This means that the target database will be dismounted and logs will be replayed in the recovered database.
- Recovery databases are not supported by this restore process. However, you can restore a database to an alternative location and move the restored data to an RDB.

Only active DAG database copies are supported when using Windows Backup. You cannot back up volumes containing passive copies.

The plugin for Windows Server Backup in Exchange has not been designed to support the backup of DAG database copies. It will back up a DAG member only if all its database copies are active. If there are any passive copies on the server, it will still perform the backup and copy the data, but the consistency check will fail, and therefore, the backup cannot be used for a restore. This is because passive copies are not mounted in the same way by the Store as active databases. Passive copies are accessed by the Exchange Replication service in order to replay transaction logs that are replicated from servers that host their corresponding active copies.

Exploring System Center Data Protection Manager 2012

With System Center 2012, Microsoft has brought the whole System Center family closer together, reinforcing the message that the suite is the best way to monitor, manage, automate, and protect any Microsoft environment. Part of this suite is the System Center Data Protection Manager 2012.

DPM is a server-based application that allows the backing up and restoring of data to/from disk or tape for computers in AD domains. It performs synchronization and replication, and creates recovery points to provide protection and fast recovery of data for servers such as Exchange, SharePoint, SQL, file servers, virtual servers, and Windows workstations.

When Microsoft first introduced DPM 2006, two key problems were its target. They were:

- The need for a better backup solution and restore functionality focusing on disk instead of tape
- The need for a better way to centralize remote backups

Although DPM 2006 was focused on protecting file servers, it was still possible to use DPM 2006 to protect Exchange Server computers by using Windows NT Backup, or another third-party backup solution to back up Exchange to disk, and then protect the resulting backup file using DPM 2006.

This was obviously not the best solution for Exchange, so DPM 2007 was designed with much better application awareness, including Exchange, SharePoint, and SQL.

With DPM 2010, the main improvement from an Exchange perspective was the support for Windows Server 2008 and Exchange 2010 DAGs, but it also included many other improvements.

While the new DPM 2012 has not received a makeover as significant as the other products in the suite, there are some major improvements in this version. For example, there are new centralized management capabilities that make life easier for backup administrators; the scoped console and the way in which role-based access control is implemented are other good improvements, as is the integration with Windows Azure that allows IT admins to back up data to an off-site storage managed by the Windows Azure Online Backup Service. More important is the fact that DPM 2012 SP1 supports Exchange 2013.

When used with Exchange, DPM provides data protection for databases and the ability to recover data at the mailbox or database levels. The DPM protection agent on a server running Exchange makes use of Windows Server VSS capabilities in order to take a snapshot of an entire database at the same time. This ensures a consistent view of the data and helps prevent data corruption caused by the recovery of tables (or rows within a table) independent of related data that is needed to correctly reconstruct the database.

Similar to DPM 2010, DPM 2012 protects Exchange databases that are contained in a DAG. If you change a database status from active to passive, or vice versa, you do not have to make any changes on the DPM server as it will continue to back up the data from the same node without any failures. Although you can protect DAG members using different DPM servers, note that one DAG member can only be protected by a single DPM server.

> All versions of DPM, including 2012, only provide bulk restore and do not provide single item restore of Exchange data.

Using DPM to protect Exchange

In order to protect Exchange using DPM, the first task that needs to be performed is to install the actual DPM server. Before beginning the deployment process, you should check that your deployment meets the configuration and hardware requirements defined in the DPM Deployment Guide.

Installing the DPM server

Microsoft does not recommend installing DPM on the system volume as this will create complications if you need to rebuild the DPM server.

The DPM installer starts by gathering user input during the beginning of the setup. It then verifies that certain prerequisites are met and installs any components that might not be installed but are needed. For its database, DPM requires a dedicated 64-bit version of SQL Server 2008 R2, SQL Server 2008 R2 SP1, or SQL Server 2012 in Standard or Enterprise edition. During setup, you can choose if you want DPM Setup to install SQL Server 2008 R2 locally, or you can specify a remote instance of SQL Server.

Allocating storage

The next step is to create a set of disks and a storage pool, where DPM will store the replicas and recovery points of all protected data. Although you do not have to dedicate an entire disk to DPM, any volume used must be dedicated to DPM.

DPM can use any of the following for the storage pool:

- Direct-attached storage (DAS)
- Fiber Channel Storage area network (SAN)
- iSCSI storage device or SAN

Installing DPM Agents on Exchange servers

After installation, DPM scans AD trying to find servers that it can protect. Choose the Exchange servers you want protected using the Protection Agent Installation Wizard. Then, you will have to install the DPM protection agent on all these servers so DPM can back them up. This agent can be installed using the DPM Administrator Console, Active Directory Group Policy, or System Center Configuration Manager 2012, or manually done from the DPM setup media or ISO image.

Creating and configuring protection groups

To make efficient use of bandwidth and storage, you should develop recovery goals that take into consideration the nature of each data source to be protected. In order to define these goals, you have to determine the following:

- **Synchronization frequency**: This defines how often a DPM agent captures snapshots of data and transmits the changes to the DPM server. This reflects how much data will possibly be lost in case of an outage or disaster with the data source.

- **Recovery point schedule**: This defines how frequently DPM creates recovery points for the protected data. Compared to a traditional backup application, the opportunities you have to recover data are similar. For example, if daily incremental backups and a weekly full backup are performed, there are seven points of recovery. These points are created whenever a full backup is performed or when data gets synchronized by the agent. Therefore, synchronizing every half hour throughout the day would provide 48 recovery points per day.

- **Retention range**: This defines how long DPM will retain protected data for recovery. DPM allows administrators to define both short- and long-term protection policies in order to help control recovery.

- **Protection groups**: These are used by DPM to define its protection policies. This is basically a policy of what is protected and how it is protected. The same protection group can cover data from different data sources such as SQL and Exchange if these servers are located in a physical office or attached to a common project.

DPM considerations

When designing and configuring DPM to protect Exchange, you should be aware of the following:

- After creating a protection group, additional performance settings such as compression or network bandwidth usage throttling can be configured with the aim of optimizing performance on slow network links.

- When creating or adding new databases to a protected Exchange server, these get automatically protected by DPM.

- If you relocate files associated with a protected database to a new location, it will no longer be protected and the replica will become inconsistent. If this happens, a consistency check needs to be run on the replica to resume protection.

- If you dismount a protected database, the protection job associated with that database will fail. On the other hand, protection jobs associated with other databases will continue to run.

- If you rename a protected database, no special steps need to be performed as protection will continue.

Replacing a backup with database availability groups

Since the introduction of DAGs in Exchange 2010 and the improvements made to Single Item Recovery, many believe that backups are no longer needed.

Exchange 2013 includes multiple features, which when deployed and configured appropriately, can provide native data protection. This in turn might eliminate the need for traditional backups of your data, or at least reduce their frequency. The following scenarios describe the most common uses for backups as well as the Exchange 2013 feature that meets each of these needs:

- **Disaster Recovery**: In the event of failures, DAGs enable high availability and allow for fast failover with no data loss. DAGs can also extend multiple sites in order to provide resilience against possible datacenter failures.

- **Recovery of deleted items**: A very common scenario is when users delete items from their mailboxes and later need them back. This typically involves finding a backup that contains the deleted data, if any, restore it, extract the items, and provide them to the user. Using the **Recoverable Items** folder and **In-Place Hold**, it becomes possible to retain all modified and deleted items for a set period of time, making recovering these items faster and easier. This reduces the burden on IT staff and enables end users to recover the items themselves.

- **Long-term data storage**: Occasionally, backups serve as an archive, with tapes typically being used to keep point in time snapshots of data for a long period of time. Exchange archiving, message retention, and multiple-mailbox search features all provide a way of efficiently preserving data for long periods of time in a manner that is end user accessible.

- **Point in time snapshot**: If an organization requires a point in time copy of mailbox data, lagged copies can be used to achieve this. A lagged copy is useful in the unlikely event of logical corruption replicating across databases in a DAG, which would result in the necessity to return to a previous point in time. Lagged copies can also be useful for scenarios where mailboxes or user data is accidentally deleted.

All of these built-in Exchange 2013 high availability features help minimize data loss and downtime when facing a disaster and reducing the messaging environment cost of ownership. By combining these features, organizations might be able to eliminate, or at least reduce their dependency on traditional backups, and reduce its associated costs. However, all of this comes at a cost: storage.

As an example, it may be practical to perform no mailbox database backups at all if:

- An Exchange DAG has been deployed with at least:
  - Three member servers with a copy of all databases each in case of a single-host failure
  - Two different physical locations in order to protect against site failure
  - One lagged copy in case of data corruption
- Single item recovery is enabled to meet the recovery point objective of the organization
- Appropriate restrictions are implemented to avoid data loss by administrative error

If all of these conditions are met, database backups may not be required. While a DAG prevents a database, server, or datacenter failure from causing data loss and downtime, single item recovery allows administrators to recover items deleted by users up to a certain point in the past.

However, many organizations have policies in place that state that mailbox items should be recoverable for three months, six months, one year, or even more. Let us consider the six months example. This means that single item recovery would need to be configured to retain all deleted items for six months or 26 weeks approximately. Now let us assume that on average:

- Users send and receive 50 messages per working day with an average size of 75 KB

- Users delete 80 percent of mailbox items

- Users edit 10 percent of the remaining mailbox items (remember that single item recovery also saves changes to items)

In this scenario:

- 5 working days * 50 e-mails = 250 e-mails/week

- For purges:
    ◦ 250 e-mails/week * 26 weeks = 6500 e-mails/retention period
    ◦ 6500 e-mails * 80% = 5200 e-mails
    ◦ 5200 e-mails * 75 KB = 380 MB

- For versions:
    ◦ 250 e-mails/week * 26 weeks = 6500 e-mails/retention period
    ◦ (6500-5200) e-mails * 10% = 130 e-mails
    ◦ 130 e-mails * 75 KB = 10 MB

This means that keeping single item recovery enabled for one mailbox for six months will increase a user's mailbox size by approximately 390 MB. If we now expand this to every user in the organization, we might be talking about more storage than what is available.

Depending on organizational policies, DAGs and single item recovery might indeed overcome the necessity for backups as a means to recover mailbox items, or at least reduce the frequency of backups. However, backups should always be performed, at least as a disaster recovery mechanism. Also, remember that by using single item recovery, administrators can search for and recover individual items, but not entire folders.

Another issue of not running backups is log truncation. As we have already discussed, when a full or incremental backup is run, transaction log files that are no longer needed for recovery are truncated. If a database is not backed up, log truncation does not occur. In order to prevent the log files from building up when backups are not performed, circular logging needs to be enabled. When circular logging is used together with continuous replication, **Continuous Replication Circular Logging (CRCL)** is used. This differs from ESE circular logging that is managed and performed by the Exchange Information Store service; CRCL on the other hand is managed and performed by the Exchange Replication service. Another difference is that ESE circular logging overwrites the current log whenever needed, meaning it does not generate additional log files. The problem with this approach is that, when in continuous replication, log files are required for log shipping and replay. As such, when CRCL is used, the current log file does not get overwritten and log files are generated for the purpose of log shipping and replay.

CRCL is managed by the Replication service so that logs are not deleted if they are still needed for replication. The Information Store service and the Replication service communicate between themselves using remote procedure calls to determine which logs can be safely deleted. With non-lagged highly available database copies, the following requirements must be met for truncation to occur:

- CRCL is enabled or the log has been backed up
- The log file is below the checkpoint
- The other copies of the database agree with the deletion
- All lagged copies of the database have inspected the log file

With lagged copies, the following requirements must be met for truncation to occur:

- The log file is older than `TruncationLagTime` + `ReplayLagTime`
- The log file is below the checkpoint
- The log file is deleted on the active copy of the database

> As such, it is extremely important to closely monitor the health of database replication when using CRCL, as any problems with it will stop the transaction logs from being truncated and built up.

Planning for disaster recovery

For most organizations, messaging services are business-critical. If it is not available, productivity lowers and business and revenue opportunities might be lost. Even if e-mail is not business-critical to an organization, it is very likely that the loss of messaging services would still create a considerable disruption.

> As even the most well-designed and maintained environment is not immune to disasters, it is crucial to have a good disaster recovery plan in order to be able to quickly restore messaging services.

Planning for disaster recovery is a complex process that depends on numerous decisions made during the planning of Exchange 2013. To start the planning process, we generally need to:

- Be aware where we may have to recover from
- Consider the established service-level agreements
- Consider the significance of having disaster recovery in mind when deploying Exchange
- Understand the dependency on AD by Exchange
- Understand Exchange database technology

It is also critical that we develop a good disaster recovery strategy as it will influence the overall Exchange design and backup strategy.

If an Exchange organization comes across an issue that requires a server recovery, there are typically three recovery options:

- **Server restore**: We can perform a server restore from a full server backup and then restore its databases (unless it is part of a DAG).
- **Server rebuild**: We can completely rebuild the server, which involves performing a new installation of Windows as well as Exchange in recovery mode and then restoring its databases.
- **Standby server**: We can also use a standby recovery server, which involves keeping recovery servers available with Windows and other software already installed. This might reduce the time it takes to rebuild a failed server in some scenarios.

In some cases, however, a complete server restore is not necessary and administrators might only have to restore a mailbox database. The following sections will cover the most common scenarios.

Recovering a mailbox

Similar to Exchange 2010, a **Recovery Database** (**RDB**) is a special type of mailbox database that allows administrators to mount a backup-restored database and extract data from it. After extraction, data can either be merged into a user's mailbox or exported to a folder. RDBs enable administrators to recover data from a copy of a database, or back up the data without disturbing users' access to their mailboxes. This process is often used when recovering items that users deleted from their mailboxes and need them recovered, usually after the retention period has expired. Another scenario where an RDB is useful is when mailboxes from a particular database, or the entire database, need to be restored.

Recovery databases are very different from the standard mailbox databases:

- They can only be created using the Shell.
- E-mails cannot be sent to or from an RDB as SMTP, POP3, and IMAP4 protocol access is blocked.
- Client access using Outlook or OWA is blocked. MAPI is supported, but only by specific recovery tools and applications.
- Mailboxes in an RDB cannot be connected to user accounts. In order to allow users to access mailbox data in an RDB, the mailbox needs to be exported to a folder or merged into a user's mailbox.
- Mailbox management policies are not applied to RDBs. This prevents items from being deleted during recovery by the system.
- Online maintenance does not run on RDBs.
- It is not possible to enable circular logging for RDBs.
- Only one RDB can be mounted per Mailbox server at any time.
- RDBs do not count towards the per server database limit.
- RDBs cannot have database copies.
- You cannot back up RDBs.
- Recovered databases mounted as RDBs are not tied in any way to their original databases.

Before you can start using an RDB, certain requirements have to be met. An RDB cannot be used to recover databases from previous versions of Exchange. Also, the target mailbox used for data merge and extraction has to be part of the same AD forest as the database in the RDB.

RDBs can be used in several situations to recover data, such as:

- **Dial tone recovery (same server)**: We can extract data from an RDB after we restore the original database from backup as part of a dial tone recovery.

- **Dial tone recovery (different server)**: We can use a different server for the dial tone database and then recover data from the RDB after we restore the original database from backup.

- **Mailbox recovery**: We can recover a user's individual mailbox from backup after the deleted mailbox retention period has already passed. We then extract the data we need from the restored mailbox and merge it into the user's mailbox or copy it to a target folder.

- **Item recovery**: We can also use a backup to restore data that has been deleted from a user's mailbox.

RDBs are not designed for full server restores, multiple concurrent database restores, or for scenarios that require rebuilding or changing the AD topology.

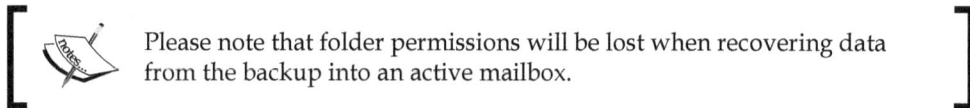

> Please note that folder permissions will be lost when recovering data from the backup into an active mailbox.

As mentioned previously, you have to use Shell to create a recovery database. After it is created, you can move a recovered or restored mailbox database into the recovery database and then extract data from it. During extraction, the data can be merged into a user's mailbox or exported to a folder.

The following example creates a recovery database named RDB1 on the Mailbox server EXMBX1:

```
New-MailboxDatabase -Name RDB1 -Server EXMBX1 -EdbFilePath "D:\DBs\
Recovery\RDB1\RDB1.EDB" -LogFolderPath "L:\Logs\Recovery\RDB1" -Recovery
```

To verify that you have successfully created a recovery database, run one of the following cmdlets to display configuration information for the recovery database:

```
Get-MailboxDatabase RDB1 | Format-List
```

```
Get-MailboxDatabase -Server EXMBX1 | Where {$_.Recovery -eq $True} |
Format-List
```

Now that the RDB has been created, you need to copy or restore the database and log files that contain the recovered data in the RDB folder structure (D:\DBs\Recovery\ RDB1\ and L:\Logs\Recovery\RDB1\ in this example). If the database is in a dirty shutdown state, then you need to use Eseutil /R to put it in a clean shutdown state.

After you have mounted the RDB using the `Mount-Database RDB1` cmdlet, you can restore the content from a mailbox in the `RDB1` database. The following example restores data from a source mailbox with the display name of Chuck Swanson (excluding the `DeletedItems` folder) on mailbox database `RDB1` to the archive mailbox of `chucks@letsexchange.com`:

```
New-MaiboxRestoreRequest -SourceDatabase RDB1 -SourceStoreMailbox
"Chuck Swanson" -TargetMailbox chucks@letsexchange.com -ExcludeFolders
#DeletedItems# -TargetIsArchive
```

Recovering a lost server

Recovering an Exchange server is a task that most administrators fear, but nonetheless, it is a critical task that should be well documented and tested as every organization should be prepared for any type of disaster recovery scenario.

If an Exchange server fails and becomes unrecoverable, it needs to be replaced. To achieve this, you can perform a server recovery operation. There are a myriad of reasons that can cause an Exchange server to have to be recovered. This can be due to a failed install, a natural disaster, a failed CPU, a failed disk, and so on. It is a fact that all the great improvements are made to Exchange in terms of high availability and resilience. However, it is still vital to have recovery plans for any kind of scenario that can lead to the requirement of recovering an Exchange server.

Similar to previous versions of Exchange, you can recover a failed server using the `Setup /mode:RecoverServer` switch in Exchange 2013. As we saw in the beginning of this chapter, most of the settings for a server running Exchange are stored in AD, making its recovery easier. The `/mode:RecoverServer` switch forces the `Setup` process to read configuration information from AD for a computer account with the same name as the server you are running `Setup` from. After configuration information is gathered, the original Exchange services and files are installed on the server, and the settings and roles that were stored in AD are applied to the server.

In this topic, we will go through the steps involved in recovering a lost Exchange 2013 server.

Before you start recovering an Exchange server, make sure that:

- The account you are using has Exchange Organization Management and Active Directory Domain Admin permissions
- It is running the exact Windows version and edition as the lost server
- It has the same drive letters as the failed server for mounted databases
- It has the same hardware characteristics and configuration as the failed server

If the server you are recovering had Exchange installed in a folder different from the default folder, you must use the `/TargetDir` parameter and specify the folder of the Exchange binary files. If this parameter is not used, Exchange is installed in the default `%programfiles%\Microsoft\Exchange Server\V15` folder.

If you cannot remember where Exchange was installed, you can check in Active Directory. The following are the steps to do so:

1. Log in to a Domain Controller.
2. Open `adsiedit.msc`.
3. Navigate to the following location (replacing everything in between <...> by what is correct for your environment):

   ```
   CN=<ExchangeServerName>,CN=Servers,CN=First Administrative
   Group,CN=Administrative Groups,CN=<ExchangeOrgName>,CN=Microsoft
   Exchange,CN=Services,CN=Configuration,DC=<DomainName>,CN=<Com>
   ```

4. Right click on the Exchange server object and click on **Properties**.
5. Search for the **msExchInstallPath** attribute that states the installation path.

Now that you know where Exchange was previously installed, you can proceed with the recovery process as follows:

1. Reset the failed server's computer account in Active Directory:
   1. Open **Active Directory Users and Computers**.
   2. In the console tree, navigate to the folder that contains the computer that you want to reset.
   3. In the details pane, right click on the computer account and then click on **Reset Account**.
2. Install Windows Server and name the new server with the exact name as the failed server. If the name is different, recovery will not succeed.
3. Add the server to the same domain.
4. Install all the necessary operating system components and prerequisites.
5. Open a command prompt with elevated rights.
6. Navigate to the Exchange 2013 installation files and run the following command (remember to use the `/TargetDir` parameter if necessary):

   ```
   Setup /mode:RecoverServer /IAcceptExchangeServerLicenseTerms
   ```

7. When the setup has completed, reapply any custom settings that you previously made and restart the server.
8. After thorough testing, you can place the recovered server into production.

Recovering a server that was part of a DAG is a similar process with just a few differences. Let us assume the server being recovered is called EXMBX1.

1. First, start by removing any mailbox database copies that existed on the server being recovered, as shown in the following cmdlet:

   ```
   Remove-MailboxDatabaseCopy <DB 1 Name>\EXMBX1

   Remove-MailboxDatabaseCopy <DB 2 Name>\EXMBX1

   Remove-MailboxDatabaseCopy <(...)>\EXMBX1
   ```

2. Next, you need to remove the failed server from the DAG. If it is offline and cannot be brought online, add the ConfigurationOnly switch to the following cmdlet:

   ```
   Remove-DatabaseAvailabilityGroupServer <DAG Name> -MailboxServer
   EXMBX1
   ```

3. Reset the failed server's computer account in Active Directory.

4. Install Windows Server and name the new server with the exact same name as the failed server. If the name is different, recovery will not succeed.

5. Add the server to the same domain.

6. Install all the necessary operating system components and prerequisites.

7. Log back on to the server and open a command prompt with elevated rights.

8. Navigate to the Exchange 2013 installation files and run the following command (remember to use the /TargetDir parameter if necessary):

   ```
   Setup /mode:RecoverServer /IAcceptExchangeServerLicenseTerms
   ```

9. When the setup is complete, reconfigure any custom settings that were previously present on the server and then restart the server.

10. Add the recovered server back to the DAG using the following command line:

    ```
    Add-DatabaseAvailabilityGroupServer <DAG Name> -MailboxServer
    EXMBX1
    ```

11. After adding the server back to the DAG, reconfigure its database copies using the following command line:

    ```
    Add-MailboxDatabaseCopy <DB Name 1> -MailboxServer EXMBX1
    -ActivationPreference <x>

    Add-MailboxDatabaseCopy <DB Name 2> -MailboxServer EXMBX1
    -ActivationPreference <y>

    Add-MailboxDatabaseCopy <(...)> -MailboxServer EXMBX1
    -ActivationPreference <z>
    ```

12. In Shell, run the following cmdlets to verify the health and status of the recovered DAG member:

```
Test-ReplicationHealth EXMBX1
Get-MailboxDatabaseCopyStatus -Server EXMBX1
```

Explaining database portability in disaster recovery situations

Database portability is a feature that allows administrators to move a database from an Exchange 2013 server and mount it on another Exchange 2013 server in the same organization. You can then reconnect users to mailboxes in the moved database. Database portability is important because it allows administrators to recover from a server failure by moving database files to another server, and as such, restore service to users.

Database portability allows you to move a mailbox database from one server to another as long as either the **Cumulative Update** (**CU**) level is the same or the destination server is running a later CU version. For example, you can move a database from a server that is running Exchange 2013 CU1 to a server running Exchange 2013 CU2. However, you cannot move a database from Exchange 2013 CU2 to Exchange 2013 CU1.

> Databases from previous Exchange versions cannot be moved to a Mailbox server running Exchange 2013.

There are some scenarios where database portability is not the best solution, such as when a Mailbox server is part of a DAG. In this scenario, you will probably be able to activate the database on another DAG member that holds a replica of the database.

In order to move user mailboxes to a recovered database using database portability, you have to use Shell:

1. The first step is to copy the database and its log files to the target server where you want to mount the database. This can be done by simply copying the files (if they can be accessed) by restoring them from backup or by reassigning the storage used by the old server to the new server.

2. Next, check that the database state is a clean shutdown. If this is not the case, perform a soft recovery to commit any uncommitted log files into the database so that there is no data loss. If you do not have all the required log files, you cannot complete the soft recovery process (skip this step). This means you are likely to experience data loss. So that all uncommitted logs get committed to the database, run the following command where <Enn> is the log prefix for the database into which you are replaying the log files:

   ```
   Eseutil /R <Enn>
   ```

3. Create a database on the new server. The following example is for illustration purposes only:

   ```
   New-MailboxDatabase -Name DB1-Recovered -Server EXMBX5
   -EdbFilePath D:\DBs\DB1-Recovered\DB1.edb -LogFolderPath L:\Logs\
   DB1-Recovered
   ```

4. Enable **This database can be over written by restore** using the following cmdlet:

   ```
   Set-MailboxDatabase DB1-Recovered -AllowFileRestore $True
   ```

5. Move the database and log files to the appropriate location.

6. Mount the database as follows:

   ```
   Mount-Database DB1-Recovered
   ```

7. Next, modify the users' account settings so they point to the mailboxes on the new database. To move all users at the same time from the old to the new database, run the following cmdlet:

   ```
   Get-Mailbox -Database DB1 | Set-Mailbox -Database DB1-Recovered
   ```

8. Trigger delivery of any messages that remain in a queue, as follows:

   ```
   Get-Queue <Queue Name> | Retry-Queue -Resubmit $True
   ```

Once AD replication is complete, users are able to access their mailboxes on the new server. Outlook clients will be redirected via Autodiscover, and Outlook Web App users will also be automatically redirected to the new server. If something such as a network outage stops AD from being able to replicate this information, users will not be able to connect to their mailboxes on the database until replication completes.

Dial tone portability

Dial tone portability is an Exchange feature that enables limited business continuity for failure scenarios where a database, server, or the entire site is affected. It provides users with a temporary mailbox, allowing them to send and receive e-mails while their original mailbox is in the process of being restored. This temporary mailbox can either be on the same Mailbox server or on any other Mailbox server in the organization (as long as it contains databases with an identical schema version), allowing users' mailboxes that were previously on the failed server to be hosted on an alternative server. Clients who support Autodiscover will then automatically be redirected to the new server without the need to manually update the user's profile. Once the user's original mailbox has been restored, the recovered mailbox and the dial tone mailbox can be merged into a single and up-to-date mailbox.

Using dial tone portability is a process called **dial tone recovery**.

There are typically three options when carrying out dial tone recovery:

- **Using the server with the failed database**: If the server with the failed database remains operational, we can perform a dial tone recovery on that same server. This results in less downtime as we do not have to move database files around or reconfigure client profiles that do not support Autodiscover.

- **Using an alternative server**: If the server fails and has to be rebuilt, the easiest and quickest way to provide users with basic messaging functionality is by creating a dial tone database on a different server and moving the users' mailbox configuration to the new server using database portability. As this involves moving the dial tone database to the recovered (original) server, it adds more time to the entire recovery process and is more complex than the previous example. The server that hosts the dial tone database needs to have sufficient resources in order to support the added load, and users' clients that do not support Autodiscover have to be reconfigured so they point to the dial tone server.

- **Using and staying on an alternative server**: This option is similar to the previous one with the exception that we do not revert to the original server. This is recommended in situations where it is not viable, or possible, to recover the failed server. Here, users remain on the alternative server after the recovery has completed. Again, the server that hosts the dial tone database needs to have sufficient resources in order to support the added load. Users' clients that do not support Autodiscover have to be reconfigured so they point to the dial tone server.

The preceding options all follow the same steps:

1. **Create dial tone database**: The new dial tone database enables users with a mailbox on the failed database to be able to send and receive e-mails by pointing them to the new database without moving the mailbox. Remember that if the dial tone database is created on a different server, we have to move the mailbox configuration to the new server.

2. **Restore old database**: Using the most recent backup, we restore the failed database. If we use the same server, we need to restore the database to an RDB.

3. **Swap dial tone database with restored database**: Once we restore the failed database, we swap it with the dial tone database, giving users the ability to access data in the restored database and send and receive e-mails. We have to move the mailbox configuration back to the original server if users were moved to a dial tone database on a different server.

4. **Merge databases**: In order to get data out of the dial tone database and into the restored database, we use the `New-MailboxRestoreRequest` cmdlet to merge the data.

The EAC cannot be used to perform a dial tone recovery, so we need to use Shell. The steps to perform this are as follows:

1. Ensure that any file of the database being recovered gets preserved in the event you need them for additional recovery operations.

2. Create a dial tone database using the following command line:

```
New-MailboxDatabase -Name DB1-DT -EdbFilePath D:\DBs\DialTone
\DB1-DT.edb
```

3. Rehome mailboxes from the database being recovered to the new dial tone database using the following command line:

```
Get-Mailbox -Database DB1 | Set-Mailbox -Database DB1-DT
```

4. Mount the database so users can access it and send and receive e-mails:

```
Mount-Database DB1-DT
```

5. Create a recovery database and restore the database and log files to it.

6. Previous to mounting the restored database, all existing log files need to be copied from the failed database to the recovery database log folder so they can be replayed.

7. Mount and dismount the recovery database using the following command line:

```
Mount-Database RDB1
```

```
Dismount-Database RDB1
```

8. After it is dismounted, move the database and its log files to a safe location. This is to prepare to swap the database recovered with the dial tone database.

9. Dismount the dial tone database using the following command line (users will experience downtime):

```
Dismount-Database DB1-DT
```

10. Move the database and its logs from the folder containing the dial tone database into the recovery database folder.

11. Move the database and its logs from the safe location into the folder of the dial tone database and mount it using the following command line (this ends the downtime for users):

```
Mount-Database DB1-DT
```

12. Mount the recovery database using the following command line:

```
Mount-Database RDB1
```

13. Export data from the recovery database using the `Get-Mailbox` and `New-MailboxRestoreRequest` cmdlets and import it into the recovered database. The following example imports all e-mails sent and received using the dial tone database into the production database:

```
Get-Mailbox -Database DB1-DT | New-MailboxRestoreRequest
-TargetMailbox RDB1
```

14. After the restore is complete, dismount and remove the recovery database using the following command line:

```
Dismount-Database RDB1

Remove-MailboxDatabase RDB1
```

Recovering Public Folders

As we saw in *Chapter 3, High Availability with the Mailbox Server*, **Public Folders** (PF) have been reengineered in Exchange 2013 and now use a mailbox infrastructure which allows them to make use of DAGs for high availability and storage technologies of normal mailbox databases. Since PFs have significantly changed for the first time in many years, it is crucial to plan for the recovery of deleted PF data.

Recovering deleted items

With PFs now being in a mailbox, recovering items that have been deleted from a PF is identical to using the Dumpster to recover items deleted from any user's mailbox.

The **Recover Deleted Items** feature for PFs is by default enabled in Outlook 2007 and above, which is the minimum required client for Exchange 2013 anyway. Items deleted from a PF go directly to the Dumpster where they remain based on the retention settings set on the PF (or the inherited default settings). As such, in order to recover deleted items, a user clicks on **Recover Deleted Items** in Outlook, which will display a new window listing all the items that can be recovered. After selecting which items to recover and clicking on **Recover Selected Items**, these will be moved back to their original folder.

Recovering deleted items post retention

When it comes to recovering deleted PF items that have already passed their retention period, the only available option is to restore them from a backup just like with normal user mailboxes.

After restoring the database hosting the PF content mailbox to a recovery database, we use the `New-MailboxRestoreRequest` cmdlet, just as used before, to extract data from the recovery database into another PF mailbox using the following command line:

```
New-MailboxRestoreRequest -SourceDatabase "Recovery Database Name" -
SourceStoreMailbox "mailbox with deleted PF" -TargetMailbox "target
mailbox to restore data to" -AllowLegacyDNMismatch -IncludeFolders
"deleted PF name"
```

> Ensure that your Exchange 2013 servers have CU2 installed in order to avoid the *712.22 Issue - Public Folder Permissions Loss After PF Mailbox Move* bug.

Recovering deleted Public Folders using Outlook

Outlook can be used to easily recover deleted PFs as long as the following conditions are true:

- The user recovering the PF has *Owner* permissions on the PF being recovered

- The deleted items retention period has not expired for the deleted PF

- If the recovered PF is a root folder, the user restoring it also needs *Owner* permissions at the *Root* level

- If the recovered PF is a *Child* folder, the user restoring it also needs *Owner* permissions on the *Parent* folder

Assuming all of the preceding conditions are met, or are not applicable, a user or administrator can recover the PF using the usual **Recover Deleted Items** feature in Outlook. However, note that any root PF recovered using Outlook gets restored to the *Primary Public Folder* mailbox. If its original mailbox was a different one, you can move it using the following cmdlet:

```
New-PublicFolderMoveRequest -Folders \<Folder> -TargetMailbox "Target
Mailbox"
```

If the root PFs contained subfolders that were recovered, you will likely need to move the child PF to the secondary mailbox. This is because moving the root PF does not change the content mailbox for its child folders. In order to move these to their respective content mailboxes you need to use the `Move-PublicFolderBranch.ps1` script.

If you need to recover deleted child PFs or a parent PF and its child folders, it is easier to use Shell, as we will see in the next sections.

> Any deleted root PF that is recovered using Outlook should retain its original permissions. If it also had child PFs, the child folder permissions will be replaced and inherited from their parent PF.

Recovering deleted Public Folders using PowerShell

While recovering a single PF might be easy using Outlook, Shell is much better in certain scenarios. For example, if you need to restore a PF to the root path or you are not the owner of the PF that was deleted and you need it to be recovered, it is easier to use Shell.

Let us assume I deleted a PF named **Exchange** that I want to recover. First, we need to find out where exactly it is currently located within the Dumpster. To do this, we run the following cmdlet:

```
Get-PublicFolder "\NON_IPM_SUBTREE" -Recurse | Where {$_.Name -match
"Exchange" | Format-List Identity
```

```
Machine: EXAIO.letsexchange.com                    _  □  X

[PS] C:\>
[PS] C:\>Get-PublicFolder "\NON_IPM_SUBTREE" -Recurse | Where {$_
.Name -match "exchange"} | FL Identity


Identity : \NON_IPM_SUBTREE\DUMPSTER_ROOT\83b6fc41-4692-4d63-b1d
           e-dd629a937cc1\Exchange


[PS] C:\>_
```

To recover this particular PF from the Dumpster back to the PF root (or to wherever you want to recover it to), we simply update its path by running:

```
Set-PublicFolder "\NON_IPM_SUBTREE\DUMPSTER_ROOT\<ID>\Exchange" -Path "\"
-Verbose
```

```
Machine: EXAIO.letsexchange.com

[PS] C:\>
[PS] C:\>Set-PublicFolder "\NON_IPM_SUBTREE\DUMPSTER_ROOT\83b6fc4
1-4692-4d63-b1de-dd629a937cc1\Exchange" -Path "\" -Verbose
VERBOSE: [13:04:14.973 GMT] Set-PublicFolder : Runspace context:
Executing user: letsexchange.com/Users/Administrator, Executing
user organization: , Current organization: , RBAC-enabled:
Enabled.
VERBOSE: [13:04:14.973 GMT] Set-PublicFolder : Active Directory
session settings for 'Set-PublicFolder' are: View Entire Forest:
'False', Default Scope: 'letsexchange.com', Configuration
Domain Controller: 'DC1.letsexchange.com', Preferred Global
Catalog: 'DC1.letsexchange.com', Preferred Domain Controllers:
'{ DC1.letsexchange.com }'
VERBOSE: [13:04:14.973 GMT] Set-PublicFolder : Beginning
processing Set-PublicFolder
VERBOSE: [13:04:14.973 GMT] Set-PublicFolder : Instantiating
handler with index 0 for cmdlet extension agent "Admin Audit Log
Agent".
VERBOSE: [13:04:14.973 GMT] Set-PublicFolder : Current ScopeSet
is: ( Recipient Read Scope: {{, }}, Recipient Write Scopes: {{,
}}, Configuration Read Scope: {{, }}, Configuration Write
Scope(s): {{, }, }, Exclusive Recipient Scope(s): {}, Exclusive
Configuration Scope(s): {} )
VERBOSE: [13:04:15.035 GMT] Set-PublicFolder : Searching objects

"\NON_IPM_SUBTREE\DUMPSTER_ROOT\83b6fc41-4692-4d63-b1de-dd629a93
7cc1\Exchange" of type "PublicFolder" under the root "$null".
VERBOSE: [13:04:15.035 GMT] Set-PublicFolder : Previous
operation that ran on:
'Microsoft.Exchange.Data.Storage.PublicFolderSession
'.
VERBOSE: [13:04:15.035 GMT] Set-PublicFolder : Processing object

"\NON_IPM_SUBTREE\DUMPSTER_ROOT\83b6fc41-4692-4d63-b1de-dd629a93
7cc1\Exchange".
VERBOSE: [13:04:15.051 GMT] Set-PublicFolder : Admin Audit Log:
Entered Handler:Validate.
VERBOSE: [13:04:15.067 GMT] Set-PublicFolder : Admin Audit Log:
Entered ClassFactory:InitializeConfig.
VERBOSE: [13:04:15.067 GMT] Set-PublicFolder : Admin Audit Log:
Exited ClassFactory:InitializeConfig.
VERBOSE: [13:04:30.103 GMT] Set-PublicFolder : Admin Audit Log:
Exited Handler:Validate.
VERBOSE: Setting public folder
"\NON_IPM_SUBTREE\DUMPSTER_ROOT\83b6fc41-4692-4d63-b1de-dd629a93
7cc1\Exchange".
VERBOSE: [13:04:30.170 GMT] Set-PublicFolder : Resolved current
organization: .
VERBOSE: [13:04:30.201 GMT] Set-PublicFolder : Searching objects
"\" of type "PublicFolder" under the root "$null".
VERBOSE: [13:04:30.201 GMT] Set-PublicFolder : Previous
operation that ran on:
'Microsoft.Exchange.Data.Storage.PublicFolderSession
'.
VERBOSE: [13:04:30.248 GMT] Set-PublicFolder : Saving object
"\NON_IPM_SUBTREE\DUMPSTER_ROOT\83b6fc41-4692-4d63-b1de-dd629a93
7cc1\Exchange" of type "PublicFolder" and state "Unchanged".
VERBOSE: [13:04:30.248 GMT] Set-PublicFolder : Previous
operation that ran on:
'Microsoft.Exchange.Data.Storage.PublicFolderSession
'.
VERBOSE: [13:04:30.248 GMT] Set-PublicFolder : Admin Audit Log:
Entered Handler:OnComplete.
VERBOSE: [13:04:45.937 GMT] Set-PublicFolder : Admin Audit Log:
Exited Handler:OnComplete.
VERBOSE: [13:04:45.937 GMT] Set-PublicFolder : Ending processing
Set-PublicFolder
[PS] C:\>_
```

The PF has now been recovered and can be accessed by users straightaway. This method also restores any deleted child PF or an entire branch of PFs. Just follow this procedure to restore the root PF, and all its content and child folders will be restored as well.

Recovering deleted Public Folders post retention

Recovering PFs within a retention period is easy as we have just seen. However, recovering PFs that have already been deleted from the Dumpster is not as easy. First, we need to do a backup restore of the database containing the affected PF. Once the database is restored to a recovery database, we use Shell to extract and restore content from it. However, to recover any PF mailbox data you must create the "target" folders in the target mailbox, meaning that at the time of writing this book the recovery process does not create the folder structure automatically, and if the target folder does not exist, the process will fail.

> Once again, please ensure that your Exchange 2013 servers have CU2 installed in order to avoid the *712.22 Issue - Public Folder Permissions Loss After PF Mailbox Move* bug.

Let us consider the same scenario where we deleted the **Exchange** PF that has now expired and cannot be recovered from the Dumpster. In order to recover this PF from the restored database, after we do a backup restore, we need to have a folder with the same name of **Exchange** in the target PF mailbox to which we are restoring data to. This is a current limitation of the restore process that will be addressed in the future.

Now we restore the database into a recovery database and then create a new PF named **Exchange** in a PF content mailbox by using the following command line (assuming it does not already exist):

```
New-PublicFolder -Mailbox <Mailbox Name> -Name Exchange
```

Next, we run the following:

```
New-MailboxRestoreRequest -SourceDatabase <Recovery Database> -
SourceStoreMailbox <recovered mailbox with affected PF" -TargetMailbox
<mailbox where data is being recovered to> -AllowLegacyDNMismatch -
IncludeFolders Exchange
```

Once the restore is complete, we can run the cmdlet to check if we are able to successfully restore the content we wanted by using the following command line:

```
Get-MailboxrestoreRequest | Where {$_.Status -eq "Completed"}
```

To check if the restore is complete, run the following cmdlet and check the value of `ItemsTransferred`:

```
Get-MailboxrestoreRequest | Where {$_.Status -eq "Completed"}
 | Get-MailboxRestoreRequestStatistics | Select *Items*
```

The affected PF, as well as all its content, has now been recovered and can be accessed by users.

Summary

In this chapter, we explored multiple Exchange features that, when working together, might reduce the necessity for traditional backups or even, in some cases, eliminate them altogether. Using single item recovery together with In-Place Hold will ensure deleted and modified items are kept easily available in case they need to be recovered. Another advantage is that even end users can recover them. However, this usually comes at a high cost: *storage*.

DAGs have also reduced the likelihood of needing backups to perform a restore of data. Having multiple database copies ensures that a database, server, or even datacenter failure is quickly recoverable by activating databases on another server. By using lagged copies, we can even protect ourselves against the rare event of data corruption.

Nonetheless, backups will still be used by most companies as not everyone is able to support the requirements needed to run a backup-less environment. As such, we had a look at what should be backed up for each Exchange role and how we can perform several types of recovery for most disaster recovery scenarios.

In the next chapter, we will explore the changes and improvements made in Exchange 2013 around monitoring. More specifically, we will explore the new managed availability monitoring engine.

8
Monitoring Exchange

Throughout this book we have been exploring how to design Exchange 2013 with high availability in mind. However, this task does not finish once an Exchange environment is fully built and backups are configured. It is also critical for organizations to continuously monitor Exchange. Users often complain that their e-mail is slow and administrators struggle to identify where and why a slowdown is occurring or even if one is actually occurring. Addressing these concerns as early as possible, ideally before an issue occurs, is the best policy to minimize costs and avoid business disruption.

Comprehensive monitoring of Exchange within organizations is a vital prerequisite to ensure maximum security to the company as well as achieve a high level of performance and availability. Monitoring is also necessary to enable continued efficiency of company operations unconstrained by server performance issues.

Some of the most basic metrics that need monitoring include CPU utilization, free disk space, available memory, and transport queues, and so on. However, Exchange is made up of so many services and components that it is simply impossible to monitor everything manually.

There are two main objectives of Exchange monitoring: optimizing its performance and ensuring its availability. In Exchange 2013, Microsoft introduced major improvements in server health and performance as we will see throughout this chapter.

Introducing Managed Availability

In the previous releases, administrators used **System Center Operations Manager** (**SCOM**), or another third-party solution, when they needed a comprehensive monitoring solution for Exchange. This involved collecting data and performing actions based on that data if necessary. When Microsoft started developing Exchange 2013, a focus area was to improve end-to-end monitoring in a way that it would work seamlessly for any Exchange deployment, from the largest deployment (Office 365) to the smallest one. By maintaining and developing Exchange Online throughout the past years, Microsoft has learned a lot. As an example, even though there were approximately 1,100 alerts in Exchange 2010 Management Pack, only 150 of those were shown to be useful in Office 365. As such, many were disabled for Exchange Online. The lessons learned from Office 365 led Microsoft to take a different approach towards monitoring.

Exchange 2013 introduces **Managed Availability** or **Local Active Monitoring** (**LAM**) as it is used internally by Microsoft Corporation. Managed Availability is a built-in monitoring engine that ties together internal monitoring and recovery features in order to help prevent failures. This is achieved by proactively restoring services, automatically initiating server failovers, or by alerting administrators to take action. It focuses on monitoring and managing the user experience to help keep the service permanently available, instead of focusing simply on component and server uptime.

This new model decentralizes monitoring. Previously, there used to be an SCOM agent deployed on each server and all measurements would be streamed to a central SCOM server, which would then assess all the measurements taken and establish if something was healthy or not. However, this is not ideal in high-scale environments with alerts sometimes taking longer to be raised, as channeling all this data to a central location does not scale well. Instead of having each server acting as an isolated island, each server now executes their own probes, they monitor themselves, and take action to self recover or escalate if needed.

Managed Availability focuses on the user and measures three main aspects that constitute the end user experience: availability, experience (sometimes measured as latency), and whether errors are occurring. Let us use OWA as an example to better understand these three aspects. Availability is simply whether the user can access the OWA web page or not. If they are unable to, the experience is broken and that generates a service desk escalation. If they are able to log into OWA, latency measures what the experience is like, such as whether the interface loads and whether the users can access their e-mails. As users are able to log in, latency then measures, for example, how fast the e-mail is rendered in the browser.

Exploring Managed Availability components

Managed Availability is integrated into both Exchange 2013 server roles and is made up of two processes: the Exchange Health Manager service (MSExchangeHM, MSExchangeHMHost.exe) and the Exchange Health Manager Worker process (MSExchangeHMWorker.exe).

Managed Availability is made up of three main components:

- The first one is the **probe engine** that has the responsibility of taking measurements on the server, which are then passed on to the next component

- The second one is the **monitor** that contains the logic behind what is considered to be healthy and makes decisions on whether something is considered healthy or not

- The third one is the **responder engine**, which first tries to recover a component when it is detected as unhealthy

Managed Availability has a multistage recovery process which can vary from scenario to scenario. As an example, the first attempt it makes could be to restart an affected application pool, the second attempt to restart the service, the third to restart the server, and the final attempt to take the entire server offline so that it cannot accept any more traffic. If all these recovery attempts fail, then it escalates the problem through an event log notification. The following diagram shows the components and the recovery process of Managed Availability:

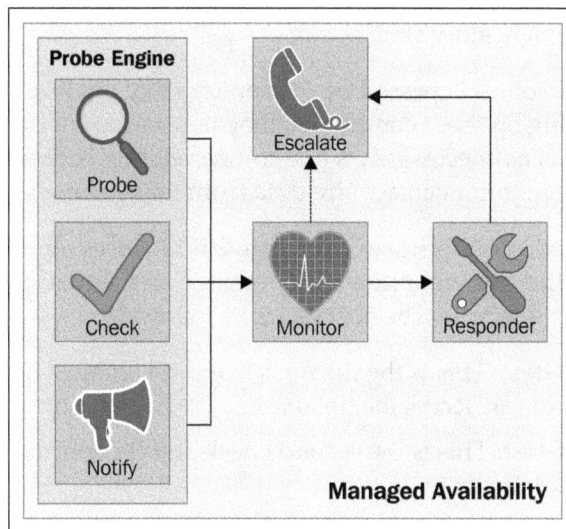

Probes

The infrastructure of probes is made up of three frameworks:

- **Synthetic transactions**: These execute synthetic user transactions to measure the perception of the service. These are similar to the test cmdlets.

- **Checks**: These are the passive monitoring mechanisms that measure the actual customer traffic.

- **Notifications**: An example is the notification that the administrators receive in the **Exchange Admin Center** (**EAC**) when a certificate expires.

Exchange 2013 contains a new type of mailbox, called **health mailboxes**, and they are used to perform synthetic transactions by the probes. There is typically one health mailbox per database copy. If, for any reason, these get corrupted or are deleted by mistake, they get recreated automatically when the health manager service starts. So if this is the case, simply restart this service.

To view these hidden mailboxes you can use Active Directory Users and Computers. Enable **Advanced Features**, and navigate to **Microsoft Exchange System Objects | Monitoring Mailboxes**. Alternatively you can use the following cmdlet:

```
Get-Mailbox -Monitoring
```

Monitors

Monitors are Managed Availability's central components. They define what data is collected, what each features' state of health is, and the actions to be taken in order to restore a feature to a healthy state.

The data that probes collect is passed on to monitors that analyze it for specific conditions. Depending on these conditions, they determine if a component is healthy or unhealthy. There is not necessarily a one-to-one relation between probes and monitors, as a single monitor can acquire data from many probes.

As already mentioned, monitoring in Exchange 2013 focuses on the user experience. To accomplish this, there are monitors at different layers, and each check performs detection at different intervals. The checks are as follows:

- **Mailbox self-test**: This is the first check and it validates if the local interface or the protocol can access the database.

- **Protocol self-test**: This is the second check and it confirms if the local protocol is functioning.

- **Proxy self-test**: This is the third check. It runs on CASs and validates whether the proxy functionality for the protocol is functioning.

- **All-inclusive check**: This is the last check and it validates the end-to-end user experience.

Different layers are used in order to deal with dependencies. For example, if the mailbox self-test and the protocol self-test probes fail at the same time, which does not necessarily mean that the store is down, but that the Mailbox server's local protocol is not working. On the other hand, if the protocol self-test passed but the mailbox self-test failed, it indicates a problem at the storage level which might mean that the store or database is offline.

From a monitoring perspective, this means finer control over the alerts that are raised. When evaluating the health of OWA, for example, Exchange is more likely to delay raising an alert if the mailbox self-test fails and the protocol self-test passes. However, it will raise an alert immediately if both monitors are unhealthy.

> Using the crimson channels, you can check the definitions of monitors, probes, and responders. For monitors, check `Microsoft/Exchange/ActiveMonitoring/MonitorDefinition` log.

Practically all monitors collect one of the following types of data:

- Some monitors change their status based on **direct notifications**.

- Most monitors are based on **probe results**. These turn unhealthy when some probes fail, either based on a number of successive failures or based on a number of failures over an interval of time.

- Some monitors use **performance counters** and merely establish if a counter is above or below a defined threshold for the required time.

Monitors have a `TypeName` property that indicates what data they collect and the threshold that needs to be reached for it to be considered unhealthy. The following table describes the most common types:

TypeName value	Description
`OverallPercentSuccessMonitor`	Analyzes probe results and calculates the success percentage over the past `MonitoringIntervalSeconds` property. It turns unhealthy if the calculated percentage of success is less than `MonitoringThreshold`.
`OverallConsecutiveProbe FailuresMonitor`	Analyzes the last X probe results as stipulated in `MonitoringThreshold`. It turns unhealthy if all are failures.
`OverallXFailuresMonitor`	Analyzes probe results over the past `MonitoringIntervalSeconds` property. It turns unhealthy if at least X results as stipulated in `MonitoringThreshold` are failures.
`OverallConsecutiveSample ValueAboveThresholdMonitor`	Analyzes the last x performance counter results as stipulated in `SecondaryMonitoringThreshold` over the past. It turns unhealthy if at least x counters are over the threshold stipulated in `MonitoringThreshold`.

The following screenshot shows some of these properties for `ECPProxyTestMonitor`:

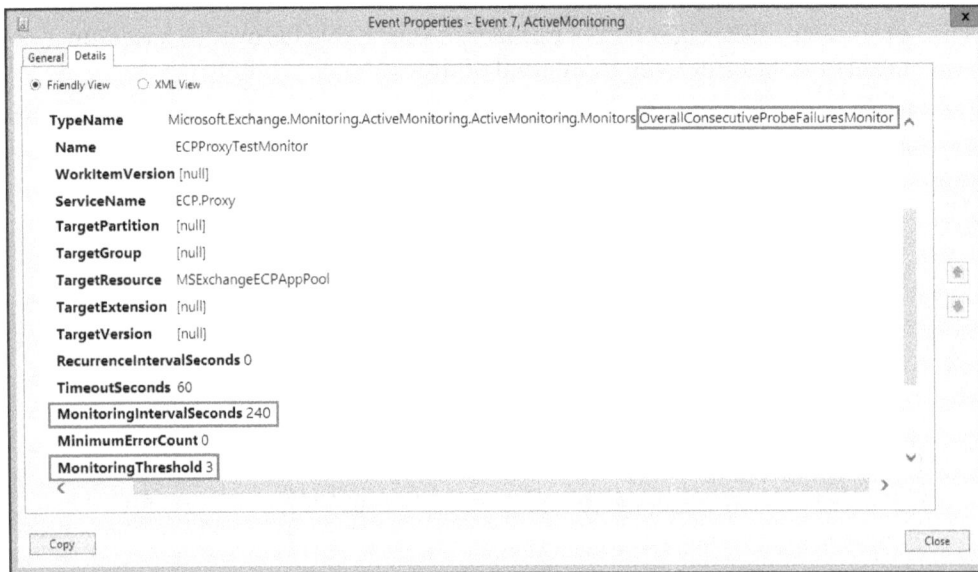

For a monitor to become unhealthy, another event must happen. The code for each individual monitor that checks the threshold only runs every few seconds, stipulated by a property called `RecurrenceIntervalSeconds`.

> A threshold is checked only when the monitor runs.

If the threshold is met, the monitor turns unhealthy as soon as it runs. `Get-ServerHealth` will then report for the first 60 seconds (usually) that the monitor is in a **degraded** state even though monitors do not have this concept of being degraded; they only have two states: healthy or unhealthy.

The **health set** (a group of related monitors) that the monitor belongs to is defined by its `ServiceName` property as you can see in the preceding screenshot. If any of the health set's monitor is in an unhealthy state, the entire health set becomes unhealthy as observed using SCOM or `Get-HealthReport` (both these cmdlets are explored further in the chapter).

Responders

When a monitor establishes that a component is unhealthy, it generates an alert which triggers a responder. When the responder engine gets alerted, it first tries to recover the component using the multistage recovery process already discussed.

There are several types of responders:

- **Restart responder**: This stops and restarts the services
- **Reset AppPool responder**: This recycles IIS application pools
- **Failover responder**: This takes a Mailbox server out of service
- **Bugcheck responder**: This initiates bug checks
- **Offline responder**: This takes protocols out of service
- **Online responder**: This puts servers back into service
- **Escalate responder**: This, using event logging, escalates issues
- **Specialized Component responders** : Some components have also specialized responders that are unique to them

The offline responder, which is load balancer-agnostic, is used to remove a protocol from being used on the CASs. When this responder is invoked, the protocol does not reply to a load balancer's health check, thus causing the load balancer to remove the protocol or the server from its pool. Similarly, when the monitor turns healthy again, the online responder is automatically initiated and allows the protocol to reply to the load balancer health check, causing the load balancer to re-add the protocol or server back into its pool. This, of course, is for load balancers that are aware of Exchange-managed availability.

> The offline responder can be manually invoked using the `Set-ServerComponentState` cmdlet, enabling administrators to manually put servers in the maintenance mode.

When the escalate responder gets invoked, a Windows event is generated, stating that a health set is healthy/unhealthy. These events are used to alert administrators and manipulate the monitors inside SCOM. Basically, managed availability decides when to generate an alert in SCOM, making the decision as to when an escalation to an administrator should occur.

The type of responder that gets executed and the timeline in which it is executed is defined by the monitors and is known as a recovery sequence for a monitor. Let us go back to our OWA example and assume that a probe for the OWA protocol triggers the monitor to become unhealthy. The current time is saved (let us call it T), and the monitor then starts a recovery process based on the current time and defines recovery actions at certain intervals within the recovery process. For this example, the recovery sequence would be:

1. At $T=0$, the responder Reset AppPool gets initiated.
2. If at $T=5$ minutes, the monitor has not returned to healthy, the Failover responder is executed and databases are failed over to a different server.
3. If at $T=8$ minutes, the monitor has not returned to healthy, the Bugcheck responder is triggered and the server gets rebooted.
4. If at $T=15$ minutes, the monitor is still unhealthy, the Escalate responder is executed.

The recovery sequence does not stop when the monitor becomes healthy, as the last action does not have to complete before the next one starts. Also, a monitor can have many time intervals with each interval triggering one or more responders as shown in the following diagram:

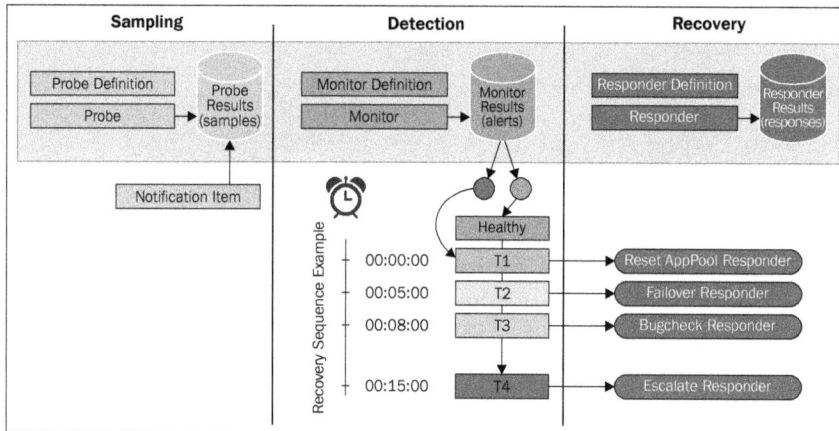

Monitors have the `StateTransitionXML` property that states at which stages
different responders are executed. For the `ECPProxyTestMonitor`, these are:

```
<StateTransitions>
<Transition ToState="Degraded" TimeoutInSeconds="0"/>
<Transition ToState="Unhealthy" TimeoutInSeconds="420"/>
<Transition ToState="Unhealthy1" TimeoutInSeconds="480"/>
<Transition ToState="Unhealthy2" TimeoutInSeconds="900"/>
<Transition ToState="Unrecoverable" TimeoutInSeconds="3600"/>
</StateTransitions>
```

The transition states in the preceding code are used only internally, as a monitor
only has two states from an external perspective as already explained: healthy
or unhealthy. This process of initiating different responders at different stages
is known as a **responder chain**. As thresholds continue to be reached, stronger
responders execute at each step until the monitor establishes that it is healthy
or until an administrator is notified. If the code for a monitor runs while it is
in one of these states and the threshold is no longer reached, then no other
responders will get executed and `Get-ServerHealth` (which will be discussed
shortly) will again report the monitor as being healthy.

Health

Hundreds of health metrics are polled and analyzed by Managed Availability
on every Exchange 2013 server every second. If something wrong is found, it is
usually fixed automatically. However, there are issues that Managed Availability
simply cannot fix on its own of course, so they are escalated to an administrator
through event logging, and if deployed, SCOM. If an administrator gets involved in
investigating the issue, the starting point is usually the cmdlets `Get-HealthReport`
and `Get-ServerHealth`.

`Get-ServerHealth` retrieves health data in a raw format while `Get-HealthReport` uses this data to provide a current snapshot of the health. These two cmdlets can operate at multiple layers, for example:

- They can display the health of a server detailed by health set
- They can be used to analyze, in more detail, a health set and display each monitor's status
- They can summarize the health of a group of servers like a load-balanced array of CASs or DAG members

Health sets are grouped into units called **health groups**, which are used for reporting within SCOM. There are four health groups:

- **Customer Touch Points**: This reports on components with direct user interaction such as OWA
- **Service Components**: This reports on components with no direct user interaction such as OAB generation
- **Server Components**: This reports on physical resources of a server such as memory and disk
- **Dependency Availability**: This reports on a server's ability to use its dependencies such as AD

`Get-HealthReport` tells us the status of all the health sets present on a server, as shown in the following screenshot:

```
 Machine: EXCAS1.letsexchange.com          _ □ X

[PS] C:\>
[PS] C:\>Get-HealthReport EXCAS1

Server    State      HealthSet     AlertValue LastTransi MonitorCo
                                              tionTime   unt
------    -----      ---------     ---------- ---------- --------
EXCAS1    NotAppl... AD            Healthy    30/11/2... 10
EXCAS1    NotAppl... EDS           Healthy    30/11/2... 10
EXCAS1    Online     Fronten...    Healthy    30/11/2... 11
EXCAS1    Online     HubTran...    Healthy    30/11/2... 29
EXCAS1    NotAppl... Monitoring    Healthy    30/11/2... 9
EXCAS1    NotAppl... DataPro...    Healthy    30/11/2... 1
EXCAS1    NotAppl... Network       Unknown    01/01/0... 1
EXCAS1    NotAppl... FIPS          Healthy    30/11/2... 3
EXCAS1    Online     Transport     Healthy    30/11/2... 9
EXCAS1    NotAppl... RPS           Healthy    30/11/2... 2
EXCAS1    Online     UM.Call...    Healthy    30/11/2... 7
EXCAS1    NotAppl... UserThr...    Healthy    30/11/2... 7
EXCAS1    NotAppl... Search        Healthy    30/11/2... 9
EXCAS1    NotAppl... AntiSpam      Healthy    30/11/2... 3
EXCAS1    NotAppl... Security      Healthy    30/11/2... 3
EXCAS1    NotAppl... IMAP.Pr...    Healthy    30/11/2... 3
EXCAS1    NotAppl... Datamining    Healthy    30/11/2... 3
EXCAS1    NotAppl... Provisi...    Healthy    30/11/2... 3
EXCAS1    NotAppl... POP.Pro...    Healthy    30/11/2... 3
EXCAS1    NotAppl... Outlook...    Healthy    30/11/2... 9
EXCAS1    NotAppl... Process...    Healthy    30/11/2... 9
EXCAS1    NotAppl... Store         Healthy    30/11/2... 6
EXCAS1    NotAppl... Transpo...    Healthy    30/11/2... 3
EXCAS1    NotAppl... Mailbox...    Healthy    30/11/2... 6
EXCAS1    NotAppl... EventAs...    Healthy    30/11/2... 2
EXCAS1    NotAppl... MRS           Healthy    30/11/2... 3
EXCAS1    NotAppl... Message...    Healthy    30/11/2... 3
EXCAS1    NotAppl... Central...    Healthy    30/11/2... 3
EXCAS1    NotAppl... UM.Prot...    Healthy    30/11/2... 3
EXCAS1    Offline    ECP.Proxy     Unhealthy  30/11/2... 4
EXCAS1    NotAppl... OWA.Pro...    Healthy    30/11/2... 3
EXCAS1    NotAppl... Calenda...    Healthy    30/11/2... 3
EXCAS1    Online     RPS.Proxy     Healthy    30/11/2... 13
EXCAS1    Offline    RWS.Proxy     Unhealthy  30/11/2... 10
EXCAS1    NotAppl... PushNot...    Healthy    30/11/2... 3
EXCAS1    Online     Outlook...    Healthy    30/11/2... 4
EXCAS1    NotAppl... EWS.Pro...    Healthy    30/11/2... 3
EXCAS1    NotAppl... ActiveS...    Healthy    30/11/2... 3
EXCAS1    NotAppl... ECP           Degraded   30/11/2... 1
EXCAS1    Online     Autodis...    Healthy    30/11/2... 1
EXCAS1    Online     ActiveS...    Healthy    30/11/2... 1
```

As you can see from the preceding screenshot, the **ECP** health set is currently in a **Degraded** state, most certainly caused by the fact the **ECP.Proxy** health set is **Unhealthy**.

As already explained, similar monitors or monitors that are tied to a particular component are grouped into health sets. The health of a health set is determined by the "weakest" of the monitors within the health set. For example, if there are five monitors in a particular health set and one is unhealthy, then the entire health set is considered unhealthy.

We can also see that the state for **ECP.Proxy** is **Offline**, as shown in the following screenshot, meaning the offline responder has already been actioned:

```
Machine: EXCAS1.letsexchange.com                           —  □  x

[PS] C:\>
[PS] C:\>Get-HealthReport EXCAS1 -HealthSet ECP | FL

RunspaceId               : 2689c6e8-c377-460a-ba8c-1255d4f6bb5d
Server                   : EXCAS1
State                    : NotApplicable
HealthSet                : ECP
HealthGroup              : CustomerTouchPoints
AlertValue               : Unhealthy
LastTransitionTime       : 30/11/2013 10:30:46
MonitorCount             : 1
HaImpactingMonitorCount  : 0
Entries                  : {EacCtpMonitor}
Identity                 : ECP\EXCAS1
IsValid                  : True
ObjectState              : New



[PS] C:\>
[PS] C:\>Get-HealthReport EXCAS1 -HealthSet ECP.Proxy | FL

RunspaceId               : 2689c6e8-c377-460a-ba8c-1255d4f6bb5d
Server                   : EXCAS1
State                    : Offline
HealthSet                : ECP.Proxy
HealthGroup              : ServiceComponents
AlertValue               : Unhealthy
LastTransitionTime       : 30/11/2013 10:57:14
MonitorCount             : 4
HaImpactingMonitorCount  : 1
Entries                  : {PrivateWorkingSetWarningThresholdExce
                           eded.msexchangeecpapppool, ProcessProc
                           essorTimeErrorThresholdExceeded.msexch
                           angeecpapppool, ExchangeCrashEventErro
                           rThresholdExceeded.msexchangeecpapppoo
                           l, ECPProxyTestMonitor}
Identity                 : ECP.Proxy\EXCAS1
IsValid                  : True
ObjectState              : New


[PS] C:\>
```

In the preceding screenshot, we can see **HealthGroup** of each health set. **MonitorCount** tells us that **ECP.Proxy** relies on four monitors. So let us check which of these four monitors is unhealthy. To do this, we use the Get-ServerHealth cmdlet as shown in the following screenshot:

```
                    Machine: EXCAS1.letsexchange.com        _  □  x

[PS] C:\>
[PS] C:\>Get-ServerHealth EXCAS1 -HealthSet ECP.Proxy | Select Na
me, CurrentHealthSetState, TargetResource, AlertValue, ServerComp
onentName


Name                         : PrivateWorkingSetWarningThresholdExceede
                               d.msexchangeecpapppool
CurrentHealthSetState        : Offline
TargetResource               : msexchangeecpapppool
AlertValue                   : Healthy
ServerComponentName          : EcpProxy

Name                         : ProcessProcessorTimeErrorThresholdExceed
                               ed.msexchangeecpapppool
CurrentHealthSetState        : Offline
TargetResource               : msexchangeecpapppool
AlertValue                   : Healthy
ServerComponentName          : EcpProxy

Name                         : ExchangeCrashEventErrorThresholdExceeded
                               .msexchangeecpapppool
CurrentHealthSetState        : Offline
TargetResource               : msexchangeecpapppool
AlertValue                   : Healthy
ServerComponentName          : EcpProxy

Name                         : ECPProxyTestMonitor
CurrentHealthSetState        : Offline
TargetResource               : MSExchangeECPAppPool
AlertValue                   : Unhealthy
ServerComponentName          : EcpProxy


[PS] C:\>
```

At this stage, we know that it is the **ECPProxyTestMonitor** that is detecting
a problem with ECP. The health set **ECP.Proxy** monitors the EAC proxy
infrastructure's availability on the CASs. When the **ECP.Proxy** is unhealthy,
this means there is an issue that might be preventing you from using the EAC.

This probe might fail for different reasons such as the following:

- The application pool hosted on the CAS is not working correctly
- Incorrect monitoring account credentials
- Domain controllers not responding

So far we know that the problem lies within the ECP application pool as the
TargetResource property displayed in the preceding screenshot is very clear.
However, this might not be the case with every issue you face. If we did not know
that the problem was with the ECP application pool, we could check the Microsoft/
Exchange/ActiveMonitoring/MonitorDefinition crimson channel where the
definition of each monitor is written. A quick search for ECPProxyTestMonitor
reveals the monitor we are looking for. The SampleMask property is a substring
that all probes for this monitor have in their names. In this example, this property
is ECPProxyTestProbe/MSExchangeECPAppPool.

As such, if we now go to the probes' definition channel, `Microsoft/Exchange/ActiveMonitoring/ProbeDefinition`, and search for `MSExchangeECPAppPool`, we will find the probe that is detecting the issue:

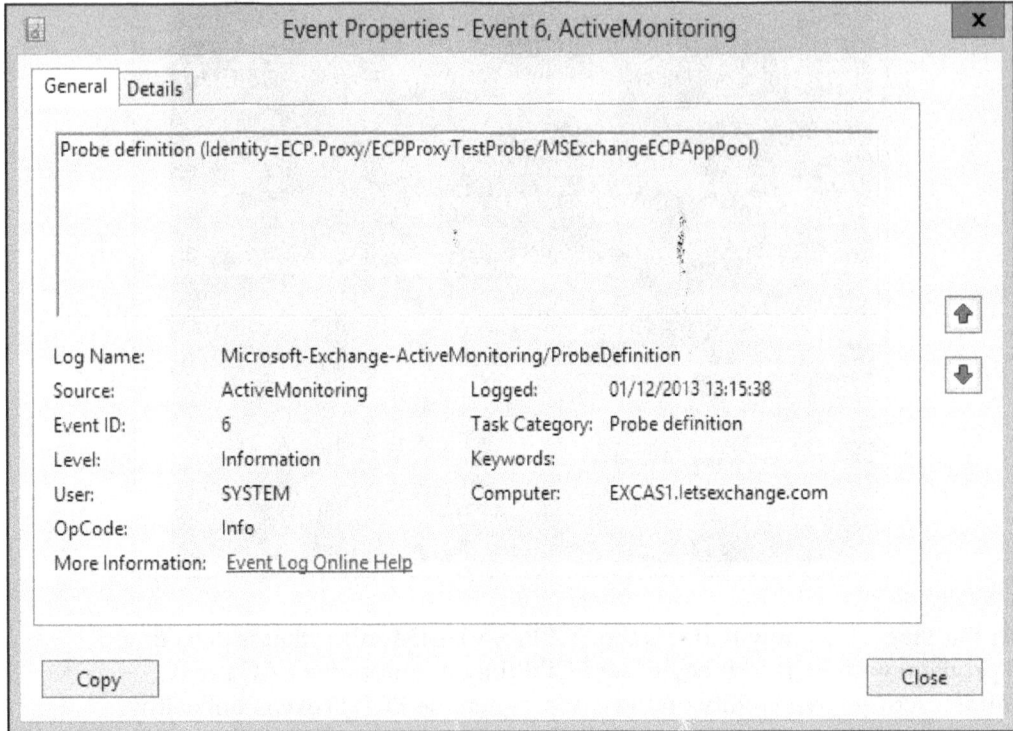

```
Event Properties - Event 6, ActiveMonitoring                    X

General | Details

  Probe definition (Identity=ECP.Proxy/ECPProxyTestProbe/MSExchangeECPAppPool)




  Log Name:        Microsoft-Exchange-ActiveMonitoring/ProbeDefinition
  Source:          ActiveMonitoring      Logged:          01/12/2013 13:15:38
  Event ID:        6                     Task Category:   Probe definition
  Level:           Information           Keywords:
  User:            SYSTEM                Computer:        EXCAS1.letsexchange.com
  OpCode:          Info
  More Information: Event Log Online Help


  Copy                                                            Close
```

Under the probe's definition properties, **ServiceName** will state the health set for this probe, and more important for us is the **TargetResource**. It will inform the object that the probe is validating, in this case `MSExchangeECPAppPool`.

We already have this information from the previous steps. However, this might not be the case every time you troubleshoot; you might have to perform these steps in order to check exactly what the probe is validating.

We can also use the `Get-MonitoringItemIdentity` cmdlet to list all the probes, monitors, and responders in a given health set. If we run it against the `ECPProxy` health set, we see that there is only one probe in this health set. This might not be the case in every scenario, so the preceding steps are useful in some cases. The following screenshot shows all the responders, monitors, and probes associated with the `ECPProxy` health set:

```
[PS] C:\>
[PS] C:\>Get-MonitoringItemIdentity ECP.Proxy -Server EXCAS1 | FT
ItemType, Name -AutoSize

ItemType   Name
--------   ----
   Probe   ECPProxyTestProbe
 Monitor   ECPProxyTestMonitor
 Monitor   PrivateWorkingSetWarningThresholdExceeded.msexchang...
 Monitor   ProcessProcessorTimeErrorThresholdExceeded.msexchan...
 Monitor   ExchangeCrashEventErrorThresholdExceeded.msexchange...
Responder  ECPProxyTestRecycleAppPool
Responder  ECPProxyTestOffline
Responder  ECPProxyTestOfflineFailedEscalate
Responder  ECPProxyTestEscalate
Responder  PrivateWorkingSetWarningThresholdExceeded.msexchang...
Responder  PrivateWorkingSetWarningThresholdExceeded.msexchang...
Responder  ProcessProcessorTimeErrorThresholdExceeded.msexchan...
Responder  ProcessProcessorTimeErrorThresholdExceeded.msexchan...
Responder  ProcessProcessorTimeErrorThresholdExceeded.msexchan...
Responder  ExchangeCrashEventErrorThresholdExceeded.msexchange...


[PS] C:\>
```

Machine: EXCAS1.letsexchange.com

The next step is to rerun the probe that is associated with the unhealthy monitor. An additional method would be to use the information provided in the Exchange 2013 Management Pack Health Sets TechNet page, which tells us that the probe responsible for checking this application pool is `ECPProxyTestProbes`.

So, we use the `Invoke-MonitoringProbe` cmdlet to rerun it and check **ResultType**, as shown in the following screenshot:

```
                Machine: EXCAS1.letsexchange.com        - □ x

[PS] C:\>
[PS] C:\>Invoke-MonitoringProbe ECP.Proxy\ECPProxyTestProbe -Serv
er EXCAS1 | FL


RunspaceId           : 2689c6e8-c377-460a-ba8c-1255d4f6bb5d
Server               : EXCAS1
MonitorIdentity      : ECP.Proxy\ECPProxyTestProbe
RequestId            : 97f22787-3848-48a0-8dd4-e00a454b22a8
ExecutionStartTime   : 30/11/2013 11:03:18
ExecutionEndTime     : 30/11/2013 11:03:18
Error                : Unknown app pool name:
Exception            : System.InvalidOperationException: Unknown
                       app pool name:
                          at Microsoft.Exchange.Monitoring.ActiveM
                       onitoring.ClientAccess.CafeLocalProbe.DoWor
                       k(CancellationToken cancellationToken)
                          at Microsoft.Exchange.WorkerTaskFramewor
                       k.WorkItem.Execute(CancellationToken
                       joinedToken)
                          at Microsoft.Exchange.WorkerTaskFramewor
                       k.WorkItem.<>c__DisplayClass2.<StartExecuti
                       ng>b__0()
                          at System.Threading.Tasks.Task.Execute()
PoisonedCount        : 0
ExecutionId          : 34517756
SampleValue          : 0
ExecutionContext     : probe defined timeout=60000ms, actual
                       timeout=60000ms, http request
                       timeout=59000ms

FailureContext       :
ExtensionXml         :
ResultType           : Failed
RetryCount           : 0
ResultName           : 97f22787384848a08dd4e00a454b22a8-ECPProxyTe
                       stProbe
IsNotified           : False
ResultId             : 47940
ServiceName          : InvokeNow
StateAttribute1      :
StateAttribute2      :
```

In the output, **ResultType** is still **Failed**, so further troubleshooting might be necessary. If the value was **Succeeded** instead, the issue would have been only a momentary error and would no longer exist.

> The crimson channel where probes log information to is Microsoft/Exchange/ ActiveMonitoring/ProbeResult.

The following event is the one previously logged by our `Invoke-MonitoringProbe` action. Basically, it displays the same information as that of the previous screenshot:

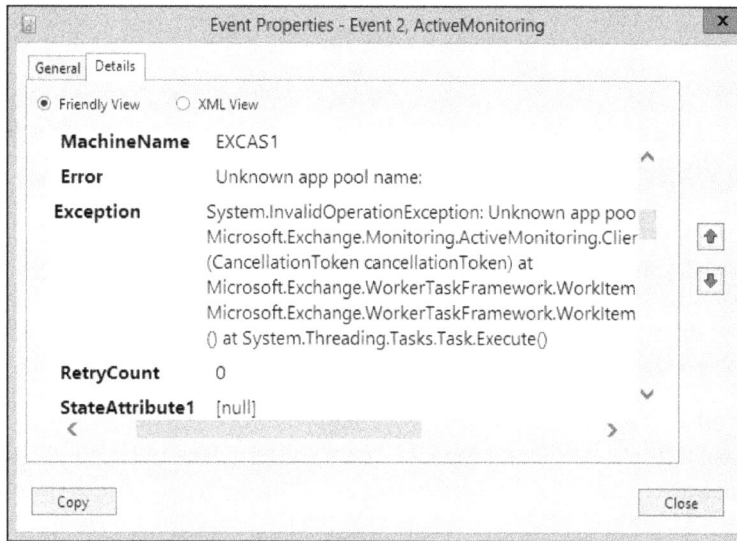

Some of the most useful probe result properties are as follows:

- **ServiceName**: This specifies the probe's health set
- **ResultName**: This is the name of this probe, plus an identifier of the code the probe executes
- **Error**: This is the error the probe returns in case it fails
- **Exception**: This is the callstack of the error if there was one
- **ResultType**: This is an integer indicating one of the following:
    - 1 indicates Timeout
    - 2 indicates Poisoned
    - 3 indicates Succeeded
    - 4 indicates Failed
    - 5 indicates Quarantined
    - 6 indicates Rejected
- **ExecutionStartTime**: This is the time the probe started
- **ExecutionEndTime**: This is the time the probe completed
- **ExecutionContext**: This is the additional information about the probe's execution
- **FailureContext**: This is the additional information about the probe's failure

> Some probes may use additional fields to provide further details regarding the failures. Usually the `Error` and `Exception` fields provide very useful information regarding what exactly is causing the error. Unfortunately, this is not always the case as we can see from the preceding screenshot.

In this scenario, the issue was caused by manually stopping the ECP application pool. As expected, the `ECPProxyTestRecycleAppPool` responder (as you can see from the following screenshot) restarted this application pool after a couple of minutes and everything went back to normal. The issue only remained because I manually stopped it again and again.

When Managed Availability performs a recovery action such as failing over a database or restarting a service, it logs an event in the crimson channel `Microsoft/Exchange/ManagedAvailability/RecoveryActionResults`. The following example shows Managed Availability automatically recovering from the ECP application pool error that we have been troubleshooting in this chapter.

An **EventID** of **500** means that a recovery action has begun:

```
Event Properties - Event 500, ManagedAvailability                    X

 General  Details

  Recovery Action Started. (ActionId=RecycleApplicationPool,
  ResourceName=MSExchangeECPAppPool, Requester=ECPProxyTestRecycleAppPool, InstanceId=
  131130.111711.43041.002, ExpectedToFinishAt=2013-11-30T11:17:41.4304156Z

  Log Name:        Microsoft-Exchange-ManagedAvailability/RecoveryActionResults
  Source:          ManagedAvailability        Logged:        30/11/2013 11:17:11
  Event ID:        500                        Task Category:  Recovery
  Level:           Information                Keywords:
  User:            SYSTEM                     Computer:      EXCAS1.letsexchange.com
  OpCode:          Info
  More Information:  Event Log Online Help

     Copy                                                            Close
```

While an **EventID** of **501** shows the action that was taken has completed:

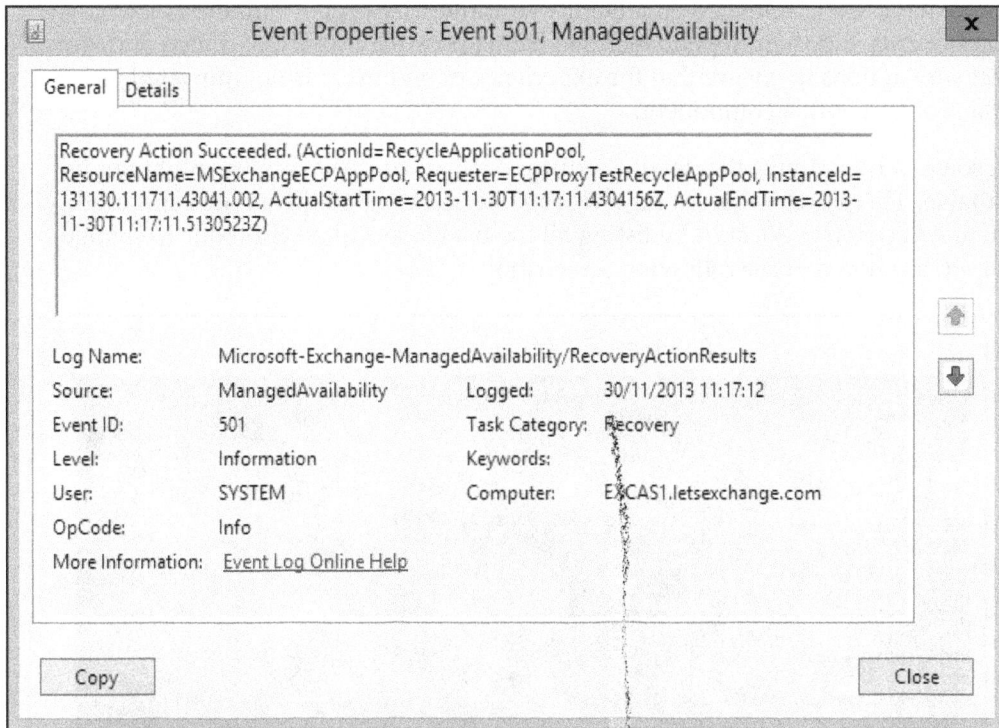

The preceding logged event provides us with some useful properties for this recovery action:

- The first sentence mentions if the recovery action was successful or not.
- **ActionId** shows what action was taken, **RecycleApplicationPool** in this example. Other common values are `RestartService`, `RecycleAppPoolComponentOffline`, or `ServerFailover`.
- **ResourceName** shows the object (such as service or a server) that was affected by the action, **MSExchangeECPAppPool** in this case.
- **Requester** is the name of the responder that took the action, **ECPProxyTestRecycleAppPool** in this case. Usually this will give you an indication of the problem.
- **ActualEndTime** is the time when the action got completed.

Customizing Managed Availability

As we have seen, Managed Availability continuously probes numerous Exchange components and their dependencies to detect possible problems. It then performs recovery actions to ensure that the experience of end users is not impacted because of a problem with a component.

In some deployments, the default settings of Managed Availability might not be suitable. Therefore, let us see how we can check these default settings and modify them if necessary. We start by listing all the health sets that are on our Exchange server, as shown in the following screenshot:

```
Machine: EXCAS1.letsexchange.com

[PS] C:\>Get-HealthReport -Server EXCAS1 | Select HealthSet

HealthSet
---------
AD
EDS
FrontendTransport
HubTransport
Monitoring
Autodiscover.Protocol
ECP.Proxy
OAB
OutlookMapi.Proxy
ECP
ActiveSync
Autodiscover.Proxy
ActiveSync.Proxy
EWS.Proxy
OAB.Proxy
OWA.Proxy
OWA
Compliance
```

We then use the Get-MonitoringItemIdentity cmdlet to list all the probes, monitors, and responders in the ECP.Proxy health set as we have already done.

In some cases, there will be multiple probes with the same name associated with the same component because a probe is created for each resource. For example, in a Mailbox server, you will see **OutlookRpcSelfTestProbe** multiple times, one for each database present on the server.

We can also list the resources for which monitoring item identities are created:

```
Machine: EXCAS1.letsexchange.com                    _  □  X

[PS] C:\>
[PS] C:\>Get-MonitoringItemIdentity ECP.Proxy -Server EXCAS1 | FT
 ItemType, TargetResource, Name -AutoSize

 ItemType TargetResource          Name

    Probe MSExchangeECPAppPool     ECPProxyTestProbe
  Monitor MSExchangeECPAppPool     ECPProxyTestMonitor
  Monitor msexchangeecpapppool     PrivateWorkingSetWarningThresh...
  Monitor msexchangeecpapppool     ProcessProcessorTimeErrorThres...
  Monitor msexchangeecpapppool     ExchangeCrashEventErrorThresho...
Responder MSExchangeECPAppPool     ECPProxyTestRecycleAppPool
Responder MSExchangeECPAppPool     ECPProxyTestOffline
Responder MSExchangeECPAppPool     ECPProxyTestOfflineFailedEscalate
Responder MSExchangeECPAppPool     ECPProxyTestEscalate
Responder msexchangeecpapppool     PrivateWorkingSetWarningThresh...
Responder msexchangeecpapppool     PrivateWorkingSetWarningThresh...
Responder msexchangeecpapppool     ProcessProcessorTimeErrorThres...
Responder msexchangeecpapppool     ProcessProcessorTimeErrorThres...
Responder msexchangeecpapppool     ProcessProcessorTimeErrorThres...
Responder msexchangeecpapppool     ExchangeCrashEventErrorThresho...


[PS] C:\>_
```

All the preceding information is useful so that we know exactly what we need in order to customize the monitoring.

Enabling or disabling a health set

Managed Availability provides the ability to configure overrides for individual servers or for the entire environment in order to customize monitors, probes, and responders. Each override can be configured to be applied only to a specific server version or for a specified duration. The *-ServerMonitoringOverride and *-GlobalMonitoringOverride cmdlets are used to create, remove, or view overrides. There are two types of overrides: local and global.

Local overrides are used to customize a server-specific Managed Availability component (not available globally) or a component on a specific server. These are managed with the *-ServerMonitoringOverride cmdlets and are stored in the local registry of the server:

```
HKEY_LOCAL_MACHINE\SOFTWARE\Microsoft\ExchangeServer\v15\
ActiveMonitoring\Overrides\
```

Every 10 minutes, the health manager service reads the configuration information stored in this registry path and loads any changes. For changes to be loaded immediately, you can simply restart this service.

Global overrides are used to customize a Managed Availability component across multiple servers. These are managed with the `*-GlobalMonitoringOverride` cmdlets and are stored in the following AD container:

```
CN=Overrides,CN=Monitoring Settings,CN=<Org Name>,CN=Microsoft Exchange,
CN=Services,CN=Configuration,DC=<domain>,DC=<com>
```

Let us assume that, for example, your organization does not use the EAC. As such, you may want to disable monitoring for this feature. A more realistic example would be disabling monitoring for POP or IMAP, but since we have been dealing with the EAC, let us continue. To do this, we first need to determine the list of monitors associated with the EAC. Using the TechNet web page **Appendix A: Exchange Health Sets**, we can see that `ECP.Proxy` is the only health set associated with EAC. So, as before, we run `Get-MonitoringItemIdentity` to list all the monitors associated with the `ECP.Proxy` health set:

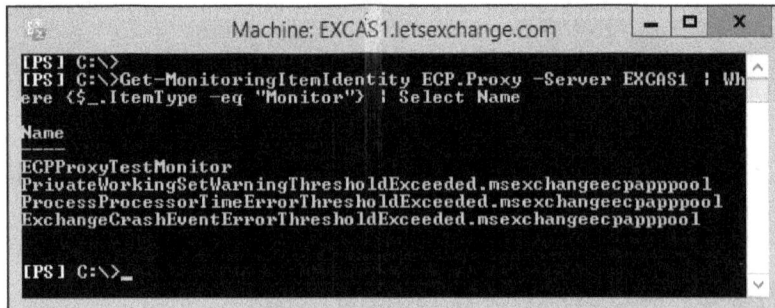

```
Machine: EXCAS1.letsexchange.com                    _  □  X

[PS] C:\>
[PS] C:\>Get-MonitoringItemIdentity ECP.Proxy -Server EXCAS1 | Wh
ere {$_.ItemType -eq "Monitor"} | Select Name

Name
----
ECPProxyTestMonitor
PrivateWorkingSetWarningThresholdExceeded.msexchangeecpapppool
ProcessProcessorTimeErrorThresholdExceeded.msexchangeecpapppool
ExchangeCrashEventErrorThresholdExceeded.msexchangeecpapppool

[PS] C:\>_
```

Let us store these monitors in a variable so that we can work with them more easily:

```
$ECPmonitors = Get-MonitoringItemIdentityECP.Proxy -Server CAS1 | Where
{$_.ItemType -eq "Monitor"}
```

Now, for each of these monitors we need to create a global override using the `Add-GlobalMonitoringOverride` cmdlet. As we have all of them in a variable, instead of doing them one by one, we can simply pipe them to this cmdlet and set the `Enabled` property to `0` (disabled) as follows:

```
$ECPmonitors | Where {Add-GlobalMonitoringOverride -Item Monitor
-Identity $($_.HealthSetName+"\"+$_.Name) -PropertyName Enabled
-PropertyValue 0 -Duration 60.00:00:00
```

The `Duration` parameter specifies the length of time to keep the monitoring override as a time span: dd.hh:mm:ss. In the preceding example, `60.00:00:00` specifies 60 days.

To verify whether the global overrides have been created, run the following command:

```
Get-GlobalMonitoringOverride | FT Identity, ItemType, PropertyName,
PropertyValue
```

Let's say, we simply want to update the timeout value for the probe that was failing in our previous scenario. Using the `Microsoft/Exchange/ActiveMonitoring/ProbeDefinition` crimson channel, we can find the details of the `ECPProxyTestProbe` probe:

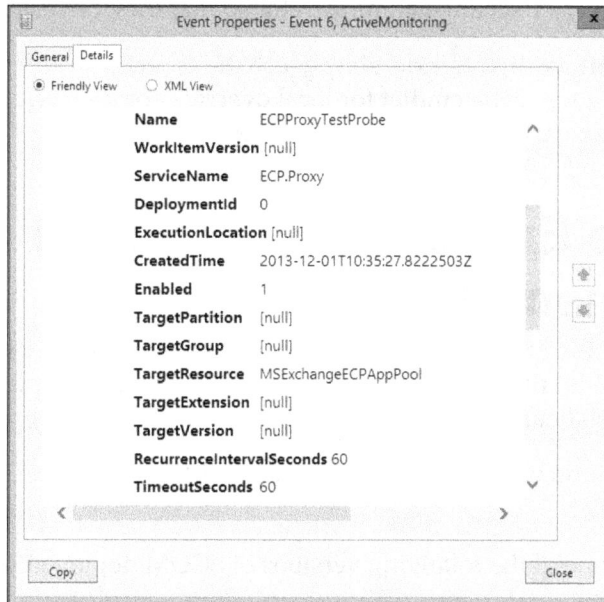

To change the timeout interval from `60` to `120` seconds, for example, first we need to determine which Exchange version our servers are running so that the override automatically applies to all servers with the same version:

```
Get-ExchangeServer | Select Name,AdminDisplayVersion
```

Then, we use the following cmdlet to create the global override:

```
Add-GlobalMonitoringOverride "ECP.Proxy\ECPProxyTestProbe" -ItemType
Probe -PropertyNameTimeoutSeconds -PropertyValue120 -ApplyVersion
"15.0.775.38"
```

In the preceding two examples, we used `Duration` in one and `ApplyVersion` in the other. By using the parameter duration, the override will only be in effect for the period stated (with 60 days being the maximum duration allowed).

The `ApplyVersion` override will be in effect for as long as the version of the Exchange server matches the value stated. In this case, we created the override for a version of `"15.0.775.38"` or CU3. While the Exchange server version remains the same, the override will be applied, meaning that once the server is upgraded to a different version, the override will stop working.

Therefore, if you want an override to apply for a longer period, use the `ApplyVersion` parameter but remember to update your override(s) once you upgrade your servers. It is recommended to keep all these changes well documented and accessible to every Exchange administrator so that they can easily be referred to.

If you decide to remove an override, simply use the `Remove-ServerMonitoringOverride` cmdlet for local overrides or `Remove-GlobalMonitoringOverride` for global overrides.

Using the Exchange 2013 SCOM Management Pack

Independent of all the great improvements made in Exchange 2013 in terms of monitoring, SCOM is still a very useful solution to gather and display information related to the health of an Exchange environment.

Before you import and use the **Management Pack (MP)**, ensure the following conditions are met:

- You have one of the following versions of SCOM deployed in your organization:
    - SCOM 2012 RTM or later
    - SCOM 2007 R2 or later
- SCOM agents have been deployed to Exchange servers
- The SCOM agents are running under the local system account
- The SCOM agents are configured to act as a proxy
- The user account you use is part of the Operations Manager Administrators role

This MP contains around 75 monitors covering the health of customer touch points (such as "is OWA working?"), Exchange components, clustered scenarios, and dependency monitoring (such as "is AD healthy?").

As we already discussed, Managed Availability allows Exchange to detect and try to automatically recover from issues before an administrator gets notified. This means both less alert noise and reduced administrative overhead. The following screenshot shows the only three views that are available with this MP:

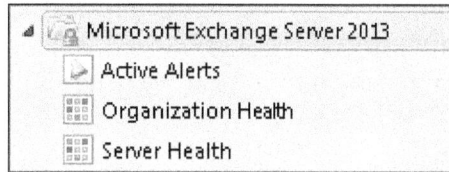

This is a simple MP: it contains a few classes, 3 views (displayed earlier), and around 75 monitors for the health sets already explored. All monitors are simple event-based monitors that use events logged in the `Microsoft/Exchange/ManagedAvailability/Monitoring` event log by each Exchange server (remember that each Exchange server is now responsible for its own monitoring).The MP has only 75 monitors because it dynamically determines the set of monitors to be used by communicating with Managed Availability.

In terms of scalability, this means that MP has a low impact on any Operations Manager environment and it does not require a separate Management Group for scalability purposes.

The Exchange 2010 MP had the correlation engine service that ran on the Root Management Server and that interconnected the health data from all Exchange components being monitored. In this new MP, there is no longer a correlation engine as each Exchange server is responsible for monitoring its own health and reports it via the Operations Manager agent.

This MP does not use any performance counters to collect information as Managed Availability covers performance scenarios. Nonetheless, Exchange PerfMon counters are still available, which allows administrators to create their own performance collection rules if desired.

It is important to highlight that there are no reports in this MP. However, administrators are able to use some of the SCOM built-in reports to track availability or define SLAs, for example.

If you want to disable a particular monitor, you can still do this by simply creating an override in Operations Manager as usual. However, if you want to change a threshold for a monitor, this is done through PowerShell in the Managed Availability engine as we have already discussed.

It is important to review every new cumulative update of Exchange as it might contain updated or new monitoring logic. This way you can determine if it will have any impact on your monitoring. A great place to check this is on the Microsoft Exchange Team Blog at `http://blogs.technet.com/b/exchange`.

In terms of interoperability, this MP is a completely new MP, meaning it does not upgrade the Exchange 2010 MP. As expected, you can run both the 2010 and the 2013 MPs side by side during a transition from your Exchange 2010 environment to 2013.

Summary

Exchange monitoring has changed significantly in Exchange 2013. The new Managed Availability service performs numerous health assessments for every server, periodically testing multiple components to establish their viability and determine the health of the components or the entire server. When an issue is detected, a multistep process is initiated and corrective actions are performed to try and bring the server back into an operational state. If Managed Availability is not able to return the server into a healthy state, then it alerts the administrators.

Managed Availability focuses on the experience of end users to guarantee that if issues occur, the user experience is impacted as minimally as possible, if at all.

While SCOM is passive only and requires human intervention, Managed Availability is fully automated, with both being customizable. One of the key differences between the two is not the monitoring itself but the automated actions.

In the next and final chapter, we will explore key infrastructure components and systems that also need to be made highly available so they do not affect Exchange's availability.

9
Underlying Infrastructure

Designing a highly available Exchange environment is not just in the hands of the messaging team, which unfortunately can be frustrating for some administrators or architects. Exchange is completely dependent on a variety of other services and systems that are usually administered and maintained by other teams. This chapter provides an overview of what should be done in order to improve the high availability of Active Directory, **Domain Name System** (**DNS**), network, storage, and virtualization platforms so that the likelihood of a failure with any of these systems causing an outage with Exchange is mitigated.

Active Directory

Since Exchange 2000 dropped its own directory service, **Active Directory** (**AD**) became a central prerequisite for any deployment of Exchange. In fact, Exchange is the Microsoft application that, by far, makes the most extensive use of AD. As such, a highly available AD is paramount to guarantee Exchange's availability.

Although only a single **domain controller** (**DC**) is needed for each domain, doing so makes it a single point of failure. To prevent this, you should always add additional DCs to increase AD's availability. AD uses a two-way replication model, where DCs replicate between them synchronously in order to ensure consistency among all DCs in the domain. AD also uses **multimaster replication**, where any DC can send or receive updates of information stored in AD.

> To achieve high availability for your AD infrastructure, simply deploy multiple DCs per domain/site.

Data for a domain is replicated to every DC within that domain, but not beyond it. If a DC is also configured as a global catalog server, it contains several properties for all the objects in all the domains across the **AD forest** (in broad terms, a forest is a collection of one or more domains that trust each other). By default, this includes attributes that are more frequently used in search operations to enable users to search objects located in another domain. Not all the attributes of every object get replicated to global catalogs; only attributes commonly used in search operations, for example, first and last names.

Exchange uses global catalogs for the e-mail-based lookups of names, e-mail addresses, and other mail-related attributes. For example, global catalogs are used by Exchange to expand a distribution group's membership.

> Exchange requires each AD site where Exchange is deployed to have at least one global catalog server.

Although one global catalog per site might be enough for small sites hosting just one or two Exchange servers, as the number of Exchange servers (and users) grows and the need to ensure availability increases, you will need to deploy more global catalogs. This will be necessary to handle the load generated by Exchange and its users so that the messaging service continues in case one global catalog fails. Therefore, if you do not provide enough global catalog capacity, Exchange servers will not function smoothly, no matter how well configured and powerful Exchange servers are. Do not assume that the relatively light load on global catalogs caused by ordinary operations such as client logons will remain the same once Exchange is deployed. This is far from the truth; demand on global catalogs expands intensely with Exchange in place.

Without going in-depth into the realm of AD capacity planning for Exchange, it is important to understand that proper capacity planning is vital for a highly available Exchange environment. After all, if your global catalogs cannot reply to Exchange requests in a timely manner, your user experience will be affected, or worse. AD sizing remains the same as it was for Exchange 2010. For Exchange 2013, Microsoft recommends deploying a ratio of one AD global catalog processor core for every eight Mailbox role processor cores handling active load, assuming 64-bit global catalog servers. For example, in a site with four Exchange servers each with four processor cores, you have 16 cores dedicated to Exchange. As such, you should deploy two 64-bit processor cores for global catalogs. Two servers each with two cores would be better for availability as dividing the load across two global catalogs means that if one fails, Exchange will continue working.

> You should always invest in global catalogs as there is nothing better at stopping Exchange from working than the unavailability of a global catalog server.

Another aspect to consider is positioning global catalogs alongside Exchange. As a rule of thumb, you should have a global catalog on every WAN segment supporting Exchange to ensure that a network outage has a minimal effect on Exchange from an AD perspective. However, this might not always be possible — branch offices come to mind.

> Exchange Server 2013 cannot make use of **Read-Only Domain Controllers** or **Read-Only Global Catalog servers**, so make sure you plan for full global catalog and domain controllers for Exchange.

When a DC fails for any reason, you should first repair it and then recover its data. AD is capable of recovering lost data because it uses log files to recover lost data together with replication to recover data from other DCs in the domain.

There are a variety of tools that you can use to repair a DC and recover AD, but these are not in this book's scope. The point to take from this section is that it is important to deploy multiple DCs and global catalogs. This will ensure that a failure in one does not affect Exchange, and so its recovery becomes easy and painless.

As with Exchange, it is very important to monitor AD so that any possible issue can be dealt with as soon as possible before it escalates and causes more serious problems to users and Exchange. These are some of the tools that can be used to monitor AD:

- **Event log**: You can use the event log to gather information about software, hardware, and system problems.
- **Performance logs and alerts**: You can configure alerts when certain thresholds have been exceeded.
- **Replication monitor** (Replmon): This tool provides the low-level status and performance information regarding AD replication between DCs, and it is available as part of the Windows 2000 Resource Kit.

> Replmon has been deprecated since Windows Server 2008 and replaced by the new Replication Status Tool, as described in the following points.

- `Repadmin.exe`: This command-line tool helps diagnose AD replication problems between DCs. You can use this tool to view the replication topology from the perspective of each DC. Additionally, you can use it to manually create the replication topology, force replication between DCs, and view the replication metadata. You can also use `Repadmin.exe` to monitor the relative health of an **Active Directory Domain Services (AD DS)** forest. The `Repadmin.exe` tool is built into Windows Server 2008 and above, if you have the AD DS or the **Active Directory Lightweight Directory Services (AD LDS)** server roles installed. It is also available if you install the Active Directory Domain Services Tools that are part of the **Remote Server Administration Tools (RSAT)**.

- **Active Directory Replication Status Tool (ADREPLSTATUS)**: This tool analyzes the replication status for DCs in an AD domain or forest and displays replication results in a user interface. While this tool does not offer the same level of functionality as `Repadmin`, such as the ability to zstart replication or change replication settings, it is a great tool for gathering visual information quickly and finding replication errors.

- **SCOM**: The Active Directory Domain Services Management Pack for SCOM provides reactive and proactive monitoring of AD. It monitors events that various AD components and subsystems write to the event logs. It also monitors the AD's overall health and alerts administrators to any critical performance issues.

Domain name system

DNS provides the indispensable service of name resolution in TCP- or IP-based networks. DNS is used to map host names to IP addresses and vice versa. It can also be used to store and retrieve other information about a host, such as the services it provides.

The two most important changes in the Windows architecture between Windows NT 4.0 and Windows 2000 were AD and the use of DNS for name resolution. AD extended the Windows 4.0 directory into a fully-extensible, scalable directory service. Windows NT Server and earlier versions depended on NetBIOS names and implemented **Windows Internet Name Service (WINS)** to resolve computer names to IP addresses. Windows 2000 Server introduced DNS as the name resolution mechanism.

DNS is the backbone of AD and another crucial system for Exchange as it is the principal name resolution mechanism of any Windows server and client. DCs use DNS to dynamically register information about their configuration and about the AD system. Other Windows systems such as Exchange which are part of the domain query DNS to locate AD-related information. If DNS is not functioning correctly, domain-wide outages will occur and DC replication will stop. Users will be unable to log on to the domain or to join the domain from a workstation or server in the absence of DNS. Non-Microsoft applications are similarly affected by the loss of DNS services, because everything from web browsing to e-mail and enterprise applications rely on DNS for mapping host names to IP addresses. As a result, the security and availability of DNS is critical.

In a network in which AD is deployed, DNS services are often installed on DCs. This simplifies administration of DNS and AD by allowing the AD and DNS domain namespaces to be simultaneously maintained. However, in some cases, this might not be possible, and the DNS service has to be installed on a stand alone server. This could be to provide load balancing, for security reasons, or even to support an infrastructure that does not have AD deployed.

Integrating DNS with Active Directory

Once you have installed AD, you have two options for storing and replicating DNS zones:

- **Standard zones**: DNS stores its zones in `.dns` files located in the `systemroot\System32\Dns` folder of each DNS server. These files are then synchronized between DNS servers using a separate replication method called **zone transfer**.

- **Directory-integrated zones**: AD-integrated DNS enables AD replication and storage of DNS zone databases. In this case, the zone data is stored as an AD object that gets replicated as part of the domain replication.

> Only DNS servers that run on DCs can load AD-integrated zones.

To use directory-integrated zones, you need to assign the Active Directory-integrated zone type when creating the zone. The AD objects representing these zone records are created in Microsoft DNS within the System container. You can view this by enabling **Advanced Features** in the **Active Directory Users and Computers** window. This information is replicated to all DCs in the domain that are configured as DNS servers. With AD-integrated DNS zones, all DCs configured as DNS servers function as primary name servers.

For networks deploying DNS to support AD, directory-integrated DNS is strongly recommended from an availability perspective. With standard zones, DNS updates are done using a single-master update architecture where an authoritative DNS server is nominated as the primary source for the zone, which represents a single point of failure. In case this server becomes unavailable, updates from DNS clients are not able to be processed. On the other hand, with directory-integrated DNS, dynamic updates to DNS are performed using a multi-master update architecture where any authoritative DNS server, such as a DC running the DNS service, is considered a primary source for the zone. As the zone's master copy is maintained in AD, which is fully replicated to all DCs in the domain, any of these DCs can update the zone. With the multi-master update architecture of AD, any of these primary servers can process DNS clients' requests to update the zone as long as a DC is available and reachable on the network.

> The same applies as before: to guarantee DNS high availability, simply deploy multiple DNS servers per domain/site. By integrating DNS with AD, you guarantee both AD and DNS availability when you deploy multiple DCs that are also configured as DNS servers.

Microsoft recommends using the DNS server provided with Windows Server to support AD and to provide all other DNS functionality. However, many environments may have non-Microsoft DNS implementations in place and may wish to implement Exchange before or without migrating to Microsoft DNS. **Berkeley Internet Name Domain (BIND)** DNS is probably the most common example.

Do not assume that hosting AD and Exchange using BIND DNS is a bad idea. As long as all of the necessary records and zones are in place, everything will work just fine. BIND is quite capable of working with AD and Exchange. However, you have to ensure it is highly available, otherwise it will impact the availability of your messaging environment.

Explaining the importance of a network

Users rely on their applications, from word processing software to e-mail clients such as Outlook, and these applications and their data have to be available to be useful, else productivity will suffer. Outlook and OWA do not just rely on DNS and Exchange to work. Without a properly configured and healthy TCP/IP network, nothing will work. Yes, users can "work" in offline mode, but for how long?

Outlook and OWA must be able to process Exchange data, and that data must be available to users. When considering Exchange availability, we have to evaluate the network design in order to locate any potential single points of failure or bottlenecks that may interrupt the messaging service. If any are found, redundancy should be added or changes to the network topology should be made to mitigate these.

Consider a network connection, for example, between two Exchange servers separated by a switch. Normally, they would be connected through a single link to the switch, which presents a chain of points that could fail and affect service. To improve availability, it is recommended to add a second network card to Exchange servers (a recommendation for many years now) and establish a redundant connection from the new card to another switch port (even better would be a port on a second switch).

Messaging availability is dependent on correct network design choices that make use of relevant technologies and best practices to help ensure application availability.

Networks are often not designed to accommodate the needs of key applications such as Exchange because organizations simply do not understand the implications of availability. Some organizations do not define what their needs are and only have numerous vague requirements that state *applications must always be up and running* or *the network may never go down*. Even if these goals are technically achievable, they are rarely affordable, and it is not necessarily what the organization is looking for.

More important is to ensure an appropriate network for the required workload. Bandwidth and latency are typically the main issues for Exchange. Ethernet LAN bandwidth, for example, has moved away from 10/100 Mbps to 1 Gbps and will eventually move up to 10 Gbps.

When it comes to availability, redundancy is as important as speed. Enterprise networks have to be designed to avoid single points of failure between storage, servers, and users. This includes, for example, using redundant network links for failover and greater performance. Redundant links, maintained by different service providers, can also be used across WANs.

Enterprises are becoming more distributed, with multiple datacenters, remote users, and branch offices. As a consequence, the ability to remotely access applications is becoming increasingly important, almost to the level of application availability. Application acceleration and WAN optimization solutions are becoming increasingly more popular. WAN optimization usually combines TCP/IP traffic manipulation (such as fewer application handshakes and jumbo frames) with data compression in order to transfer more data within the same given bandwidth. These technologies are typically deployed in an attempt to save money by avoiding an increase in the available bandwidth. In addition, WAN optimization allows organizations to consolidate resources by moving servers/services from remote sites back into a main datacenter. Applications such as Exchange can then potentially be deployed to the entire user community using a single, highly available network.

> When using WAN optimization devices, please ensure they do not interfere with Exchange traffic, as these are known for causing issues with Exchange replication traffic of DAGs.

Using high available storage

High available (HA) storage is very important for any Exchange deployment. Although with DAGs and AutoReseed a disk failure might not be as serious as before, losing a disk that holds Exchange data can still be very damaging for some organizations.

Redundancy is the key feature of HA storage, and is achieved by storing data in more than one place to eliminate single points of failure. HA storage systems can be used anywhere from a single server to a complex virtual environment. There are typically two ways to achieve high available storage: RAID and enterprise-level storage clusters.

RAID was initially defined as **Redundant Array of Inexpensive Drives**. However, RAID was indeed expensive initially, so I became **Independent**. Since the costs of disks have come down significantly, RAID has become more popular, and is now embedded in most desktop and server motherboards. Storage RAIDs were mainly designed to offer better performance, improve fault tolerance, and for easier management of storage, as they present several hard drives as a single volume making storage management simpler.

The three fundamental RAID techniques are as follows:

- **Mirroring**: Stores the exact data across two or more hard drives, which provides both redundancy and read speed. Redundancy as when a single drive fails, the second drive still has the data; and great read throughput and performance as it is able to process two read requests concurrently. Write operations are not faster than a single drive because data has to be written to both drives at the same time. The disadvantage of mirroring is that the end capacity is typically half the total capacity of all drives, which can become expensive.

- **Striping**: Simply distributes data throughout multiple drives. It scales well on read and write operations, but it provides lower read throughput than mirroring when trying to process multiple tasks simultaneously. In this case, the end volume's capacity is the same as the total capacity of all drives in the array. Striping is not very often used by itself as it does not provide any fault tolerance, meaning that a single drive failure causes all data to be lost. As such, it is commonly used together with mirroring or with parity.

- **Striping with parity**: Brings fault tolerance into striping, but at the expense of capacity and a performance penalty on write operations. Data is still distributed across multiple drives but with additional parity data stored in one or more drives. Parity allows the reconstruction of a RAID volume if one or two (depending on the configuration) drives fail. Regardless of the capacity and performance hit of using parity, it provides more available volume capacity than mirroring while providing fault tolerance, which makes it a reliable and cost-effective large-capacity storage solution.

Other than the RAID techniques we just explored, there are several RAID types which are defined by **level** numbers. At the "simple" level, there are RAID levels 0 through 6, but there are also a number of composite RAID types comprising multiple RAID levels. The following are the three most common RAID levels used with Exchange to provide both resilience and performance at the storage level:

- **RAID level 5**: This is an example of striping with parity. The parity is distributed across all drives, providing increased performance when compared to using a single drive for parity (used in some RAID levels). In an array with "N" drives (the minimum being 3), the total volume capacity is "N-1" drives.

- **RAID level 6**: This is similar to the previous example, but in this case with dual distributed parity for greater fault tolerance by using the capacity of two drives to store parity. Historically, RAID 6 was only used in high-end RAID systems; however, it is now more common as storage becomes cheaper. Dual parity allows for two drives in the array to fail without the loss of data. In an array with "N" drives (the minimum being 4), the total volume capacity is "N-2" drives.

- **RAID level 10 (composite of 1 and 0)**: Sometimes called 1+0 or simply 10, this is the most common and recommended composite RAID type used. When doing both mirroring and striping, the recommendation is for mirroring to be done before striping; this provides better fault tolerance as it can mathematically withstand more drive failures. At the same time, its performance does not degrade as much when a single drive fails. On the other hand, RAID 0+1, which performs striping before mirroring, is considered to be inferior and is not recommended. RAID 10 is commonly used with Exchange as it provides good read and write performance as well as resilience.

At the enterprise level, organizations often combine RAID with storage clusters. An HA storage cluster is made of at least two separate storage nodes (often made of multiple disks in a RAID configuration) running under the control of specialized software. If one of the nodes fails, the other one will immediately take over. To make this solution effective and efficient, it requires high-end software and hardware.

There are a variety of storage architectures, but exploring these is out of the scope of this book. An example is a storage architecture that uses replication with automatic failover/failback technology, which allows the **Storage Area Network (SAN)** to operate uninterrupted in the event of a node failure, as is shown in the following diagram:

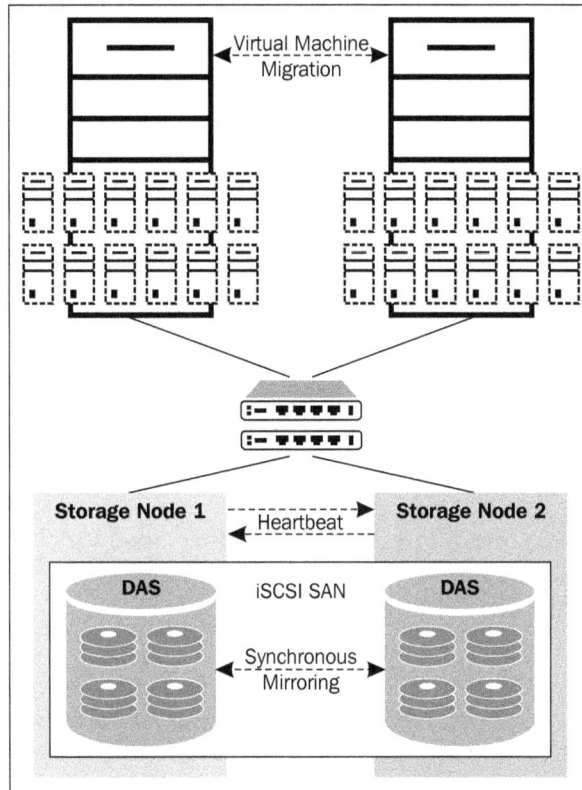

Automatic failover technology allows administrators to deploy a dual node SAN in an active/active configuration to ensure fault tolerant and highly reliable storage. Data is load balanced across both nodes. In case of a failure, all storage traffic originally destined to the failed node is routed to the remaining node. Both nodes monitor each other continuously and failover happens with no manual intervention.

A **heartbeat** guarantees data is synchronized between both nodes in an HA configuration. It prevents single point of failures by establishing which node takes priority, while maintaining synchronization between nodes.

Storage architectures such as this often manage synchronous mirroring and automatic failover on a per-volume basis. Since the volume's identity does not change even during a node failure, Exchange experiences continuous data availability.

Benefiting through virtualization

The demand to virtualize tier-1 applications such as Exchange continues to increase as organizations push towards virtualized environments to improve efficiency, reduce operational and capital costs, and improve the management of their IT infrastructure. Exchange virtualization seems to deliver another benefit, **dual-level of resiliency**, where the messaging environment is protected against failures by both Exchange and virtualization platform features, as we will soon explore. But can virtualization really help make Exchange deployments more resilient?

Virtualization has been a hot technology since around 2008, and many claims have been made regarding all the advantages that it brings. A typical one is that virtualization can help make IT infrastructures more resilient to failure. Virtualization has three characteristics that show potential for enhancing resilience:

- Multiple operating system images are able to share the same physical resource in isolation.

- Virtual machines can allow applications developed for another processor architecture to run effectively, which can be helpful when providing resilience for legacy applications.

- Virtualization allows for applications to access a group of distinct resources that are presented as a single resource. Besides convenience for the application, this has the advantage of resources being grouped for throughput or resilience through RAID.

At the same time, virtualization carries an inherent risk that is also seen as an advantage: **server consolidation**. Before virtualization, the risk is spread across the network. If one server fails, the loss is restricted to that server. With virtualization, there is the same number of servers but with less physical servers (virtual machine hosts). The failure of one host has a much greater impact as several virtual machines will be simultaneously affected.

Backup and restore

Effective backup and restoration of applications and data is essential for any resilient infrastructure. Virtualization offers several advantages in this area, which are as follows:

- **Virtual machines are not hardware-aware**: Restoring a physical server can be problematic due to hardware differences between the original and the restoration server, typically in a disaster situation. This does not happen when restoring a virtual machine.

- **Virtual images are easier to restore**: As virtual images include all aspects of the virtual server, they are easier to restore when compared to conventional images that are very dependent on the hardware configuration they are being restored to.

- **Virtual images are easy to move from one host to another**: The nature of virtualization means that a virtual machine can easily be moved from one host to another. This means that a host upgrade can be easily handled and that virtual machines can easily and quickly be brought back online during a disaster.

High availability

Hyper-V and VMware build upon some of the virtualization-inherent resiliency factors discussed earlier in order to bring high availability into virtual systems. These typically monitor the activity and responsiveness of virtualized systems, detecting when failures occur and restarting failed virtual machines automatically on a different host within the same shared resource pool.

But going back to our original question, does virtualization really provide resilience? The answer depends on the scenario being considered. For example, if we consider a failure within the primary datacenter, virtualization helps in:

- Migrating and recovering failed virtual machines
- Automatically recovering from hardware failures with minimal or no downtime
- Balancing sever workloads and reducing processing bottlenecks
- Monitoring systems at the logical partition level

Within the primary datacenter environment, it is safe to say that virtualization definitely adds to resilience. However, traditional aspects of information availability cannot be forgotten. For example, virtual systems are vulnerable to flood, fire, and power outage as much as conventional systems.

In a scenario where the primary datacenter becomes unavailable and Exchange must be switched to a recovery datacenter, the answer is not as clear, as virtualization may add to complexity and result in an increased recovery time. However, a properly designed Exchange environment together with a well-designed virtual infrastructure will help overcome this.

> Virtualization does not equal resilience, but it helps to increase the availability of any Exchange environment.

Hyper-V and VMware

Microsoft supports running both Exchange 2013 roles in production on hardware virtualization software, subject to the following conditions:

- The hardware virtualization software is running Windows Server with Hyper-V, Hyper-V Server, or a third-party hypervisor such as VMware that is part of the Windows Server Virtualization Validation Program.

> Deploying production Exchange servers in Windows Azure is not supported at the time of writing this book.

- The Exchange guest virtual machine is deployed on Windows Server 2008 R2 SP1 (or later) or on Windows Server 2012.

> Most hypervisors have the ability to capture a virtual machine's state when it is either running or turned off, which is called a snapshot. This feature enables administrators to take several snapshots and revert virtual machines to any of its previous states. The problem is that snapshots are not Exchange aware, and using them will have unexpected consequences for Exchange. While snapshots may not create problems for fairly stateless servers such as the CAS role, reverting a DAG member to a previous snapshot will. Doing this often causes its database copies to not be recognized within the DAG, or it may even prevent the server from rejoining the domain or the cluster. As a result, taking snapshots of Exchange virtual machines is not supported.

While Hyper-V and VMware meet the deployment, manageability, and performance requirements necessary to virtualize an Exchange 2013 environment, the unique nature of Exchange means the choice of whether or not to virtualize it should be considered carefully. Performance analysis and capacity planning of any existing Exchange deployment is always recommended to determine if your organization's current or new Exchange environment is suitable for virtualization and to plan for processor, memory, storage, and network resources that have to be configured for each Exchange virtual machine.

Combining Exchange Mailbox servers that are part of a DAG with host-based migration technology and failover clustering is also supported now. As our main concern in this book is high availability, it is important to determine these requirements as a first step. You should deploy the same Exchange roles across multiple hosts to allow for load balancing and high availability. Therefore, never deploy either of the following on the same host: Mailbox servers that are members of the same DAG or all CASs.

The next sections explore two of the most common Exchange deployment scenarios in a virtualization platform.

Single Exchange on a virtual cluster

For smaller organizations that require only a single Exchange 2013 server but still need a high level of availability, a good option is to run Exchange as a virtual machine on top of a Hyper-V or VMware physical cluster. The following diagram shows two Hyper-V cluster nodes connected to a centralized SAN storage, but this could be iSCSI or **Fiber Channel** (**FC**). With Windows Server 2012 Hyper-V, this can also be an SMB 3.0-based storage.

The Exchange virtual machine has a number of virtual disks to store data and other relevant Exchange information that is stored on different LUNs and spindles in the SAN. If one of the physical cluster nodes fail, any virtual machine currently running on that failed node will experience some downtime. The diagram showing two Hyper-V cluster nodes connected to a centralized SAN storage is as follows:

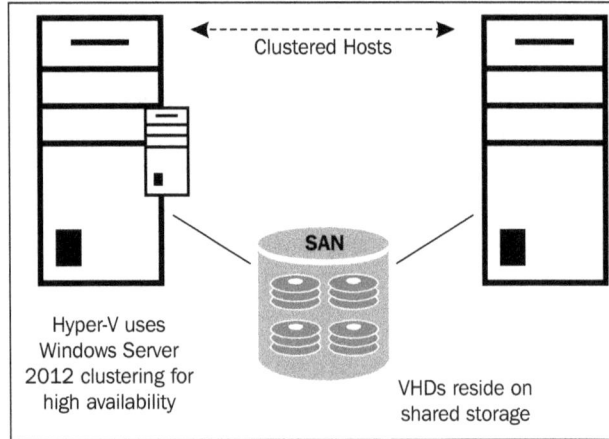

The virtual machines, however, will restart automatically on the other node in that cluster without administrator intervention and with minimal downtime, as shown in the following diagram:

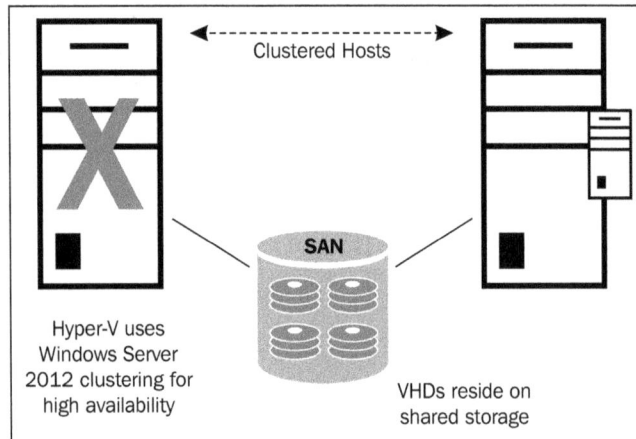

The cluster will try to start the virtual machines from the failed host on another available cluster node as quickly as possible, but you may want to ensure that the Exchange virtual machine starts first. With this in mind, you can set the **Change Startup Priority** setting in Hyper-V for the Exchange virtual machine to **High**. This ensures that even under contention, the Exchange virtual machine will successfully start and receive the resources it needs, taking resources from other currently running virtual machines, if required.

Resilient Exchange on a virtual cluster

When two or more virtual machines running Exchange are configured as a DAG, one virtual machine will take over if any one of the others fail. With DAGs, Exchange can work as a cluster-aware application to provide better availability and resiliency for Exchange mailboxes in a virtualized environment.

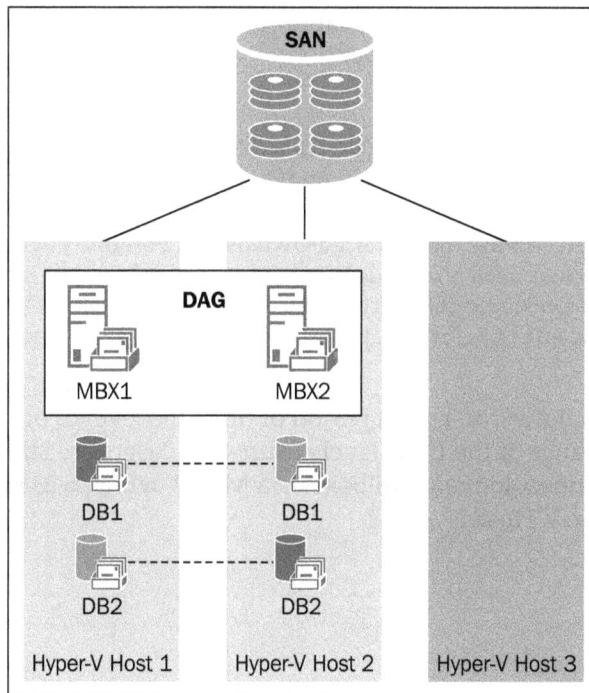

In this example, a Hyper-V cluster with three nodes is connected to a shared storage on which the Exchange VHDX files are stored. Exchange has no requirement for shared storage, but Hyper-V requires some form of shared storage to store the virtual disks of the virtual machines for resiliency through failover clustering.

On top of this cluster, there are two virtual machines hosting the Mailbox role and configured in a DAG. The virtual machines are split across the hosts, with **MBX1** on **Hyper-V Host 1** and **MBX2** on **Hyper-V Host 2**. This is the preferred distribution as the failure of either host running the Exchange virtual machines will not bring the entire Exchange DAG down.

Let us assume we now lose **Hyper-V Host 1**. **MBX1** would be temporarily lost, but would automatically restart on another available node on the cluster, **Hyper-V Host 3** in this case. When restarting the virtual machines from **Hyper-V Host 1**, Failover Cluster Manager looks at the available resources in the cluster and places the restarting virtual machines on the most appropriate host (if multiple are available), again all without administrator intervention.

> Use the **Change Startup Priority** setting to ensure that upon failover, Exchange 2013 virtual machines start in advance of other less important virtual machines.
>
> You can also use the **Preferred Owners** and **Possible Owners** settings to specify which hosts failed virtual machines should be moved to. Also, to ensure certain virtual machines stay apart on different hosts, use the `AntiAffinityClassNames` property of the failover cluster.

Though **MBX1** was down for a short period of time, the level of built-in high availability in Exchange at the DAG level ensures that users are still able to access information and connect to their mailboxes via **MBX2**, which was running during the outage of **Hyper-V Host 1**.

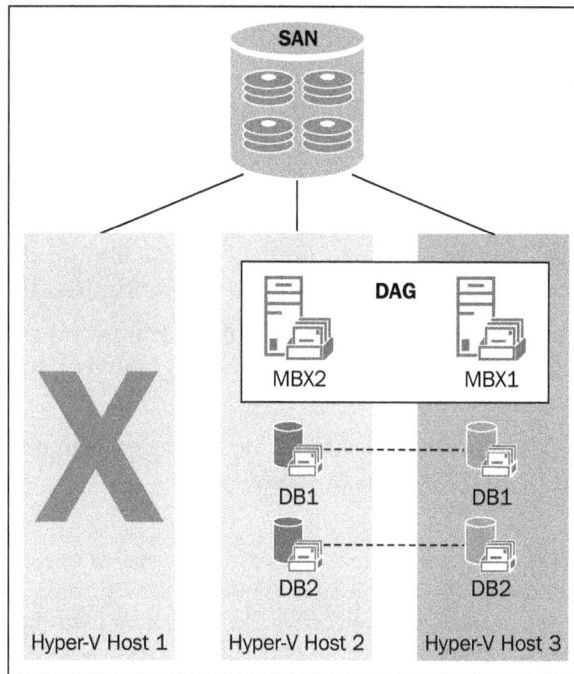

This dual layer of availability, by combining Exchange-level availability with host-level availability, means that users will not be impacted and both virtual machines will be fully online within a few minutes. Administrators can then rebalance the databases within the DAG, thereby restoring the highest levels of availability that were experienced before the outage.

While in this example we have focused on the DAGs, this is equally applicable to CASs to distribute the CAS functionality across multiple virtual machines.

Other features

With the Exchange virtual machines now stored on a Hyper-V cluster, individual virtual machines can be moved around the cluster using **live migration**. Live migration allows administrators to transparently move from one node of the cluster to another, running virtual machines without dropping network connectivity and without any perceived downtime.

When performing live migration of DAG members, you should follow these key points:

- If the server is offline for more than five seconds, it will be evicted from the cluster. As such, ensure that the hypervisor and host-based clustering use the live migration technology to help migrate virtual machines with no perceived downtime.

- If you raise the heartbeat timeout threshold, you should thoroughly test it to ensure that migration succeeds within the configured timeout period.

- On the live migration network, enable jumbo frames on each host's network interface. Also, make sure the switch handling network traffic is configured to support jumbo frames.

- Allocate considerable bandwidth for the live migration network to ensure that it completes as quickly as possible.

> Exchange server virtual machines can make use of host failover and migration capabilities as long as they do not save and restore their state when moved or taken offline. When failing over the virtual machine to another host, it must perform a cold boot. Migrations must either shutdown the virtual machines or be performed online using live migration.

Although Hyper-V has been the main focus of the past few sections, VMware vSphere also provides identical availability options. Some of the features of the vSphere platform that can help achieve a higher level of availability for Exchange include:

- **Virtual machine portability**: Exchange servers are no longer bound to specific hardware. This allows administrators to easily adjust CPU, memory, and storage requirements, or upgrade virtual machines to newer hardware.

- **VMware vSphere High Availability (HA)**: This protects servers from hardware and guest operating system failures. If a VMware host or any critical component within the host fails, causing virtual machines to go offline, vSphere HA automatically powers on the virtual machines on another host. By combining vSphere HA with DAGs, we can mitigate both hardware and software failure risk for maximum availability.

- **VMware vSphere Distributed Resource Scheduler (DRS)**: This balances workloads and speeds up recovery. As host utilization increases and available resources decrease, DRS migrates virtual machines to balance resource utilization across a vSphere cluster. DRS can also help to recover more quickly after a server hardware failure. For example, if a host fails, vSphere HA reboots the virtual machine on another host. When the failed host is replaced, DRS migrates virtual machines to keep workloads balanced across the vSphere cluster.

Summary

In this final chapter, we explored several systems that Exchange is completely dependent on. Active Directory, DNS, storage, network, and hardware are the most obvious ones. Ensuring they are resilient and highly available is fundamental to achieve a high level of availability for Exchange.

While in small environments all these systems might fall under the remit of the same team, this is typically not the case in larger environments. Relying on other teams and their systems to design a highly available messaging infrastructure might be frustrating, but it remains critical nonetheless. Therefore, it is crucial for all these teams to work together to address any possible issues and pitfalls before starting to deploy Exchange 2013.

Microsoft Exchange Server 2013 High Availability aims at providing you with a number of clear illustrations and concepts to help you understand how this new version of Exchange works and how you can achieve the most out of it in terms of availability and resilience. We explored all the roles, components, and features that should be considered to help you successfully design, configure, and maintain a highly available Exchange 2013 environment.

It is hard to imagine what the next version of Exchange will bring. Some administrators dream of the merge of Exchange and Lync into one solution, and although I share the same dream, I still think that is at least half a decade away. With every release, Microsoft is capable of surprising us with great improvements and new features. It is safe to assume the next release will come around 2016, but how different it will be is another story, almost impossible to guess.

Index

[PACKT] enterprise ✖
PUBLISHING   professional expertise distilled

Thank you for buying
Microsoft Exchange Server
2013 High Availability

About Packt Publishing

Packt, pronounced 'packed', published its first book "Mastering phpMyAdmin for Effective MySQL Management" in April 2004 and subsequently continued to specialize in publishing highly focused books on specific technologies and solutions.

Our books and publications share the experiences of your fellow IT professionals in adapting and customizing today's systems, applications, and frameworks. Our solution based books give you the knowledge and power to customize the software and technologies you're using to get the job done. Packt books are more specific and less general than the IT books you have seen in the past. Our unique business model allows us to bring you more focused information, giving you more of what you need to know, and less of what you don't.

Packt is a modern, yet unique publishing company, which focuses on producing quality, cutting-edge books for communities of developers, administrators, and newbies alike. For more information, please visit our website: www.packtpub.com.

About Packt Enterprise

In 2010, Packt launched two new brands, Packt Enterprise and Packt Open Source, in order to continue its focus on specialization. This book is part of the Packt Enterprise brand, home to books published on enterprise software – software created by major vendors, including (but not limited to) IBM, Microsoft and Oracle, often for use in other corporations. Its titles will offer information relevant to a range of users of this software, including administrators, developers, architects, and end users.

Writing for Packt

We welcome all inquiries from people who are interested in authoring. Book proposals should be sent to author@packtpub.com. If your book idea is still at an early stage and you would like to discuss it first before writing a formal book proposal, contact us; one of our commissioning editors will get in touch with you.

We're not just looking for published authors; if you have strong technical skills but no writing experience, our experienced editors can help you develop a writing career, or simply get some additional reward for your expertise.

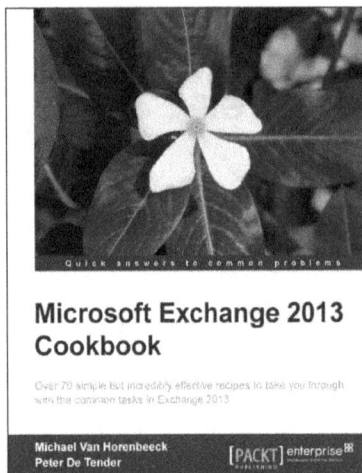

Microsoft Exchange 2013 Cookbook

ISBN: 978-1-78217-062-4   Paperback: 354 pages

Over 70 simple but incredibly effective recipes to take you through with the common tasks in Exchange 2013

1. Deploy Microsoft Exchange 2013 in the real world

2. Understand the key changes with regards to previous versions

3. Design and plan an implementation or migration towards Exchange 2013

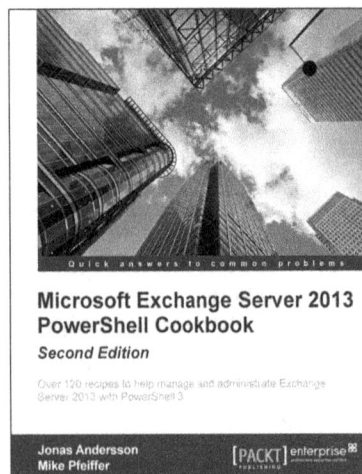

Microsoft Exchange Server 2013 PowerShell Cookbook
Second Edition

ISBN: 978-1-84968-942-7   Paperback: 504 pages

Over 120 recipes to help manage and administrate Exchange Server 2013 with PowerShell 3

1. Newly updated and improved for Exchange Server 2013 and PowerShell 3

2. Learn how to write scripts and functions, schedule scripts to run automatically, and generate complex reports with PowerShell

3. Manage and automate every element of Exchange Server 2013 with PowerShell such as mailboxes, distribution groups, and address lists

Please check **www.PacktPub.com** for information on our titles

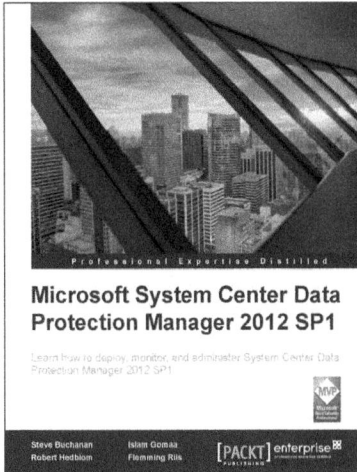

Microsoft System Center Data Protection Manager 2012 SP1

ISBN: 978-1-84968-630-3   Paperback: 328 pages

Learn how to deploy, monitor, and administer System Center Data Protection Manager 2012 SP1

1. Practical guidance that will help you get the most out of Microsoft System Center Data Protection Manager 2012

2. Gain insight into deploying, monitoring, and administering System Center Data Protection Manager 2012 from a team of Microsoft MVPs

3. Learn the various methods and best practices for administrating and using Microsoft System Center Data Protection Manager 2012

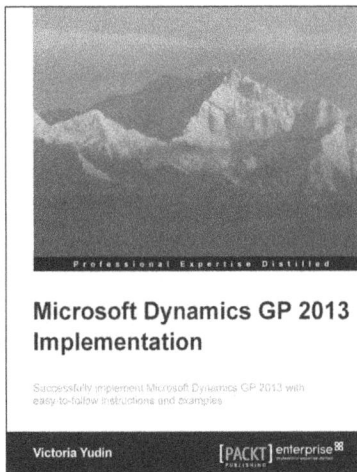

Microsoft Dynamics GP 2013 Implementation

ISBN: 978-1-78217-784-5   Paperback: 430 pages

Successfully implement Microsoft Dynamics GP 2013 with easy-to-follow instructions and examples

1. Plan, install, and implement Microsoft Dynamics GP 2013 with real-world advice from a Microsoft Dynamics GP MVP

2. Learn how to set up the core modules in Microsoft Dynamics GP effectively following detailed, step-by-step instructions

3. Discover additional tools and resources available for your Dynamics GP

Please check **www.PacktPub.com** for information on our titles

www.ingramcontent.com/pod-product-compliance
Lightning Source LLC
Chambersburg PA
CBHW061358210326
41598CB00035B/6020